Case-Based Planning

Viewing Planning as a Memory Task

Perspectives in Artificial Intelligence — *Volume 1*

Case-Based Planning

Viewing Planning as a Memory Task

Kristian J. Hammond

Department of Computer Science
The University of Chicago
Chicago, Illinois

ACADEMIC PRESS, INC.
Harcourt Brace Jovanovich, Publishers
Boston San Diego New York
Berkeley London Sydney
Tokyo Toronto

ACADEMIC PRESS, INC.
1250 Sixth Avenue, San Diego, CA 92101

United Kingdom Edition published by
ACADEMIC PRESS INC. (LONDON) LTD.
24-28 Oval Road, London NW1 7DX

This book describes work done at the Yale AI Lab under the direction of Roger Schank. This work was supported by the Advanced Research Projects Agency of the Department of Defense and monitored by the Office of Naval Research under contract N00014-82-K-0149, Office of Naval Research contract N00014-85-K-0108 and N00014-75-C-1111, NSF grant IST-8120451, and Air Force contract F49620-82-K-0010. It was also supported by Office of Naval Research contract number N00014-88-K-0295.

Library of Congress Cataloging-in-Publication Data

Hammond, Kristian J.
Case-based planning: viewing planning as a memory task.
(Perspectives in artificial intelligence; vol.1)
1. Artificial intelligence. 2. Planning.
I. Title. II. Series
Q335.H35 1989 006.3 88-34354
ISBN 0-12-322060-2

Printed in the United States of America
89 90 91 92 9 8 7 6 5 4 3 2 1

For Cynthia

Editor's Note

This book is the first in a new series by Academic Press: Perspectives in Artificial Intelligence. My goal as series editor is to make this the preferred series for important, new AI ideas that have been developed in some detail so that their power can be seen. Contributions (including monographs and edited collections) from all AI researchers will be considered for the series; high-quality PhD dissertations that stake out a significant territory will also be an important source of material. My bias is toward ideas that explain intelligence in action, not as an abstraction. That means preference for ideas that show how intelligent behavior is accomplished in a computationally effective manner, and how its building blocks relate to human knowledge and its organization. I would like the books in the series to occupy a niche between purely formal analyses that do not concern themselves with the tractability of their proposed mechanisms and purely engineering approaches that do not help us build a theory of intelligence.

This brings me to the first volume in the series – *Case-Based Planning: Viewing Planning as a Memory Task*, by Kristian J. Hammond. This book examplifies all the goals that I have for the series. It helps us understand that one of the sources of power of human intelligence in planning tasks is its use of experience and memory in ways that help it avoid the computational complexity of many planning algorithms. This view of the role of memory and experience also naturally leads to psychologically plausible theories of learning. I am very pleased to introduce the series to you through the first volume. Enjoy.

– B. Chandrasekaran

Contents

Acknowledgements x

Preface: Roger Schank xii

Preface: Drew McDermott xvii

A Guide for the Reader xix

List of Figures xxiii

1 Planning and Memory 1

1.1 Case-based planning 1

1.2 A new theory of planning 3

1.3 Learning from planning 7

1.4 The structure of case-based planning 9

1.5 Building it from the bottom 10

2 Learning from Planning 30

2.1 Learning from cases 30

2.2 CHEF: A case-based planner 32

2.3 Learning plans 49

2.4 Learning to predict failures 53

2.5 Learning critics 59
2.6 How learning from planning is different 62
2.7 How learning from planning is better 64

3 Planning from Memory **66**
3.1 Our view of memory 66
3.2 The function of memory 67
3.3 A planner's memory 69

4 Planning TOPs and Strategies **108**
4.1 TOPs in understanding and planning 108
4.2 TOPs and strategies 111
4.3 TOPs 113
4.4 CHEF's TOPs 114
4.5 Why TOPs? 129
4.6 CHEF's repair strategies 131
4.7 Strategies not used by CHEF 136

5 Modifying Plans **138**
5.1 The MODIFIER's tools 141
5.2 Different situations for altering plans 147
5.3 The introduction of failure 156

6 Repairing Plans **158**
6.1 Noticing the failure 159
6.2 Explaining the failure 164
6.3 Getting the TOP 170
6.4 Applying the strategies 174
6.5 Choosing the repair 179
6.6 Storing the plan 183

7 Planning and Planners **186**

7.1 Case-based planning as planning. 186

7.2 Case-based planning as learning. 201

8 Case-based Planning **213**

8.1 CHEF as a program 213

8.2 CHEF's gains 217

8.3 The real difference 220

A A Causal Vocabulary for TOPs **222**

B CHEF's Simulator **227**

C CHEF's Recipes **236**

C.1 CHEF's initial recipes 237

C.2 The recipes CHEF created 247

Bibliography **267**

Index **271**

Acknowledgments

I didn't go into this with the belief that it would come to an end. I was convinced it would go on forever. I thought that I could spend the rest of my days at Yale thinking about planning and memory. Fortunately, there were those around me who did not.

At the head of this group was my advisor, Roger Schank. Roger strongly and repeatedly suggested that I finish. For this and many other things, I owe Roger a professional and personal debt that I cannot imagine I'll be able to repay. I certainly am not going to try to do so within the confines of this page.

Also helping me along was Chris Riesbeck. As of this writing, I have known Chris as a friend and advisor for well over a decade. He gave me my first introduction to AI and provided both encouragement and support during the difficult times of qualifying exams, defense and thesis writing. He and his wife Max have repeatedly gone well beyond the requirements and expectations of friendship.

But Yale AI is not just Chris and Roger. Drew McDermott continues to be intellectually intimidating while Elliot Soloway remains damned enthusiastic about it all.

Larry Birnbaum gave me a great deal of help by reading and commenting on early versions of the ideas in this book. Diane Schank and Peter Childers helped smooth out the language in the final draft. My students—Jeff Berger, Tim Converse, Mitchell Marks, Greg Hajeck and Neil Hurwitz—were also a huge help to me in preparing the final draft of this book.

I would like to stop here, but that is not the Yale way. So I am forced to thank Steve Lytinen for being the world's worst best man, Colleen Seifert for being the only other member of my graduate class and Gregg Collins for the joke about the two guys and the bear. Without you three, I'd have finished years ago. And, while I deplore his eating habits, I cannot stop myself from thanking Charles Martin for his help and conversation over the past few years.

I am also compelled to thank Chris Owens and David Leake for doing their part in convincing me that I know something by occasionally listening to me and Alex Kass for working hard at trying to make me a less nasty person. Nice try, Alex.

Preface: R. Schank

Humans love to glorify themselves, and this is as true for our view of our mental abilities as it is for our view of our bodies, our buildings, and our space shuttles. We think we are terrific. Unfortunately, at least in the case of human mental abilities, we also think we are unfathomable. After all, we do so many complex operations, it must all be very mystical and impossible to pin down.

One of the most typical mental activities, our ability to plan, has received some of the greatest attention in this regard. Many complex models of human planning have been built, most attempting to reduce planning ability to a set of first principles from which plans can be derived. But, neither the mathematicization nor the mystification of human planning have shed much light on the subject. It may well be that humans plan in a way that is simpler than first meets the eye. We are neither mystical nor logical. We are case-based.

People do not reason about each problem they face as if they had never before faced a problem like it. Rather, they try to find the best plan they have heard of or previously used that is closest to the problem at hand and attempt to adapt that plan to the current situation.

Whenever there is a prior case available to reason from, people will find it and use it as a model for their future decision making. This process of case-based reasoning can be very advantageous to a decision maker when he has available a large number of cases to reason from and an indexing mechanism that makes the most relevant case come to mind when needed. This is why case-based thinking is taught in law schools and business schools; however, it is the cases that are being taught, not the reasoning technique. Everyone knows how to reason from cases; they do it quite naturally.

Why do law schools and business schools teach cases? It seems obvious that both of these subjects are inherently case-based. The law depends upon judges reasoning from prior cases and lawyers trying to find prior cases that will serve as precedents in favor of their clients. The reason for this is that the law does not account for every single possibility that might ever occur in the future of mankind. There are some principles of law, to be sure, but the nuances that determine why one case is an instance of a given principle of law, while another represents a different principle are embodied in case law, that is, in the knowledge of the common set of cases that have been decided and stored away as prototypes in the collective legal mind.

Knowing the law, in the sense of being able to practice law effectively, means knowing the cases or at least knowing where to find cases when one needs them. For law, knowledge means knowledge of cases.

The same is true in business, but for a slightly different reason. There are some principles of business that one can learn in business school. But, to make money, which is the intent of business, after all, one cannot simply follow the successful cases of the past. One has to reason from a prior case by attempting to understand what principles it teaches, apart from the particulars of the given context in which that case occurred. After all, if there were simply one successful paradigmatic case to be followed, everyone would follow it in the pursuit of success.

In business, each new case changes the world sufficiently so that the methods that were specifically applied will not work again. Those methods might work, however, in a different industry, or with a different product, or in a different city. A very standard way of conducting business, then, is to replicate what others have done, but not identically; or if you do choose identical methods, to make sure you aren't the one who will cause there to be less business for everybody.

The essence of thinking in both law and business is the storage and retrieval of cases. Learning in these subjects means learning the cases, and reasoning in these subjects means being able to make new decisions by abstracting the essentials from an appropriate prior case.

It is not law and business that are the oddballs in education or in reasoning. Neither of these subjects pretends nor should they pretend to be based upon systematic principles that would allow just those principles to be learned while particular cases are ignored. Many, more academic, fields do have such pretensions. In mathematics, for example, high school students may learn principles, but graduate students also learn the cases - in this context, prior proofs of theorems.

Case-based reasoning is the essence of how human reasoning works. In some ways this can be seen as a bad thing. After all, if I have had only one experience with a given subject, I am likely to treat a new experience of the same kind in the same way. We make decisions based on very little information, precisely because case-based reasoning fools us into believing that the prior case that we have retrieved is the best case that we could have retrieved. But, contrasted with rule-based reasoning, it is clear that case-based reasoning has its benefits. When you reason from rules, you easily lose track of the origin of those rules. You apply a script because you always have applied it. We become increasingly rigid in this way. When prior experience is indexed cleverly, when the cases we get reminded of are far afield from the current case, then reasoning from experience can lead to brand new insights. All people reason from experience. The difference between reasoners depends upon how they have coded up their prior experiences in the first place. We are not all reminded of the same things at the same time.

The trick in case-based reasoning then is to find relevant cases. We can use our own experiences or thoughts as cases if we have a relevant one, or we can make use of the experience of others to the extent that we can obtain information about such experiences. An individual's knowledge is really no more than the collection of experiences that he has had or that he has heard about. Or, to put this another way, all we really have are cases. We have so many cases available to us that finding them can be very tricky indeed. Human memory depends upon good methods of labeling cases so that they can be retrieved when needed. Whatever general principle we may abstract from a given case or set of cases serves as one of many possible labels by which that case can be retrieved. But, it is the case that matters, general principles can be derived from comparing cases and those principles can be used to label cases. But, the general principle will rarely account for enough information to be very helpful in a new situation. Being able to consider the actual case from which any principle was derived can always yield new insights.

The problem with standard problem solving programs is that each and every problem presented to them is the same in terms of the approach that must be taken. Each must be reduced to first principles and logical deductions made using those principles as a basis. This approach may seem to be suitable for mathematicians in pursuit of their professions, but not even mathematicians behave this way. Mathematicians are often parodied by other scientists as attempting to reduce everything to known and solved problems and then to proceed from there. In fact, what mathematicians do while doing mathematics, as opposed to what people seem to imagine that they do, is very much like what real people do in everyday thinking.

It is really far too difficult to attempt to be rational about every problem we face. We needn't reason logically about where the butter might be, we need merely recall where we saw it last, or if we are in a new place, where we saw it in a place that resembled the one we are in now. We don't attempt to derive the principle by which a restaurant operates, we merely recall the actions that need to be taken on our part when the time comes. Real thinking has nothing to do with logic at all. Real thinking means retrieval of the right information at the right time. It follows, then, that the most difficult part of thinking when processing an input is the creation of labels that will allow us to retrieve something we already know is marked with those labels so that we can produce it as output. Thinking of the kind that attempts to reason from first principles, hardly occurs at all.

What makes us intelligent is our ability to find out what we know when we need to know it. What we actually know is all the stories, experiences, "facts," little epithets, points of view, and so on that we have gathered over the years. Each of these is like a screen full of information in a computer. Each screen has a label, and to find that screen we must produce that label. Part of our intelligence is devoted to decoding inputs from the outside world sufficiently well so that these inputs produce labels that cause our own experiences to be brought to mind. When our own experiences come to mind, we can adapt them to a new situation if we are problem solving, reduce them to a one-liner if we are in a short conversation, or tell them whole if we have an amiable listener. We can compare two stories and attempt to find the similarities and differences. We can alter a story to invent a new one for some purpose. We can use these stories any way that we like. In the end, they are all we have.

One consequence of this model of intelligence, especially any computer implementation of that model, is that such a system runs the risk of being described as only appearing to be intelligent without actually being intelligent. In some sense, intelligence is in the eye of the beholder, and most beholders are very prejudiced by skin. If the skin of the teller of the story is fleshy and human-like, we are likely to consider the algorithm that produced that story to be an intelligent one, except perhaps in the case of the grandfather who we would agree was intelligent but is now telling the same story too often. But, if the skin is plastic, and we suspect that a computer is inside, we are likely to claim that the algorithms being used to produce the same story were somehow just unintelligent retrieval methods. All we have, machine or human, are stories and methods of finding and using those stories.

Being a knowing system means being a system that knows cases and can find them when necessary. Intelligence is the apt use of the cases that are available. To build models of intelligence, or simply to understand the nature of intelligence, we must understand how cases are stored in memory and how cases are found and adapted when needed.

Kris Hammond was thrown into this problem while he was my student at Yale. He built what has become the best example of a case-based reasoner to date. His book attacks all the important problems of indexing and retrieval, adaptation and the creation of plans. His book is, in essence, a book about creativity. It may be about creativity of a rather mundane sort, but it is important to start simple. I consider Kris' book to be a very significant work on the road to understanding and modeling the true nature of the mind.

Roger Schank
Yale University, 1988

Preface: D. McDermott

Planning is a subfield of artificial intelligence that has yet to find a coherent theory. It began as an offshoot of mechanical theorem proving, in which the goal was to constructively prove the existence of a plan to bring about a desired state of affairs. In the mid-seventies, it enjoyed a burst of attention as the result of the work of Sacerdoti and others on *hierarchical, least-commitment* planning, in which a plan is incrementally debugged, first in a vague form, and eventually in a completely specified form. But the emphasis was still on finding provably correct plans, in logically simple domains. The work said little about how to plan the behavior of real systems, such as robots. For a while, it looked as if what was most urgently required was a deeper logical analysis of the planner's environment, in hopes that the reasoning style of existing planners could be carried over. Deeper logical analyses were forthcoming, but the result was to make the standard planners look even worse.

Eventually it was realized that there could be no theory of planning without a theory of behaving. Planning is what happens when a behaving system has time to think ahead a bit. There are lots of kinds of behaving, and hence lots of kinds of planning. It is probably premature to look for a unified theory of either one. However, there are certain features we expect in most domains. A realistic system is unpredictable, because of its own complexity and its environment's complexity. A planner can probably predict bugs that are likely to occur, but it probably cannot prove that none will occur. Instead, it must be prepared to cope with them.

This picture suggests the following mechanism for planning: Given a set of tasks to carry out, the planner proposes a preliminary plan for doing that, typically drawn from an indexed library of plan schemas, and then "mentally" simulates the execution of the plan, watching for errors and inefficiencies to occur. When such problems crop up, it uses a description of the problem to index to a library of plan transformations that are likely to change the plan in favorable ways. The transformed plan is then reanalyzed.

The current momentum behind such *transformational planning* is due in large part to the work of Kris Hammond, who (starting from earlier work by Sussman and by Schank on failure-driven learning) developed the idea and tested it via the implementation described in this book. Hammond's planner operates in the domain of Chinese cooking. A recipe is a sort of plan, which can be transformed by adding ingredients, adding steps, changing cooking times, and so forth. One feels an urge to apologize for this domain, an urge which should be fought. If the domain sounds a bit frivolous, that's just the usual misguided intuition that what people do in everyday life is "too easy" for computers. In fact, a full-scale treatment of everyday behavior such as cooking is still far in the future, and this work is only a preliminary step. Hammond's planner assumes that only a single recipe is required, and that resources (utensils, ingredients) are always available. The most serious limitation is that it does not actually try its recipes and cope with the kind of feedback an actual cook gets.

But what it does do is impressive. Given a set of goals that a dish must satisfy, the planner searches for an existing recipe that satisfies as many as possible, then applies transformations (e.g., ingredient substitutions) to bring it closer to what is required. It then simulates cooking the dish, discovers problems, and applies transformations to get rid of them. Finally, it indexes the newly invented recipe for future reference. In other words, it learns.

There are two somewhat divergent directions to take this work. One can focus on the learning (what is called "case-based" reasoning by Hammond and Schank), or one can focus on the use of transformations in planning (or in design generally). The two are not linked that tightly, because there are cases where transformations are appropriate but learning is not, namely, where a plan is unlikely to be used twice. Since the dissertation this book is based on appeared, several research efforts based on the transformational-planning mechanism have begun. It is too early to see how successful this work will be, or even if there is enough commonality to hope for a theory (or, God help us, a "paradigm"). But the success of Hammond's program is encouraging.

Drew McDermott
Yale University, 1988

A Guide for the Reader

This book presents a view of planning as a task supported by a changing dynamic memory. This view attempts to integrate a model of memory, learning and planning into a single system that learns about planning by creating new plans and analyzing how they interact with the world. We call this view of planning *Case-based Planning.*

A case-based planner makes use of its own past experience in developing new plans. It relies on its memory of effects, rather than a set of causal rules, to create and modify new plans. Memories of past successes are accessed and modified to create new plans. Memories of past failures are used to warn the planner of impending problems, and memories of past repairs are called upon to tell the planner how to how to deal with them.

This view of planning from experience supports and is supported by a learning system that incorporates new experiences into the planner's episodic memory. This learning algorithm gains from the planner's failures as well as its successes. Successful plans are stored in memory, indexed by the goals they satisfy and the problems they avoid. Failures are also stored, indexed by the features in the world that predict them. By storing failures as well as successes, the planner is able to *anticipate and avoid* future plan failures.

But this work is not only concerned with memory. It is also concerned with the mechanics of plan execution, monitoring and repair. Our approach to plan repair is based on the notion of diagnosing problems through causal analysis of the steps and states that led to their occurrence. The description that results from this analysis is used to access repair strategies associated the general problem. These strategies are then transformed into specific alterations to the faulty plan at hand. Finally, the analysis is used to identify critical features that will be used to anticipate, and thus avoid, the failure in the future.

This view of planning is aimed at improving planning behavior in three areas: failure avoidance, plan repair and plan reuse. It also attempts gains over existing learning systems, in that the learning is driven by the functional needs of a planner.

Reading this book

While some people will no doubt brave the weather and try to read this text from beginning to end, I assume that most will not. In order to help those with specific interests, the following is a subject guide to reading this book.

Interested in case-based reasoning in general? For those interested in a general introduction to case-based reasoning, I suggest the first three chapters. Chapter 1 outlines a framework for case-based reasoning while Chapter 2 examines a single example of this framework in practice. Chapter 3 discusses the different uses to which memory can be put in planning and then discusses how the form of memory can be fit to follow its function.

Together, these three chapters form a general introduction to case-based reasoning and its use in planning.

Interested in planning? For those more interested in planning, I suggest that you read the first two chapters to get a general idea of the approach and then concentrate on Chapters 5 and 6. Chapter 5 describes the methods for modifying existing plans to fit new situations, while Chapter 6 outlines the plan repair techniques that I used in CHEF.

After this, you might then read the the introduction and conclusion to Chapter 4. This will give you the outline of the repair TOPs used by CHEF to organize general repair strategies. The details of each individual TOP and the particular strategies associated with each will probably interest only the most dedicated planning researcher.

Interested in plan repair? Readers who are honestly interested in plan repair should push on and read not only all of Chapter 4 but also Appendix A, in which the causal vocabulary used by CHEF to represent different problem situations are described. Though these two sections of the book are for me the most interesting, they do take a high degree of dedication to get through.

Interested in comparing how case-based planning relates to other techniques? Chapter 7 provides a discussion of the differences between case-based planning and more traditional techniques in both planning and learning. It can be read after Chapters 1 and 2.

Interested in learning? Machine learning enthusiasts will be interested in Chapters 2 and 3 as well as the second half of Chapter 7. However, the nature of case-based reasoning is such that the learning done by the planner is scattered about the entire task. As a result, I also suggest reading the last section of Chapter 6 and the last half of Chapter 7.

Interested in CHEF as a program? For those who would like to read about CHEF's record in the kitchen, I suggest reading Chapter 8, in which the program's performance is discussed. For those with a more technical bent, the details of CHEF's simulator are discussed in Appendix B.

Interested in food? Finally, for those interested in a set of machine-generated recipes, Appendix C lists the dishes developed by CHEF along with what it learned from each. I have made a few of these myself and must say that the program had a few decent ideas. I warn all readers, however, that CHEF's world was one of simulated bean sprouts and tofu, and as such its view of success was limited by the ability of a DEC 20 to hallucinate about taste, texture and smell.

An apology and the Yale Robot Joke

Before letting you go on I must apologize for one thing: there is no humor whatsoever in this book. This is a seriously dry piece of text. I really am sorry about this. And, although I know that I cannot fully compensate you for the next 200+ pages of dry text, I will make a futile attempt to do so by telling you the Yale Robot Joke.

The Yale Robot Joke

It was the year 1995 and the DOD finally decided that it wanted to see some results. So the head of research called together all of the scientists doing work in robot planning to demonstrate their work. Everyone was faced with the same task—get a robot to cross a busy street.

The first robot was a first-principles planner from Stanford. After walking to the curb, it looked left, then right and sat for 20 minutes planning and projecting until it found a provably correct plan of action. Once finished, it stepped into the road, screamed, "I thought this was a closed world", and was hit by a speeding truck.

The next robot was the JPL Mars Rover. Integrating planning and execution, it began to slowly step out into the street, probing the ground every two feet for "deadly Martian dust pits". For ten hours it probed and stepped, stepped and probed. Eventually, the sun set, the solar powered Rover ground to a halt and was immediately hit by a speeding truck.

This was quickly followed by the CMU robot pogo stick that jumped madly about, dodging trucks left and right until it hopped happily into an open manhole.

After this came the MIT situated activity device. It leapt into the road and deftly skipped between cars. It dodged traffic impressively until, pinned on each side by ice trucks, it was nailed by a van from Bee Line Movers.

And so it went. The day wore on, and after countless tries, no robot made it across the street. Finally, there was only one robot left—the Yale robot.

Unlike the others, it was not clean and shiny. It was not silvery and smooth. It was dented and bashed, with little to be said for it. But still it bravely moved up to the curb.

It looked at the battered bits of steel and wire in front of it. It listened to the faint echos of the now distant robot pogo. It looked at the expectant faces in the crowd.

Then it paused, put its scruffy robot hands in its scruffy robot pockets, eased back on its rear wheels and said, "You know, this reminds me of a story..."

Kristian Hammond
University of Chicago, 1988

List of Figures

1.1 The RETRIEVER 14

1.2 The MODIFIER 16

1.3 The STORER 19

1.4 The REPAIRER 22

1.5 The ASSIGNER 25

1.6 The ANTICIPATOR 26

2.1 Goals satisfied by STRAWBERRY-SOUFFLE 52

2.2 Avoidance goal under STRAWBERRY-SOUFFLE 53

2.3 Marking FRUIT and SOUFFLE as predictive of problems . 56

2.4 Marking LIQUID and SOUFFLE as predictive of problems 58

2.5 Repairing DUCK-DUMPLINGS with REMOVE-FEATURE 61

2.6 Storing new critic under DUCK 61

2.7 Using a new DUCK critic. 62

3.1 The definition of BROCCOLI-WITH-TOFU. 73

3.2 Goals point to plans. 76

3.3 Discrimination network of plans indexed by goals. 77

3.4 Finding plans that satisfy partially matching goals. 78

3.5 Discriminating on the features of partially matching goals. . 80

3.6 Three plans that could be used. 86

3.7 Using new DUCK critic. 88
3.8 Features linked to the memory of a failure. 92
3.9 Table of standard modification rules. 98

4.1 The Three Blocks Problem. 122
4.2 Definition of ALTER-PLAN:SIDE-EFFECT strategy 133
4.3 Definition of RECOVER strategy 134

5.1 Definition of the role specifications of STYLE-STIR-FRY . 142
5.2 Rule for adding FRUIT to SOUFFLEs. 144
5.3 Two critics for SHRIMP. 146
5.4 Merging ADD and MIX steps. 150
5.5 Merging cooking steps. 151
5.6 Removing steps for an obsolete goal. 155

6.1 Section of result table for BEEF-WITH-BROCCOLI. 160
6.2 Finding fault with BEEF-WITH-BROCCOLI. 163
6.3 Finding fault with FISH-STIR-FRIED. 163
6.4 Test and Response for RECOVER strategy 175
6.5 Definition of RECOVER strategy 176

B.1 Definition of preconditions on MIX. 228
B.2 Precondition tests associated with SHELL. 228
B.3 Definition for two normal STIR-FRY rules. 230
B.4 Definition for normal FILL rule. 231
B.5 Rules used to infer soggy broccoli. 232
B.6 Section of Result Table for BEEF-WITH-BROCCOLI. . . . 233

Chapter 1

Planning and Memory

1.1 Case-based planning

When a surgeon approaches an operation, he does not build his course of action piece by piece out of a set of primitive steps. He recalls past operations from similar situations and modifies his behavior to suit the new situation. When an architect starts a new design for a client, he does not go back to first principles and try all possible combinations of sub-plans. Instead he recalls past plans and changes them to fit his current needs. And when you get into your car to go home tonight, you will not create a new plan for buckling up, starting the car and finding a route home. You will just recall the plan that has worked before and make use of it directly.

This book outlines an approach to this kind of planning from memory, which we call *Case-based Planning.*

Case-based planning is the idea of planning as remembering.

Planning from cases means remembering successes so that they can be reused, remembering failures so that they can be avoided, and remembering repairs so that they can be reapplied. Case-based planning differs from rule-based planning in that it rests on the notion that new plans should be based on the planner's knowledge of what has succeeded and failed in the past. Questions of memory organization, indexing and plan modification are important in case-based planning because a case-based planner makes extensive use of memory. Learning is central to case-based planning because a case-based planner must reuse, and learn from, its own experiences to build new plans and to avoid past errors.

Planning is a memory task. A plan for a set of goals is not built up piece by piece from the individual plans for each goal. It is instead constructed by modifying a plan from memory that already satisfies or partially satisfies many, if not all, of the planner's goals. A planner's failures are not only *plan* failures. They are also *expectation* failures that have to be remembered so that the faulty expectations can be changed. They are indications that the knowledge the planner has of the world is faulty and should be altered in much the same way as the plan is altered. Also, plans are not disposable items that should be built and then discarded. They are valuable commodities that can be stored and recalled for later use. The problem of building and maintaining plans is a problem of the interaction between a planner's knowledge base and the world. Any problem that arises out of a disparity between what the planner knows and how the world is actually structured indicates that the model of the world, a model shaped by the planner's memories, has to be changed.

A case-based planner uses its knowledge of the world and the effects of its actions in the world to build a plan. As a result, the plan becomes a test of that knowledge. If the plan is faulty, something about the planner's knowledge is faulty. Plans are recalled from memory and allowed to interact with the world. The feedback from this interaction is then used to modify existing plans and add new plans to memory. These modifications and additions change the planner's understanding of what can happen in different situations and make it possible for the planner to understand which plans are appropriate for certain situations.

A case-based planner must make use of memory whenever possible. It must begin planning by using its memory of past failures to warn of problems. It must then search its memory of successes for a plan that can be modified to fit the goals it needs to satisfy and problems it seeks to avoid. If it has a plan failure, the planner must treat it as a failure of its understanding of the world and explain the failure so that it can repair the faulty plan and the knowledge of the world that allowed it to create that plan. Finally, it must save its successes in memory, indexed by the goals they satisfy and the problems they avoid, so that they can be used again to satisfy similar goals and avoid similar problems.

By definition, case-based planners must learn. They must learn new plans in order to store the plans they create for later use. They must learn to predict problems based on their own experiences so that they can find the plans that avoid those problems. And they must learn specific repairs to planning problems that can be applied again when similar problems arise.

A case-based planner must learn only when that learning will help the planner in later situations. A case-based planner must store new plans in memory so that it can use them again in similar situations. It must learn to associate goals with the problems it encounters while planning for them so it can anticipate and avoid those problems in the future. And it must learn new repairs for problems so that it can apply plans with less effort once the problems have been predicted.

1.2 A new theory of planning

If we consider planning problems as memory problems, a number of basic features of most theories of planning must be altered:

1. Rather than planning for individual goals and then merging the results, a case-based planner must search its memory for plans that satisfy many of its goals at once.
2. Rather than recovering from planning errors and then forgetting the results of that recovery, a case-based planner must treat these errors as opportunities to learn and more about its domain and the problems that arise in it.
3. Rather than discarding the plans that it builds, a case-based planner has to save them in memory for later use in similar circumstances.

The theory of case-based planning sees planning as an activity that tests a planner's understanding of the world. Planning and learning form a closed loop, in which planning errors lead the planner to learn more about what causes them, which gives it a better understanding of how to avoid them.

The issues involved in case-based planning are not confined to planning in the strictest sense of the word. Although plan modification and validation, which are planning issues in the narrower sense, play a role in case-based planning, the issues of memory, indexing and learning are far more basic.

In order to plan from past experience, a planner must have a rich understanding of that experience and a clear method for organizing it and incorporating it into memory. The memory structures and learning mechanisms needed to support a case-based planner must have the ability to integrate past failures and successes into memory so that the former can be avoided and the latter reused.

Case-based planning differs from other approaches to planning and problem solving (*E.g.*, [Fikes and Nilsson 71], [Korf 82], [Sacerdoti 75], [Sussman 75], [Tate 77] and [Wilensky 80]) in three areas: in initial plan building, in the reaction to plan failures and in the vocabulary for describing and storing plans. Although there is a great deal of overlap in these areas –given that the initial choice of a plan affects the way in which it is debugged and that the way in which debugged plans are stored affects the way in which they are chosen for later use– it is important to separate them and understand how different planners handle them.

1.2.1 Building an initial plan

A case-based planner builds new plans out of old plans. It stores these past planning experiences in an episodic memory that is organized by two sorts of indices: goals to be satisfied and failures to be avoided. Plans are organized around goals so that they can be retrieved when the goals that they satisfy are requested. They are also organized under the failures that the planner encountered when originally putting them together. Anticipated failures can then be avoided by finding plans that were constructed to deal with similar failures in the past.

In order to use its own memory organization, a case-based planner must begin the task of building a plan for a set of goals by considering how they will interact. By doing this, it can anticipate any failure that it has experienced before and use this anticipation to search for a plan that solves the problem it has predicted. It can also use the prediction of any positive interaction between goals to characterize its current set of goals in terms of an already existing exemplar in memory that can be accessed directly. It has to anticipate problems that will arise in order to find plans that will avoid them. This just means that a case-based planner has to be able to infer from the fact that it is raining that it will get wet if it plans to go outside and thus it must find a plan that avoids that problem instead of building and having to repair a faulty plan that does not.

> The case-based approach to finding an initial plan is to *anticipate* problems so the planner can find plans that *avoid* them.

By organizing plans around planning failures as well as goals, a planner can avoid problems it has encountered before. The planner can use the prediction of a failure that results from a goal interaction to find a plan that avoids it. This idea of using a prediction mechanism along with a memory organization that can make use of these predictions to ***anticipate and avoid*** planning problems contrasts strongly with the ***create and debug*** paradigm that has been the thrust of machine planning over the past fifteen years (*E.g.*, [Fikes and Nilsson 71], [Sacerdoti 75], [Sussman 75], [Wilensky 80] and [Wilensky 83]). The main difference between these approaches is that the ***anticipate and avoid*** approach tries to predict problems and then avoid them by finding plans in memory that deal with them, whereas the ***create and debug*** approach debugs failures only after they arise during the planning process.

1.2.2 Debugging failed plans

A case-based planner can anticipate and thus avoid failures having to do with plan interactions. It can only do this, however, with interactions it has seen before. In order to plan effectively it must be able to recover and learn from failures that it hasn't seen before and isn't able to anticipate. So, like ***create and debug*** planners, it has to have knowledge of how to identify and repair faulty plans that have failed due to unforeseen interactions between steps.

Although there are technical differences between the way plan failures are handled by a case-based planner and the way programs such as NOAH [Sacerdoti 75] or PANDORA [Wilensky 80] deal with them, the most important difference between them is that a case-based planner treats its mistakes as *expectation* failures as well as *planning* failures. Planning is a test of understanding the world. Planning failures indicate where that understanding has broken down and where it has to be fixed. They tell the planner when it needs to learn.

A planning failure occurs when a plan does not satisfy some goal that it was designed to deal with. For example, if a planner puts together a plan to get a newspaper on a rainy day that is a simple "go outside, get paper, come back" plan, it will end up getting wet. Because the planner is wet and doesn't want to be, it has had a planning failure. But because it did not expect to get wet, it has also had an expectation failure. An *expectation* failure is different from a *planning* failure. It occurs when an expected event does not take place or when an unexpected event occurs. In the newspaper situation, the *expectation* failure occurs at the same time as the planning failure, but the response to the planning failure is the alteration of a plan whereas the response to the expectation failure has to be the alteration of the planner and its understanding of the world.

A planner must respond to a *planning* failure by building a causal explanation of why the failure has occurred and then using that explanation to access replanning strategies designed for the situation in general. It must respond to an *expectation* failure by again using that explanation to add new inference rules that will allow it to anticipate the problem that it previously was unable to foresee. It should first ask itself, "What went wrong with the plan?" and then ask "What went wrong with the planning?"

In other words, a planner has to repair its expectations about the world when those expectations lead to plans that fail.

Knowledge repair is one capability which sets case-based planning apart from other theories of planning. The experiences a planner has while planning are tests of its knowledge of the world. Any failure of a plan is a failure that forces a re-evaluation of that knowledge.

> A case-based planner responds to planning failures by repairing both the faulty plan and its own faulty knowledge base that allowed it to build the plan incorrectly.

The notion of learning from expectation failures is not a new one. Schank has argued that learning occurs when an understander is confronted by expectation failures [Schank 82]. Although the failures a planner faces are *planning* failures, it learns from them only in that they are also *expectation* failures.

1.2.3 Storing plans for later use

To store a plan in memory, a planner has to understand when it will be appropriate to use again. For most planners this has meant storing plans in relation to the goals they satisfy. For a case-based planner that tries to anticipate problems and find the plans that avoid them, this is not enough. To access a plan that avoids a certain problem, the plan must have been indexed so as to allow such a connection. The basic vocabulary of plan indexing is necessarily the vocabulary of the planner's domain, and of the goals of the domain. But this vocabulary is not sufficient to allow a planner to actively avoid the problems that it anticipates. Plans must also be stored by *descriptions of the negative goal interactions they avoid.* A plan to go outside with an umbrella has to be indexed by the fact that it gets the planner outside, but also by the fact that it does so while protecting him from the rain. It has to be indexed by the fact that it ***avoids the problem of the planner is getting wet.*** This is so it can later be accessed when the need for such a plan is inferred. As with any vocabulary item based on a plan satisfying a goal, the fact that a plan successfully avoids a problem must be used to index it for later use when a goal to avoid the same or similar problems arises.

> Plans are indexed by the goals they satisfy and by the problems they avoid. This allows a planner to find plans that achieve the goals it is planning for while avoiding the problems it predicts will arise while doing so.

1.3 Learning from planning

A case-based planner must also be a learning system because it must reuse its own experiences. The learning done by a case-based planner is learning by remembering. This is a type of learning that is not addressed by either the theories of *concept learning* via induction, (*e.g.*, [Lebowitz 80], [Michalski and Larson 78] and [Winston 70]), or *explanation-driven learning* of the form described by [DeJong 83] and [Mitchell 83]. Case-based planning requires a knowledge-based learning that makes use of the planner's understanding of the world to determine what should be learned and when it should be learned. This learning breaks down into three types: *learning plans*, *learning expectations* and *learning critics.*

Plan learning is the creation and storage of new plans as the result of planning for situations that the planner has never encountered before. The planner has to build a new plan and decide what features are best for indexing it in memory. Any new plans are stored in memory, indexed by the positive goals they satisfy as well as by the negative effects they avoid. For example, a plan for going outside in the rain to get a paper would be indexed by the fact that it is a plan to retrieve a paper and by the fact that it allows the planner to avoid getting wet.

Expectation learning is somewhat more complex than *plan learning*, but is closely linked to the indexing of plans in memory. It involves learning the features in a domain that are predictive of negative interactions between plan steps. This predictive ability is used to anticipate particular problems and then to search for plans in memory designed to avoid them. These features are learned by building causal explanations of planning failures and marking the states and steps that lead to the failures as predictive of them. The fact that it is raining and the planner has a goal to pick up his paper would be marked as predictive of the problem of getting wet–because these features would be included in any explanation of *why* the plan that lacked a umbrella failed. Once predicted, this problem could be planned for by finding a plan that avoids it. Once one of these predictions is activated, problems can be avoided by searching memory for a plan that takes them into account.

Critic learning occurs when a problem in a plan can be traced back to a specific object or initial state related to a plan rather than an interaction between steps. Any repair that is made to a plan because of an idiosyncratic object can be saved and associated with the object. The fix to a specific problem can become a general repair that can be applied in later cases of the problem's occurrence. Even if an overall plan to avoid a problem cannot be found, the repair can then be reapplied to fix a plan that satisfies other goals. This would be like predicting that the rain would get someone wet in any case of going outside and then applying the repair of using an umbrella to a plan for going outside that does not already include this fix.

Case-based planning involves three types of learning:

- Learning new plans that avoid problems;
- Learning the features that predict the problems;
- Learning the repairs that have to be made if those problems arise again in different circumstances.

All three of these types of learning are supported by a planning vocabulary that describes plans in terms of the direct goals they satisfy and the interactions they deal with. Storing plans in terms of the goals they satisfy is not enough if the planner wants to reuse them. They also have to be stored in terms of the problems they avoid. This makes it possible for the planner to rediscover these past plans when it predicts the same problems again in a different planning situation.

In the sections that follow, we will attempt to build up a model of case-based planning that has these attributes. We start with the simplest possible model and add capabilities as needed to increase the planner's functionality.

1.4 The structure of case-based planning

Human behavior often seems capricious. Minds wander from topic to topic. Ideas connected by thin strands of associations follow one another as though intimately related. Past experiences that have little to do with the apparent features of a new situation present themselves as solutions to the present problem.

Any effort at cognitive modeling must begin by explaining these seemingly capricious acts. One set of approaches to this modeling task has grown out of the idea that what appears to be capricious action actually is capricious. The theories and programs that have resulted from this idea often include random number generators, random weights associative on links or random connections between conceptual structures. They treat the seemingly random leaps of human thought as truly random, as a failure in an otherwise orderly system. Unfortunately, these theories have a seductive allure because they present models that look very much like what they are trying to explain.

The key word here, however, is, "explain". These theories look like what we want to explain, but they do not explain what we want to explain. They are mere *simulations* of behavior that do nothing to explain why it arises. They are, "non-explanation explanations".

Another way of looking at human behavior is to ask what function this behavior serves. Instead of looking at behavior in a vacuum, examine it in terms of its possible use in performing a cognitive task. Let the function served by the behavior guide the examination of it. Make the function that underlies the behavior have more importance than the simulation of the I/O of the behavior itself.

The difference between these approaches is simple. It is the difference between simulating an engine by building a box that makes engine noises and modeling an engine through an examination of the function it has and how internal combustion satisfies it.

An example of this approach is the work on naturally occurring remindings done by Roger Schank. In *Dynamic Memory* [Schank 82], Schank looked at the phenomenon of remindings and argued for their use in learning. More recently, he has augmented this view and argued that remindings also play a role in the construction of explanations ([Schank and Riesbeck 85], [Schank 84a] and [Schank 86]). This work is aimed at a functional model of why people have these remindings and what they can do with them, rather than a mere descriptive simulation of how to go about generating them.

The theory of case-based planning is aimed at a functional explanation of certain aspects of human cognitive behavior. In building the theory, one eye was kept on the data concerning episodic reminding and the other on the needs of a case-based planner. As a result, the theory describes how to use past plans in the construction of new ones and how to use remindings of past failures to avoid repeating mistakes.

> The planner has remindings that are similar to those people have, but only has them because they are required to solve particular planning problems. It is reminded of past episodes for the same reason that people are reminded of past episodes: these episodes contain information that can help in planning for new problems.

1.5 Building it from the bottom

The following sections will look at the nature of case-based planning in general, arguing why planning should make use of the case-based paradigm and then looking at what it takes to build such a planner. To do this we will start with the simplest possible case-based planner -a plan RETRIEVER- and expand it with the additions required to do plan modification, plan repair and problem anticipation.

As you read the rest of this chapter, recall that we are starting with an intentionally simplified system and adding to it in order to expand its functionality. As a result, the early stages of our description will lack some features that we will later add.

1.5.1 Why case-based?

The argument for case-based planning is straightforward: we want a planner that can learn and recall complex plans rather than having to repeat work it has already done. In the case of a single plan for building a car or a house, the number of steps involved is huge. Although such plans can be built up from a set of rules or from plan abstractions each time the planner needs them, it is more economical to save entire plans and recall them for reuse when situations that require their use arise.

It is always useful for a planner to save the plans it creates, especially in those situations in which a plan includes information about how to avoid problems that the planner's base of rules tended to lead the planner into. For any planning task involving the reuse of information, the best approach is to make use of a detailed representation of the experience itself. Given that all planning tasks make use of past information, this argues that the best approach to planning in general is to find and modify past plans rather than rebuild from a set of rules each time.

> The functional justification for case-based planning is the need to learn from experience.

The needs of a case-based planner are somewhat different from those of a rule-based system in that a case-based planner relies almost entirely on its memory of past plans. A rule-based system, on the other hand, makes almost no use of its nearly nonexistent memory. The sections that follow will discuss the *functional* needs of a case-based planner, beginning with a basic planner and then expanding to deal with problems as they arise.

1.5.2 Plan retrieval

At its simplest, a case-based planner is a memory that returns to a past plan whenever it is given a new set of goals. If it cannot find a plan that satisfies all of the goals it has been handed, it returns a plan that meets most or many of them. It is trying to find what we will refer to as the *best match* between the current situation and some situation in the past for which it has a plan. There is no guarantee that the *best match* will actually be the best possible plan for use in the current situation, but our effort is to construct a memory organization that will aim in that direction. We will call this basic planner that only finds best matches a RETRIEVER. Its input is a set of goals to be achieved and its output is a plan from its memory that achieves as many of these goals as is possible.

For a planner to find the right plans, the goals that it is asked to achieve have to be used to index past instances in memory. Planning episodes have to be indexed in memory by the goals they have satisfied. An episode in which a planner flies to London should be indexed in memory as a plan to get to London and, at a more general level, as a plan to get to someplace distant. An episode in which the planner removes an inflamed appendix should be indexed as satisfying that goal but also by the more general result of removing an diseased organ. The simple plan of calling down to the hotel desk for a wake-up call has to be indexed by the fact that it satisfies the goal of getting you up in the morning. A planner has to be able to discriminate between plans on the basis of all of the goals it is trying to accomplish.

Along with goals, a planner must also know what its initial planning situation is. It must know the states that are currently true and the goals it wants to satisfy. Then plans that are designed for particular situations, not just particular goals, can be found and used. For example, a plan to retrieve a newspaper from the porch when it is raining, which would include the use of an umbrella, must be indexed in memory under the features that make its use relevant. This means indexing it not only by the goal that it satisfies, getting the newspaper, but also by the conditions under which it is appropriate to use, when it is raining. Likewise, the plan to call down to the hotel desk for a wake-up call cannot just be indexed as a good plan for satisfying the goal to wake-up at a specific time in the morning. It also has to be indexed as a good plan in the context of being in a hotel to begin with. It is not particularly effective when at home. This means having a number of plans in memory that satisfy the same goal or goals but are distinguished by different situations. The states that define these different situations must also be used by the planner to index plans in memory.

Specific goals and states alone, however, are not sufficient to find the plans that the RETRIEVER has to return. Sometimes there is no plan that satisfies a particular goal, so the *best match* has to be a plan that satisfies a similar goal. If there is not a plan to get to London, a plan that worked in getting the planner to Paris may have to be used as the planner's starting point. Or a plan to build a two-story house may have to be modified when the planner requires a plan for a three-story building. A planner's representation must include some notion of similarity between goals. This similarity can be expressed by placing similar goals into sets, by building them into an ISA hierarchy, or by dynamically evaluating their similarity on the basis of individual features. Paris and London may both be considered as foreign countries; a gall bladder that has to be removed may be thought of as belonging to the same abstract class as an appendix; or a house with two stories may be understood in terms of structural features that are shared with a three-story building. When a planner cannot find a plan that fully satisfies the goals it is planning for, it has to have some way to find a plan or plans that partially satisfy them. No matter what the method, there has to be some metric for the similarity of goals that a planner can use to judge partial matches.

But a planner has to be able to do more than just find plans. It has to be able to choose between plans. Given a set of goals, a planner needs to find the plan in memory that is the *best match* for the plan that would satisfy all the goals. In the trivial case of having a plan that satisfies all the goals, this is no problem. As soon as a planner is confronted with a set of plans that are all partial matches, however, a problem arises: how does it determine which plan out of a group of plans best satisfies a set of goals if each of the plans satisfies some of the goals?

If goals all had the same value, the solution would be that the plan that satisfies the largest number of goals would be the best match. But goals are not featureless objects that all have the same value. Some goals have more value than others. The plan RETRIEVER has to know about the relative value of goals and find a plan that qualitatively maximizes the planner's utility rather than quantitatively maximizing the number of goals satisfied.

The goals themselves have to be in some sort of *value hierarchy* that is used to determine the relative utility of different plans with respect to a set of goals. It is important to distinguish this from the *abstraction hierarchy* that is used to determine the similarity between plans. The abstraction hierarchy tells the RETRIEVER if a plan partially satisfies a goal; the value hierarchy tells it how much that goal is worth. The source of this hierarchy is not important. What is important is the notion of deciding between competing plans on the basis of their relative utility, no matter how that utility is determined.

For example, imagine a memory with two plans: one for a two-story building of glass and steel and one for a five-story building of brick. A set of goals comes in for a five-story building of steel and glass. All other factors being equal, a planner would have to decide which plan would be the best to modify, the plan that uses the materials requested or the one that has the basic structure that has been asked for. In this case, the first plan for the two-story building can be easily modified to have extra stories; the other plan would have to recreated from the bottom up. The choice of the first plan would be on the basis of the ease with which the initial plan could be changed to accommodate all of the planner's goals. The value hierarchy of the goals would be linked to the planner's own abilities. Goals that are easier to incorporate into existing plans are less important than those that are more difficult to satisfy.

In order to get a plan that is the *best match* for a set of goals, a planner needs three kinds of knowledge:

1. A memory of plans indexed by the goals they satisfy;

2. A similarity metric for judging the similarity of goals that is required for determining partial matches;

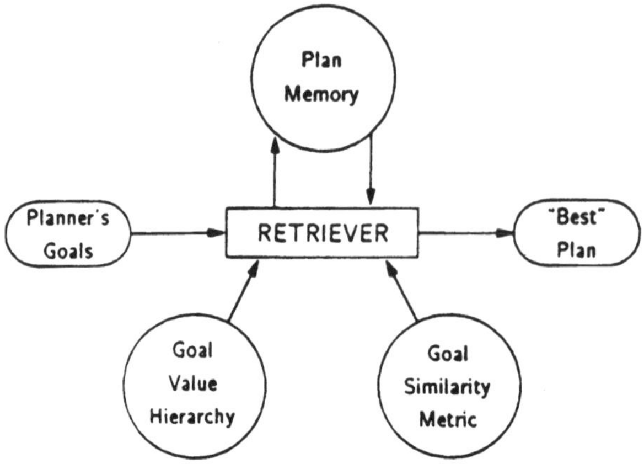

Figure 1.1: The RETRIEVER

3. A value hierarchy of goals used to judge the relative utility of plans with respect to a set of goals.

To integrate this knowledge (Figure 1.1), the RETRIEVER must function as an indexing system that uses goals and abstractions of the goals to discriminate through memory and then use its knowledge of the relative value of the different goals to decide between the overall value of competing plans. This defines a basic case-based planner that takes a set of goals and recalls a plan from memory which satisfies as many of the most important goals as possible, thus maximizing the planner's utility.

For example, in designing a building for use as an office complex there are many goals having to do with access, available floor space and cost that have to be planned for. A plan retriever has to search for a single plan that satisfies as many of the goals as possible, with the understanding that some goals are more important than others and that goals that cannot be satisfied directly can often be partially satisfied. In this case, a past instance of a known office complex that satisfies similar goals can be found and then modified to fit the exact needs of the planner. By finding a baseline plan that satisfies some goals and partially satisfies others, the planner avoids redoing the work that was already done and stored away in memory.

> To get a *best match*, the RETRIEVER needs a plan memory, a goal similarity metric (in the form of an abstraction hierarchy) and a goal value hierarchy.

But this conception isn't complete. Aside from the fact that a RETRIEVER alone is not a real planner, there is also the fact that what has been defined in this section is not quite a full RETRIEVER. It can find past plans on the basis of similarities between surface level goals, but it cannot find past plans on the basis of interactions between those goals. A planner also needs a vocabulary that describes similarities between situations not captured by the surface features alone. This problem will be examined after some discussion of the repair mechanisms from which this vocabulary emerges.

1.5.3 Plan modification

A plan retriever can only find and suggest past plans for new situations: it cannot do anything about modifying these plans to satisfy new goals. Another process, one that modifies plans to satisfy goals not already satisfied by the retrieved plan, must be added to the retrieval process. This process is called plan modification.

In order to modify a plan, a planner needs a variety of information. It needs a library of modification rules that are designed for plans and classes of goals. These rules will be sets of steps that can be added to particular plans to achieve particular goals. These modification rules do not have to be complete plans for achieving any particular goal. They can just be the modifications that are needed to alter an existing plan to achieve that goal. Access to these modification rules will allow a MODIFIER to add new steps to a plan in a way that is sensitive to the type of plan being modified and the particular goal that is being satisfied. A MODIFIER also needs information about specific objects in its domain that outlines how it should accommodate specific features of these objects while using its more general rules. This information, in the form of special purpose critics, will let it tailor the general modifications of a plan to the specific needs of the items required to achieve particular goals. Finally, a MODIFIER needs to know about what the plans it is modifying are supposed to be doing in general. This is needed so that it doesn't violate the goals of the overall plan when it modifies it to satisfy a specific goal.

> To alter old plans to meet new goals, the MODIFIER needs a set of modification rules, critics with knowledge of goal specific requirements and general plan specifications.

Thinking back to architecture, this means that to add a window to an

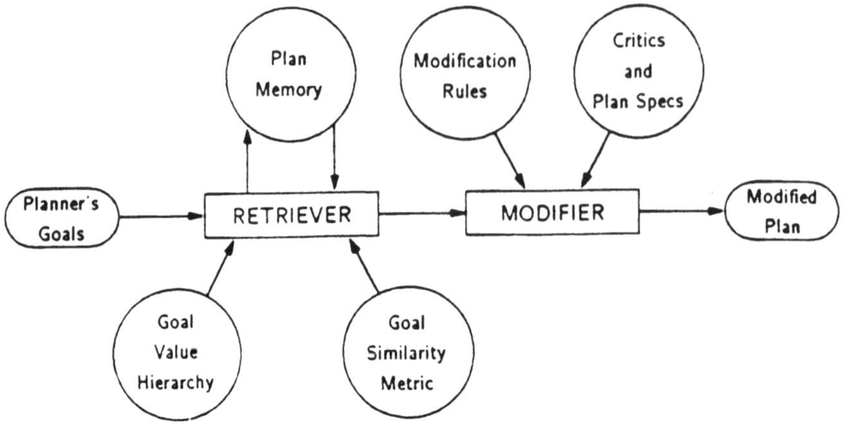

Figure 1.2: The MODIFIER

existing design, a MODIFIER would have to know the goal to be achieved (an added window) and the type of design that is being altered (an office, apartment or house). It would have to take into account the features of the particular window (the type of glass, the size or shape). The changes required for adding a window to the design for an apartment building are different from those that have to be made to a plan for a standard house. By storing modifications in terms of both the goal to be added and the type of plan begin altered, a MODIFIER can be sensitive to these differences. By also storing idiosyncratic steps that deal with the features of particular items in a domain, it can deal with those items within the context of a more general process of plan alteration.

Another example is in the domain of automotive design. Imagine a situation in which one of a planner's goals is to have different parts of a car it is designing be colored red. If the part is an exterior metal piece, the alteration to the initial plan will involve changing the color of the paint that is used to cover the part. If the part is an interior plastic part, the change will involve altering the pigments used in the initial mixing of the plastic. The different initial plans determine different alterations in response to the same goal. No one plan for changing the color will do. Different alterations, associated with the different initial plans, have to be used for the different situations.

The RETRIEVER and MODIFIER are the core of a case-based planner. The RETRIEVER takes a set of goals and finds the past plan that best satisfies them. The MODIFIER takes the plan and the goals that it fails to meet and modifies the plan to satisfy all of the goals it has been given. To do this it needs a set of modification rules, critics with knowledge of goal specific requirements and general plan specifications. (Figure 1.2). For a given set of goals the RETRIEVER finds a good plan and the MODIFIER makes it better.

1.5.4 Plan storage

The idea of case-based planning was initially justified by the need to learn. The whole notion of this kind of planning rests on the desire to alter the planner's abilities on the basis of its own experience. Within the confines of the planner that we have built so far, only one kind of learning is really possible. This is learning by remembering; that is, learning a new plan that has been built by storing it, along with existing plans, in the planner's memory.

The features that are used to store a plan must be the same as those used to access it. The knowledge that a planner needs to store a plan is exactly parallel to the knowledge it needs to find one. In part, the indices used to store plans are the goals that the plan it is storing satisfies. A planner can identify these goals using the general goal information associated with the type of plan it is building and the specific goals satisfied by the particular plan it is storing. General plans have descriptions of the nature of the goals that they satisfy.

For example, the general notion of a plan for an electrical circuit includes the idea that the input and output behavior of the circuit is important. It also includes the notion that the cost, size and durability of actual implementations are important. A particular circuit will have particular characteristics, in terms of I/O, costs of implementation, size and so forth; but it will have other characteristics as well, such as its color or its overall aesthetic character. However, only those features that relate to the goals of circuits in general or to the planner's own immediate goals are used to store the particular plan for later use. The features not relating to the goals satisfied by the plan will not be used to index the plan for a particular circuit in memory. Later, when a new set of goals is being planned for, the planner can use its current goals to search for a plan in memory that satisfies them.

By using only the goals that the plan was designed to meet rather than the entire set of states that are true as a result of running the plan, a planner can limit the features it uses to index a plan in memory while still guaranteeing that the plan is indexed under all the features that are used to retrieve plans.

But a planner cannot just store plans only by the goals they satisfy. As in the RETRIEVER, it has to attend to the circumstances under which they do so. A plan to use an umbrella to stay dry is a great plan to use when it is raining, but a less than effective one to use when the planner wants to go into a flooded basement. Plans and planning episodes have to be distinguished by the goals they satisfy *and* by the circumstances under which they do so. The circumstances that effect the choice of a plan in the initial construction have to be included in the indexing of the plan in memory.

The STORER aids in the building of later plans by storing the work that has been done by the RETRIEVER and the MODIFIER. The STORER does nothing to help in the building of a present plan. The job of the STORER is not to alter the plan that has been built. Rather, it must alter the memories of the planner itself, giving it access to a complete plan that previously had to be built from another plan and from the application of the planner's modification rules. Although this only means a savings of time at this stage, later, when the planner is given the ability to recover from its own failures, it will mean that the planner will be able to use memories of past plans to avoid repeating mistakes that waste other resources.

The vocabulary used by the RETRIEVER and STORER to access plans in memory is not yet complete. In particular, the vocabulary currently lacks any way to describe plans in terms of the problems they avoid. Both the STORER and the RETRIEVER require access to this vocabulary, giving the STORER the ability to place a plan in memory indexed by the fact that it avoids certain problems and giving the RETRIEVER the ability to find plans when it anticipates the need to avoid the same problems. We will hold-off our discussion of this vocabulary, however, until after we have outlined the process that gives rise to it: plan repair.

The learning by remembering that the STORER does is not the only kind of learning that will be done by the planner we are building. This kind of learning will be augmented with a module that does two other types of learning: it will learn the features in a situation that predict problems; and it will learn new rules for adapting particular items to the general modification plans associated with the plan types. This planner will not only remember new plans, it will also will learn to anticipate problems and build rules for adding new goals to already existing plans.

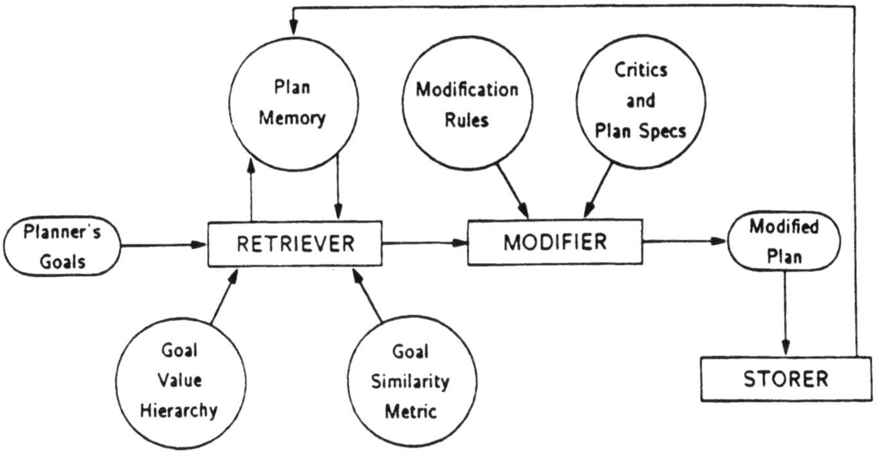

Figure 1.3: The STORER

> To place new plans in memory, the STORER needs to index them under the same features that the RETRIEVER uses to find them: the goals that they satisfy and the situations in which they are appropriate.

A basic case-based planner must incorporate these three processes:

1. A plan retriever that finds a plan from the past that is a "best match" with the current situation;

2. A plan modifier that can alter a plan with changes that are responsive to the goal being added and the plan being altered;

3. A plan storer that can place a complete plan into memory indexed by the goals that it satisfies and the conditions under which it does so.

1.5.5 Plan repair

For a planner to be practical, it has to be able to repair failed plans. No matter how good the planner is, at one time or another it will have to confront problems that arise out of its own lack of knowledge and the limits of its own heuristics. Given that the planner is going to make mistakes, we have to give it some mechanism for repairing the faulty plans it builds. This mechanism will be called the REPAIRER.

The input to the REPAIRER has to have two parts: a faulty plan and some description of the fault itself. In other words, the input must include the plan and either the desired state that it has failed to achieve or the undesired state that it has caused to come about. How a planner gets this information can vary. It can actually run its plans and examine the results. It can run simulations of the plans and use their results to diagnose errors. It can even ask an outside source if the plan will do what it wants it to. But no matter how it does it, a planner has to be able to notice and respond to its own failures.

The basic approach that we will take here is to first diagnose and then repair. The REPAIRER is going to have to have some vocabulary for describing plan failures that can be used to index methods for repairing the plan itself. This vocabulary can be a simple statement of the fact that the plan is faulty. Unfortunately, a statement like, "The plan has failed" doesn't provide a lot of guidance as to how to go about repairing it.

Given that a planner has to understand the goals it is trying to achieve and the states that are associated with these goals in order to even *recognize* planning failures, it should therefore also have access to its vocabulary of goals in order to *describe* those failures. This would allow the planner to make statements to itself like, "The engine failed to start when I turned the key." This vocabulary, however, doesn't capture all of the information that can be used to access appropriate repair methods because there could be many ways in which the states that constitute the failure could have come into being. A single type of failure such as an engine failure can be the result of many different situations, so the information about the failure of the goal provides only a little guidance as to how to deal with the problem. The best it can give is a method for responding to the failed goal in general, which may or may not be appropriate to the facts of the matter. For example, an engine may fail to start because there is no gas in the car or the battery is dead. A vocabulary that includes only the fact that the engine has failed to start could not be used to find the best strategy for dealing with the problem.

A more extensive vocabulary must include an explanation of *why* a failure has occurred along with a description of the failure itself. This would mean forming descriptions like, "The engine failed to start because a wire leading to the starter has shorted out on the body where it passes behind the side-mounted air-filter. The heat exchange from the air-filter melts the insulation on the wire." The explanation, because it points to the states and actions that participate in causing the failure, provides the focus as to what parts of a design have to be changed. Even if a specific method for fixing the particular problem doesn't already exist, one can be generated out of a method for dealing with the general problem (a side-effect of one part violating the maintenance conditions of another) and the particular states (the side-effect is excess heat, the maintenance condition is the fact of the insulation and so on). This could be used to suggest general methods that could be instantiated, using the specific facts of the current problem. This would allow a response like recovering from the side-effect (find a way to drain off the heat from the air-filter) or altering the part being interfered with to compensate for the presence of the side-effect (use a heat-resistant insulation on the wire) or changing the initial plan being interfered with (reroute the wire altogether).

No matter what vocabulary the REPAIRER uses, the idea is the same: describe the failure and use this description to find methods for dealing with it. Along with the vocabulary for describing planning failures, the REPAIRER needs a set of repair methods that can be accessed with that vocabulary. These methods should be organized such that the description of a given failure will access those and only those repair methods that have a chance of repairing that particular plan fault. This organization is the main reason that the REPAIRER describes the problem at all. This relationship between problem and repair is like the relationship between goals and plans. Plans are indexed under the goals they satisfy and repair methods are indexed under the types of problems they resolve.

A plan repairer needs access to two types of knowledge: a vocabulary for describing plan failures and a set of repair methods that correspond to those descriptions. With these it can describe problems and then use those descriptions to access the strategies for dealing with them.

There is a learning aspect of the REPAIRER that goes beyond the confines of the single plan it is repairing. That is, once the plan is repaired, it is not only a plan that satisfies a set of goals, it is also a plan that avoids a particular problem. The goals the planner was originally planning for have interacted to cause a failure. The repaired plan, because it is the repaired version of the failed plan, is now designed to cope with that interaction between goals and to avoid the failure altogether. If the REPAIRER allows the STORER to store the new plan only by the goals it satisfies directly, it will lose the information that the plan is also one to use if the planner is trying to avoid a particular problem.

The failures that a plan avoids while satisfying other goals cannot be identified by looking at a finished plan without examining the reasoning that went into constructing it. It is only during the planning process, when the plan fails and is repaired, that the problems arising out of certain interactions can be identified. The fact that a plan avoids a particular problem can only be seen by the REPAIRER, and the REPAIRER has to then tell the STORER about the goals that the repaired plan satisfies and the failures that it avoids along the way. Given this added vocabulary, the STORER can place successful plans in memory, under the goals they achieve and the problems they avoid.

> With the addition of the REPAIRER, the STORER can now index plans by the problems that they avoid as well as the goals that they satisfy.

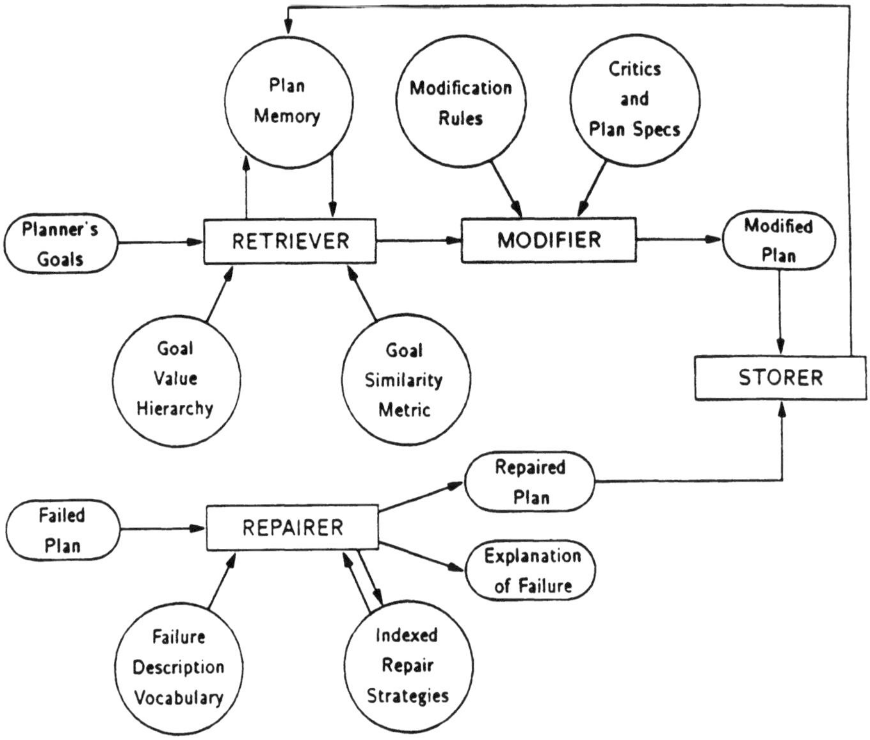

Figure 1.4: The REPAIRER

The REPAIRER is invoked only when a plan fails. Its task is to repair the plan and tell the STORER how to characterize it so that it can be found again in a similar problem situation. The REPAIRER is called only after a plan has been modified and run, only after the plan has been committed to by the RETRIEVER and MODIFIER. It requires a vocabulary for describing planning problems and a set of strategies that are indexed by the descriptions of the problems that they solve. Once it repairs a plan, it then has to hand it to the STORER for placement in memory, indexed by the goals that the plan satisfies and the problems it avoids (Figure 1.4).

> To repair failed plans and describe them to the STORER, the REPAIRER requires a vocabulary of plan failures and repair strategies that are indexed by that vocabulary.

1.5.6 Learning from failure

A case-based planner indexes the plans it builds by the problems it avoids while achieving its goals; but there is still a stumbling block to reusing that plan for similar problems in the future. This is the planner's ability to figure out when the problem is going to arise again.

The fact that a plan solves a particular problem is not useful unless the planner can anticipate that problem in the appropriate circumstances and use that prediction to find the plan in memory. The usefulness of a plan that solves a problem rests not only on having the plan indexed by the fact that it does so. It also rests on the ability to predict that the planner is going to need a plan that solves that particular problem. Having a plan that solves a problem does the planner no good if it cannot recognize the circumstances in which that problem will arise. The ability to predict when a problem is going to arise in the future, however, rests on the ability to figure out why it happened in the past. To do that the planner needs a function that can decide which features of a failed plan caused the failure to occur. Then it can extrapolate from these to the features in later situations that will predict when the problem will arise again. This function, which does the credit assignment as to which features are to blame for a failure, is called the ASSIGNER.

The job of the ASSIGNER is to look at a failed plan and decide what circumstances will be predictive of that failure in the future. The knowledge it uses can vary in much the same way that the knowledge used by the REPAIRER can vary: it can be simple and unreliable or complex and robust.

> To decide which features in a situation are to blame for a failure, the ASSIGNER needs to be able to describe the causes of the failure. The more extensive its vocabulary for this description, the more exact its credit assignment will be.

Take for example a situation in which a plane traveler has missed a ride to his hotel with a fellow traveller because he has had to wait for his baggage to come off the plane. Here is a case where a failure has occurred that can be related to the features that will predict it: checking baggage while travelling with others. When later performing a similar plan, that is, taking a flight with other people and checking baggage, a planner that can recall the failure and now plan for it by taking only carry-on luggage will be in a better position than one that could not anticipate the problem.

In the example of the failed engine: the fact that a new design for a side-mounted air filter caused a set of wires to be routed through an area of high heat should be assigned the blame for the problem. If this problem arose out of the combination of default plans, this assignment has to be such that when the goals associated with those plans are asked for again (such as the goal for a side-mounted air filter), the problem can be predicted and thus avoided.

No matter what the method, the ASSIGNER's task is to mark features in a situation as predictive of the problems that arose in that situation. Like the STORER, its function has no effect on problems that the planner is currently working on. Instead, its job is to assure that the planner is able to predict when the current problem is going to arise again in later circumstances. Its output can be a set of inference rules that are fired in the early stages of planning, links going from surface goals to predictions or a table of effects that matches features to predictions. The form of the output is not the issue here. The issue is that the planner, because the ASSIGNER is able to identify the features that predict a problem, is now able to anticipate that problem and use the goal of avoiding it to find a plan that does so. While it looks at problems along with the REPAIRER its output is not a plan, but is instead a knowledge base of possible problems that can arise and the circumstances that predict them (Figure 1.5).

1.5.7 Problem anticipation

When a plan fails, the features that participated in that failure are built into a base of rules or connections that allows the planner to anticipate problems that will arise on the basis of the goals it is planning for and the situation it is in. Another module, which anticipates problems on the basis of these features, has the task of taking these rules or connections and making the predictions.

The job of an ANTICIPATOR is to look at the planner's goals and the situation that surrounds them and decide if there is anything in the

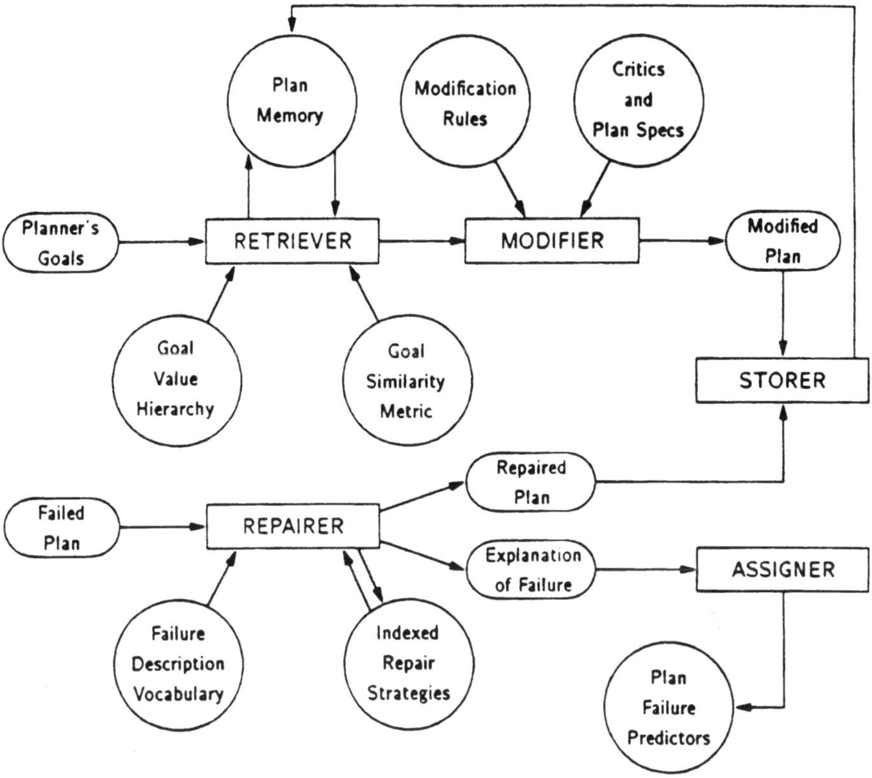

Figure 1.5: The ASSIGNER

situation that is predictive of a problem *before* any other planning is done. This is so the prediction of a problem can be used to find the plans in memory that avoid it. The whole point of an ANTICIPATOR is to provide information about problems that have to be avoided, information that will be used by a RETRIEVER to find a plan that does so, so it makes sense that an ANTICIPATOR has to be called prior to any search for plans (Figure 1.6). This problem anticipation is done prior to the initial search for a plan in order to give the planner the information about what problems it has to avoid so it can search for a plan that does so.

The knowledge that it uses is the base of information about the features that predict problems that the ASSIGNER has built up as a result of examining the planner's failures. The more failures a planner has, the better it becomes at anticipating problems and thus avoiding them.

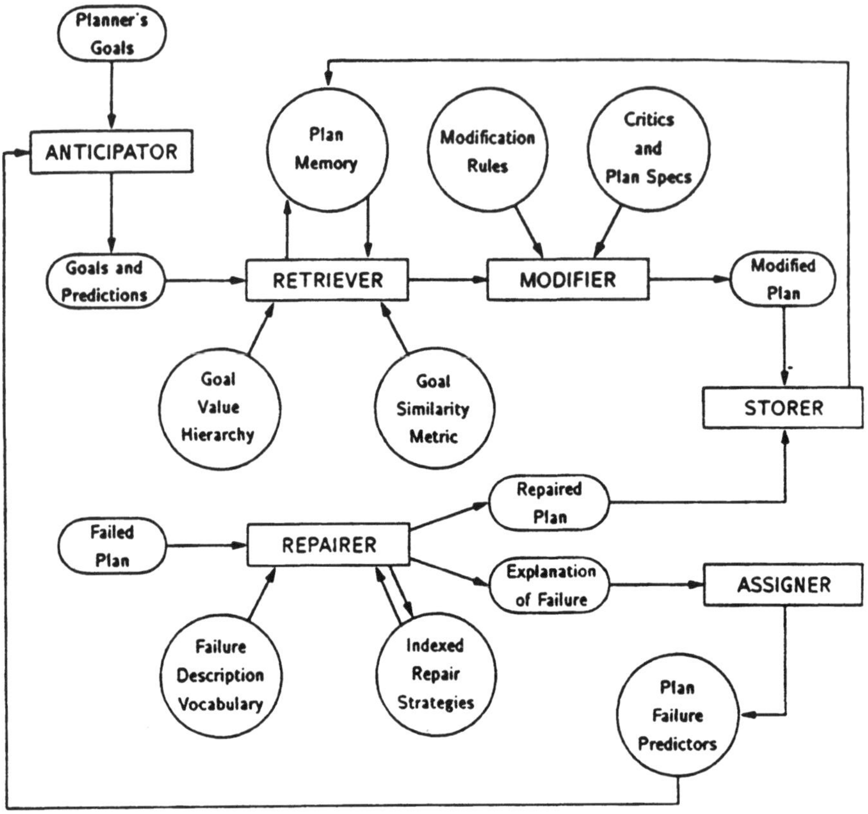

Figure 1.6: The ANTICIPATOR

> To anticipate a problem on the basis of surface features, the ANTICIPATOR needs the base of information built by the ASSIGNER.

Let us examine again the example of the traveller. The task of the ANTICIPATOR is to take the features of the situation that the planner is dealing with and recall the problems that have arisen in past situations to handle them. By being reminded of the problems caused by waiting for luggage, a planner can either find a past plan that deals with the problem or alter another plan in response to the prediction. The problem can be avoided because it can be predicted.

Likewise, when the goal to have a side-mounted air filter arises again, the prediction of the problems that result from the modifications required to satisfy this goal can be used either to find the past plan that already deals with the problem or the past repairs that were made that could also be made to a plan, so that the problem is avoided. In this way, problems that have been encountered before can be avoided. This is in contrast to a procedure in which plans are built without attending to past problems, a procedure in which the problems are repeated and must be repeatedly repaired.

There is an important relationship between plans stored in memory and the tasks of the ANTICIPATOR and the RETRIEVER. Once a problem plan has been repaired, it is stored in memory, indexed by the fact that it deals with a particular problem. At this point, however, there is no way for the planner to look at a new situation and predict that it will have to avoid that problem. So there is no way for it to find the plan in situations where the problem will come up again. Because of this, it will continue to make the same mistake because it does not know that the planning approach it used before in a similar situation led to problems. If it can figure out the causes of a failure, however, it can use this information to anticipate the problem in similar situations and look for a plan that avoids it. The ASSIGNER figures out the causes of problem. The ANTICIPATOR then uses the information built up by the ASSIGNER to predict the problem again when similar causes are present. The ANTICIPATOR notices that a problem is going to arise and then tells the RETRIEVER to find a plan that avoids it.

This communication from ANTICIPATOR to RETRIEVER is important in that it gives the RETRIEVER the added vocabulary for describing planning situations that the STORER is using to place plans in memory. The STORER, because the REPAIRER can tell it what problems a plan solves, is able to place plans in memory indexed by the fact that they do so. The RETRIEVER, because it has the ANTICIPATOR to look at the surface features of a situation and provide predictions concerning the same problems, is now able to request a plan that avoids that problem. So plans that deal with particular planning difficulties due to the interactions between plan steps can be stored and retrieved, indexed by the fact that they do so. The STORER uses information about the problems the plan solves to put it into memory and the RETRIEVER uses the predictions of the reoccurrence of those problems to get them back out.

> With the addition of the ANTICIPATOR, the RETRIEVER can search for plans on the basis of the problems that they avoid as well as the goals they satisfy.

A final point about the ANTICIPATOR: nticipation plays a role in case-based planning similar to that of *projection* in more traditional systems. They both serve to warn the planner of difficulties that might arise in running the plan. There is a substantial difference between the two concepts, however. Projection makes use of *all* of the planner's domain knowledge to simulate and thus predict any problems that might come up in a plan. Anticipation makes use of the planner's experience with failures to mke this prediction. The difference is not a subtle one: projection involves exploring all possible interactions between the results of plan steps while anticipation involves exploring only those possibilities *that have actually given rise to problems in the past.*

Given Chapman's recent result concerning the complexity of projection [Chapman 87], it seems clear that projection in its current form is an untenable approach to teasing out planning problems. This need for a new view of prediction, one that is more heuristic in nature, only serves to confirm our initial belief that anticipation on the basis of known failures is a viable alternative to the more complete, yet far less tractable approach of projection.

1.5.8 The final package

The basic case-based planner that grows out of the need to reuse plans and adapt them for new goals functions as follows: A set of goals is handed to the planner and sent directly to the ANTICIPATOR. The ANTICIPATOR, based on the knowledge built up by the ASSIGNER, makes any predictions of planning problems that it thinks will arise out of the current goals. The goals are then handed to the RETRIEVER along with the ANTICIPATOR's predictions of problems that have to be avoided. The RETRIEVER uses both to search for a plan in memory that best satisfies the goals it is trying to achieve and that avoids any problems that have been anticipated. The result is a past plan that matches some or all of the goals now being planned for.

This plan is sent to the MODIFIER, which adds or substitutes new steps to the plan in order to make it satisfy any of the planner's goals that it does not yet achieve. Once modified, the plan is run and the results checked against the goals of the planner. If there is a failure, either because a desired goal has not been achieved or because an undesired state has resulted from the plan, the plan is given to the REPAIRER.

The REPAIRER builds a characterization of the failure and uses this to find and apply one of its repair methods. The repaired plan, along with a description of the problems that had to be solved along the way, are then sent to the STORER for placement into memory. The STORER indexes the new plan by the goals it achieves and the problems it avoids. Now the plan can be used again in similar circumstances in the future.

While the REPAIRER is repairing the plan, the ASSIGNER is deciding which features in the original request, that is, which goals, interacted to cause the failure to occur. Once it has done this, it marks these features as predictive of the problem so that the ANTICIPATOR can anticipate the problem if it encounters the goals in a later input.

This planner does two things as it builds a plan. It is trying to satisfy a set of goals using its model of what plans are appropriate for different situations. But it is also testing that model of the appropriateness of those plans against the real world so that later planning will be easier and more reliable.

To serve its first function, the planner has to react to failures by repairing the present plan. To serve its second function, it has to alter its view of the world by adding new plans indexed by the problems they solve and by altering its predictions so that it can anticipate those problems and find the plans that avoid them.

The fact that planning and learning are so intimately connected in case-based planning is no accident. The power of a case-based planner is directly dependent on its ability to reuse plans, and the only way to reuse plans effectively is to take seriously the notion of learning which features in a planning situation determine when they are appropriate to use.

Chapter 2

Learning from Planning

2.1 Learning from cases

A case-based system learns by planning. It learns by storing the results of its own planning experiences in memory. This makes it a bit odd to talk about some aspects of learning from planning. A case-based planner *does* learn new plans, but learning a new plan actually involves deciding which features are important for indexing a plan that it has already built. The learning is not in the building, it is in the storing and indexing of things that already have been built.

> A case-based planner learns by correctly indexing its planning experiences in memory.

A planner can improve by recalling its past experiences, anticipating problems it has encountered before, so that they can be avoided. The task of learning in this case is not building the failure, it is deciding which features caused it in the original case and thus which features will predict it in later cases. By linking the features which are predictive of a failure to the memory of it, the planner can anticipate problems before they occur and use this anticipation to retrieve a plan in memory that solves the problem.

If a surgeon above encounters a problem while performing an operation, such as a patient's low blood pressure being reduced even further by a particular anesthetic, thus leading to heart failure, it makes sense for him to learn something from this failure. In particular it makes sense for him to learn that patients with low blood pressure will go into cardiac arrest if this anesthetic is used on them. By linking these features to the memory of the failure, the surgeon will be able to anticipate the problem when it arises and use this prediction to find a plan that avoids the problem.

Memories of past planning experience can also be helpful to a planner in dealing with the situation in which it predicts a failure but is unable to find a plan that deals with it. In these situations, the memory of the change that was made to repair a past plan in response to the same failure can often be used to repair the current plan before it is run. Just as the anticipation of a failure can point the planner to a past plan that deals with it, in the absence of that plan it could point the planner to a past repair that could be applied to whatever new plan is being devised. The problem of recalling past repairs is somewhat different than recalling past plans in that not all repairs can be transferred between plans. Like memories of plans, memories of past repairs have to be indexed by the failures that they deal with, but they also have to have some provision for the fact that not all repairs to a problem can be transferred for use on all plans in which that failure arises.

Even in this case, the problem is not to construct a new piece of information. The repair itself is constructed by the planner. It is only then that any learning mechanism comes into play. Here again, the job of the learner is to choose the features that will be used to index the information. A repair such as using an alternate anesthetic when performing appendectomies can be stored as a general repair to other plans that will be performed on low blood pressure patients. The overall appendectomy plan is saved so that it can be used again, but the specific repair of altering the anesthetic is saved as well so that it also be used to repair other plans in which the same problem is predicted.

In all three of these learning situations, the main task of the learner is to figure out which features a piece of information should be indexed under. Any generalization that is done takes the form of generalizing these features without changing the specificity of the information being stored. The plans that are placed in memory are the actual plans created by the planner. They are not generalized versions of these plans. The goals that are used to index them, however, are generalized so that the plans can be found in situations that are similar if not identical to those in which they were originally constructed.

The theory of case-based planning presented here is a theory of learning in each of these three areas. It is a theory of learning new plans, new problems and new solutions. It is a theory of learning within the context of active planning.

> A case-based planner learns new plans, the features that predict failures and past repairs to faulty plans that it can reuse. This learning is accomplished by saving the different results of the planner's own experience.

2.2 CHEF: A case-based planner

The theory of case-based planning in this book is implemented in the computer program CHEF. CHEF is a case-based planner. CHEF's approach to planning is to make use of memory whenever possible. It begins planning by using its memory of past failures to warn of problems. It then uses its memory of successes find the best plan to modify for its current goals and problems. If it has a plan failure, CHEF treats it as a failure of its understanding of the world and explains the failure so that it can repair the plan and the knowledge of the world that allowed it to create the plan. Finally, it saves its successes in memory, indexed by the goals that they satisfy and the problems that they avoid, so that they can be used again to satisfy similar goals and avoid similar problems.

CHEF's domain is Szechwan cooking. Its task is to build new recipes on the basis of a user's requests for dishes with particular ingredients and tastes. Because it is building recipes, it has a constraint that many planners do not: it has to build integrated plans for multiple goals in which all of the goals are satisfied by a single plan. This is similar to the constraint in many design domains, such as industrial design or circuit construction, in which a single object has to meet a set of specifications.

Here is an example of CHEF planning for the problem of building a stir-fry dish with beef and broccoli. In the pages that follows, all text bracketed on top and bottom by bold lines is actual output produced by the CHEF program.

The input to CHEF is a set of goals to be satisfied with a single integrated plan. In this case CHEF is given three goals: the goal to have a stir-fried dish, the goal to include beef and the goal to include broccoli. Instead of searching for individual plans that satisfy each of the goals separately and then merging them, as most hierarchical planners would do, CHEF searches its memory for a single plan that matches, or partially matches, as many of the goals as possible. In cases where multiple plans match its goals, CHEF chooses one of the plans at random.

```
Searching for plan that satisfies -
   Include beef in the dish.
   Include broccoli in the dish.
   Make a stir-fry dish.

Found recipe -> REC2 BEEF-WITH-GREEN-BEANS

Recipe exactly satisfies goals ->
    Make a stir-fry dish.
    Include beef in the dish.

Recipe partially matches ->
    Include broccoli in the dish.
          in that the recipe satisfies:
                   Include vegetables in the dish.
```

> CHEF begins planning by finding a single plan that satisfies as many of its active goals as possible.

Once the base-line plan is found, it is modified to match whatever goals it doesn't already satisfy. The modification is controlled by rules related to the kind of dish being designed (in this case a STIR-FRY dish), and by the goal that the original plan is being modified to satisfy (the goal to include broccoli). This kind of knowledge in cooking is similar to the knowledge in other design domains such as architecture. In architecture, instead of knowing how to modify STIR-FRY plans, an expert knows how to alter plans for houses and apartment buildings. Likewise, instead of knowing how to add broccoli or beef to an existing recipe, an expert would know how to add windows or doors to an existing plan.

In this case, the fact that there is a partial match between the target goal, including broccoli, and an object in the existing recipe, green beans, tells the planner that it can replace the broccoli for the green beans directly. Other structures, called *object critics*, allow it to correctly reduce the cooking time of the vegetables to account for the difference between the requirements of green beans and broccoli. They also tell the planner that it has to chop the broccoli before stir-frying it.

```
Building new name for copy of BEEF-WITH-GREEN-BEANS
Calling recipe BEEF-AND-BROCCOLI

Modifying recipe: BEEF-AND-BROCCOLI
to satisfy: Include broccoli in the dish.

Placing some broccoli in recipe BEEF-AND-BROCCOLI

- Considering ingredient-critic:
   Before doing step: Stir fry the -Variable-
    do: Chop the broccoli into pieces the size of chunks.
- ingredient-critic applied.
```

CHEF alters old plans to satisfy new goals using a set of modification rules and a set of *object critics.*

Once these modifications are made, the planner has a plan that should satisfy all of the initial goals it was asked to plan for. This plan has the same form as the initial case retrieved from memory: A set of ingredients (or props), a set of actions to be taken and a set of goals that the plan should now satisfy.

```
              BEEF-AND-BROCCOLI

              A half pound of beef
              Two tablespoons of soy sauce
              One teaspoon of rice wine
              A half tablespoon of corn starch
              One teaspoon of sugar
              A half pound of broccoli
              One teaspoon of salt
              One chunk of garlic

Chop the garlic into pieces the size of matchheads.
Shred the beef.
Marinate the beef in the garlic, sugar, corn starch,
rice wine and soy sauce.
Chop the broccoli into pieces the size of chunks.
```

```
Stir fry the spices, rice wine and beef for one minute.
Add the broccoli to the spices, rice wine and beef.
Stir fry the spices, rice wine, broccoli and beef
for three minutes.
Add the salt to the spices, rice wine, broccoli and beef.
```

There is more to CHEF's knowledge of this plan than just the steps that are included in it, however. It also knows about the goals that should be satisfied when it is run. These goals are derived from its knowledge of stir-frying and its understanding of what items are important in this recipe. So it has the understanding that running this plan should result in the following:

```
The beef is now tender.
The dish now tastes savory.
The broccoli is now crisp.
The dish now tastes salty.
The dish now tastes sweet.
The dish now tastes like garlic.
```

> CHEF derives the goals that a plan should satisfy from general plan specifications and the particulars of the current plan.

But not all plans work the first time. In this plan, the goal to have the broccoli crisp will fail, because it is being stir-fried with the beef and is cooked in the liquid that the beef produces. This was not problematic in the original BEEF-AND-GREEN-BEAN recipe because green beans are simply more robust vegetables than broccoli.

2.2.1 When plans fail

When a plan fails it is because the planner's understanding of the world has failed. It has expected that the plan would have a result that it has not had. So the explanation of a failure serves two functions: it identifies the parts of the plan that have to be altered and it identifies the places where the planner's knowledge is faulty.

CHEF discovers the failure by monitoring a simulated execution of the plan it has produced. This simulation is the program's equivalent of real world execution. The simulator consists of a set of inference rules that are used to determine the outcome of each step of the plan. Once the plan has been run, CHEF checks the final states that have resulted against its goals, looking for any failures to achieve its positive goals as well as any instances of negative states that it would like to avoid.

```
Checking goals of recipe -> BEEF-AND-BROCCOLI

Recipe -> BEEF-AND-BROCCOLI has failed goals.

The goal: The broccoli is now crisp.
is not satisfied.
It is instead the case that: The broccoli is now soggy.

Unfortunately: The broccoli is now a bad texture.
In that: The broccoli is now soggy.

Changing name of recipe BEEF-AND-BROCCOLI
to BAD-BEEF-AND-BROCCOLI
```

> CHEF checks the goals of a plan against the results of a simulation of the plan that is its equivalent of the real world.

A plan failure such as this means two things to CHEF. First, it must repair the plan itself, changing the steps so that the failure does not recur. Second, it has to repair its understanding of the world, an understanding that has been shown to be faulty in light of this failure. For both of these tasks it is important that CHEF understands exactly why the failure has come about. It is not enough that it can point to the fact that the broccoli isn't crisp and call this a failure. It must also be able to explain why this particular failure has happened. The final state that defines the failure is not enough. It must have an *explanation* of why it has occurred. It has to understand the series of steps and states that led to the failure in order to alter its plan and its understanding of the world. This explanation gives it a description of the problem that can then be used to access repair strategies fitted to that problem. Because a causal explanation is used to describe the problem, a set of fixes that are aimed at altering the causality behind the failure can be used instead of weaker methods such as back-up or total replanning.

2.2.2 Explaining plan failures

The explanation of a failure provides a causal description of why it has occurred. An explanation describes the state that defines the failure, the step that resulted in it, and the conditions that had to be true for it to come about. It is also a description of what the planner was trying to do when the failure occurred. It includes a description of the goals being served by the steps and states that caused the failure and even those being served by other steps in the plan that may have participated in the failure. It identifies what has to be changed in the plan to solve the present problem and also identifies what has to be changed in the planner's knowledge of the world so that the failure will not occur again.

CHEF explains failures using a set of inference rules that tell it about the effects of each step in its domain on each object in its domain. It uses these rules to determine what the nature of the failure is, why it has occurred, and what goals are served by the steps and states that led to the failure. These rules are the same as those used to simulate the plan, meaning that CHEF can always explain the failures it encounters. These rules are not used in the initial stage of anticipation simply because of the computational complexity of non-heuristic projection.

These rules are used to chain through the steps and states of the plan to answer a set of questions that will form the explanation of why the failure has occurred. Each of these questions is associated with a particular point in the causal chain explaining the failure. Each answer is a step from the original plan or a state caused by one of these steps. These answers are used to fill in a causal framework which will later be used to find a set of repair strategies for fixing the plan.

```
Explaining the following failures:
 It is not the case that: The broccoli is now crisp.
in that: The broccoli is now soggy.
 The broccoli is now a bad texture.
in that: The broccoli is now soggy.
In: BAD-BEEF-AND-BROCCOLI

ASKING THE QUESTION: 'What is the failure?'

ANSWER-> The failure is:  It is not the case that:  The broccoli is
         now crisp.
```

```
ASKING THE QUESTION: 'What is the preferred state?'

ANSWER-> The preferred state is: The broccoli is now crisp.

ASKING THE QUESTION:
   'What was the plan to achieve the preferred state?'

ANSWER-> The plan was:  Stir fry the sugar, soy sauce, rice wine,
         garlic, corn starch, broccoli and beef for three minutes.

ASKING THE QUESTION:
   'What were the conditions that led to the failure?'

ANSWER-> The condition was:  There is thin liquid in the pan
         from the beef equaling 4.8 teaspoons.

ASKING THE QUESTION:
   'What caused the conditions that led to the failure?'

ANSWER-> There is thin liquid in the pan from the beef equaling
         4.8 teaspoons was caused by:  Stir fry the sugar,
         soy sauce, rice wine, garlic, corn starch, broccoli
              and beef for three minutes.

ASKING THE QUESTION:
   'Do the conditions that caused the failure satisfy any goals?'

ANSWER-> The condition:  There is thin liquid in the pan from
         the beef equaling 4.8 teaspoons is a side effect
         only and meets no goals.

ASKING THE QUESTION:
  'What goals does the step which caused the condition enabling the
   failure satisfy?'

ANSWER-> The step:  Stir fry the sugar, soy sauce, rice wine,
         garlic, corn starch, broccoli and beef for three
         minutes.
         enables the satisfaction of the following goals:
         The dish now tastes savory.
         The beef is now tender.
```

At this point, then CHEF knows what steps and states combined to cause the current failure. Using its inference rules for the domain it has been able to construct a causal chain that explains why the failure has occurred. It also knows which goals were being pursued in taking the actions and creating the states that led to its failure.

CHEF explains the failures that it encounters through a causal description of why they have occurred.

2.2.3 Plan repair strategies and TOPs

This explanation serves two functions. For the short-term task of repairing the plan, it describes the planning problem in a general causal vocabulary that can be used to access some equally general plan-debugging strategies. Repair techniques are indexed in memory under causal descriptions of the situations that they are built to handle. For the long-term task of altering the planner's approach to later problems so it will not repeat its current mistake, the explanation serves to point out which features in the domain interact to cause this sort of failure to occur.

The explanation of the failure is used to find a structure in memory that organizes a set of strategies for solving the problem described by the explanation. These structures, called Thematic Organization Packets or TOPs [Schank 82], are similar in function to the critics found in HACKER [Sussman 75] and NOAH [Sacerdoti 75]. Each TOP is indexed by the description of a particular type of planning problem and each organizes a set of strategies for dealing with that type of problem. These strategies take the form of general repair rules such as REORDER steps and RECOVER from side-effects. Each general strategy is filled in with the specifics of the particular problem to build a description of a change in the plan that would solve the current problem. This description is used as an index into a library of plan modifiers in the cooking domain. The modifications found are then tested against one another using rules concerning the efficacy of the different changes and the one that is most likely to succeed is chosen.

The idea behind these structures is simple. There is a great deal of planning information that is related to the *interactions* between plans and goals. This information cannot be tied to any individual goal or plan but is instead tied to problems that rise out of their combination. In planning, one important aspect of this information concerns how to deal with problems due to the interactions between plan steps. Planning TOPs provide a means to store this information. Each TOP corresponds to a planning problem due to the causal interaction between the steps and the states of a plan. When a problem arises, a causal analysis of it provides the information needed to identify the TOP that actually describes the problem in abstract terms. But the TOPs are not there to just describe problems. Under each TOP is a set of strategies designed to deal with the problem the TOP describes. By finding the TOP that relates to a problem a planner actually finds the strategies that will help to fix that problem.

In this example, the explanation points to SIDE-EFFECT:DISABLED-CONDITION:CONCURRENT, a TOP related to the interaction between concurrent plans in which a side effect of one violates a precondition of the other. This is because the side effect of liquid coming from the stir-frying of the beef is disabling a precondition attached to the broccoli stir-fry plan that the pan being used is dry.

The causal description of the failure is used to access this TOP out of the twenty that the program knows about. All of these TOPs are associated with causal configurations that lead to failures and store strategies for fixing the situations that they describe. For example, one TOP is DESIRED-EFFECT:DISABLED-CONDITION:SERIAL, a TOP that describes a situation in which the desired effect of a step interferes with the satisfaction conditions of a later step. The program was able to recognize that the current situation was a case of SIDE-EFFECT:DISABLED-CONDITION:CONCURRENT because it has determined that no goal is satisfied by the interfering condition (the liquid in the pan), that the condition disables a satisfaction requirement of a step (that the pan be dry) and that the two steps are one and the same (the stir-fry step). Had the liquid in the pan satisfied a goal, the situation would have been recognized as a case of DESIRED-EFFECT:DISABLED-CONDITION:CONCURRENT because the violating condition would actually be a goal-satisfying state.

```
Found TOP TOP1 -> SIDE-EFFECT:DISABLED-CONDITION:CONCURRENT
TOP -> SIDE-EFFECT:DISABLED-CONDITION:CONCURRENT has 3
       strategies associated with it:
          SPLIT-AND-REFORM
          ALTER-PLAN:SIDE-EFFECT
          ADJUNCT-PLAN
```

> CHEF uses its causal description of a problem to find a TOP that has strategies which will solve it.

The TOP SIDE-EFFECT:DISABLED-CONDITION:CONCURRENT has three strategies associated with it, SPLIT-AND-REFORM, which suggests breaking the parallel plans into serial steps; ALTER-PLAN:SIDE-EFFECT, which suggests using a different plan for the initial step that caused the side-effect; and ADJUNCT-PLAN, which suggests making use of an adjunct plan that would disable the side-effect. In this example, CHEF can only find one possible instantiation, a specialization of the strategy SPLIT-AND-REFORM, so it is applied directly to the problem. The other modifications suggested have no actual instantiation, given the facts of the situation.

There are two stages to this process: finding the different changes that the strategies suggest and then actually implementing the one that CHEF judges to be the best in this situation.

The first step implemented using two different techniques. CHEF first tries to find specific versions of its strategies in a library of successful modifications it has previously made. If this fails, it uses a STRIPS-like problem solver to plan for the state suggested by the strategy.

```
Applying TOP -> SIDE-EFFECT:DISABLED-CONDITION:CONCURRENT
to failure it is not the case that: The broccoli is now crisp.
in recipe BAD-BEEF-AND-BROCCOLI

Asking questions needed for evaluating strategy:
   SPLIT-AND-REFORM

ASKING -> Can plan
           Stir fry the sugar, soy sauce, rice wine, garlic,
           corn starch, broccoli and beef for three minutes.
          be split and rejoined

Found plan: Instead of doing step: Stir fry the sugar,
 soy sauce, rice wine, garlic, corn starch, broccoli
 and beef for three minutes
 do:
 S1 = Stir fry the broccoli for three minutes.
 S2 = Remove the broccoli from the result of action S1.
 S3 = Stir fry the sugar, soy sauce, rice wine, garlic,
 corn starch and beef for three minutes.
 S4 = Add the result of action S2 to the result of action S3.
 S5 = Stir fry the result of action S4 for a half minute.
```

```
Asking questions needed for evaluating strategy:
    ALTER-PLAN:SIDE-EFFECT

ASKING -> Is there an alternative to
           Stir fry the sugar, soy sauce, rice wine, garlic,
           corn starch, broccoli and beef for three minutes.
          that will enable
           The dish now tastes savory.
          which does not cause
           There is thin liquid in the pan from the beef
           equaling 4.8 teaspoons.

No alternate plan found

Asking questions needed for evaluating strategy: ADJUNCT-PLAN

ASKING -> Is there an adjunct plan that will disable
           There is thin liquid in the pan from the beef
           equaling 4.8 teaspoons.
          that can be run with
           Stir fry the sugar, soy sauce, rice wine, garlic,
           corn starch, broccoli and beef for three minutes.

No adjunct plan found

Deciding between modification plans suggested by strategies:
  Only one modification can be implemented -> SPLIT-AND-REFORM

Implementing plan -> Instead of doing step: Stir fry the sugar,
  soy sauce, rice wine, garlic, corn starch, broccoli
  and beef for three minutes.
 do: S1 = Stir fry the broccoli for three minutes.
     S2 = Remove the broccoli from the result of action S1.
     S3 = Stir fry the sugar, soy sauce, rice wine, garlic,
     corn starch and beef for three minutes.
     S4 = Add the result of action S2 to the result of action S3.
     S5 = Stir fry the result of action S4 for a half minute.
Suggested by strategy SPLIT-AND-REFORM.
```

In this example, CHEF can only implement one of its general strategies, so the choice between possible repairs is moot. In general, this decision is made using domain-level heuristics that determine an ordering on the specific changes that CHEF is able to make to faulty plans.

CHEF tries to implement the strategies suggested by the TOP by searching for the actual plan modifications that the strategies define.

2.2.4 Anticipating failures

After changing the plan to solve immediate problems, CHEF also changes its understanding of the world so that it will be able to anticipate and thus avoid similar problems in the future. To do this CHEF must figure out what it was that caused the failure in the first place. It must decide which features in the initial situation contributed to the failure so that later requests for similar goals can be planned for. Here CHEF again makes use of the causal explanation that it has for the failure to back-chain to the features that can be used to predict this kind of problem. These features are then generalized to the highest level of description allowed by the rules which explain the situation. This means taking a feature like BEEF and generalizing it to MEAT, because the rule that explains the liquid in the pan states that stir-frying *any* meat will have this result, so the feature can be generalized up to this level. The resulting descriptions are marked as predictive of this problem. Once this is done, CHEF is able to predict and plan for a problem of this kind whenever it encounters a similar situation.

```
Building demons to anticipate failure.

Building demon: DEMONO to anticipate interaction between rules:
"Meat sweats when it is stir-fried."
"Stir-frying in too much liquid makes vegetables soggy."

Indexing demon: DEMONO under item: MEAT
by test:
    Is the item a MEAT.

Indexing demon: DEMONO under item: VEGETABLE
by test:
    Is the item a VEGETABLE.
and Is the TEXTURE of item CRISP.

Goal to be activated = Avoid failure of type
SIDE-EFFECT:DISABLED-CONDITION:CONCURRENT exemplified be the
failure 'The broccoli is now soggy' in recipe BEEF-AND-BROCCOLI.
```

```
Building demon: DEMON1 to anticipate interaction between rules:
"Liquids make things wet."
"Stir-frying in too much liquid makes vegetables soggy."

Indexing demon: DEMON1 under item: SPICE
by test:
    Is the TEXTURE of item LIQUID.

Indexing demon: DEMON1 under item: VEGETABLE
by test:
    Is the item a VEGETABLE.
and Is the TEXTURE of item CRISP.

Goal to be activated = Avoid failure of type
SIDE-EFFECT:DISABLED-CONDITION:CONCURRENT
exemplified by the failure 'The broccoli is now soggy'
in recipe BEEF-AND-BROCCOLI.
```

The demons associated with a failure are indexed by the surface features that are explained as having caused that failure. But these demons are also indexed by the states that were included as links in the overall causal chain. Liquid in the pan, for example, was the actual cause of the broccoli wilting, but was itself a by-product of the stir-frying of the meat. CHEF does not waste a piece of reasoning. Once it determines the causes of a problem, whether initial or proximate, it indexes its memory of the problem in terms of those causes. This allows CHEF greater flexibility than would indexing its recollection of a failure only in terms of the surface features associated with it. It is able to anticipate a wider range of problems without sacrificing its ties to experience.

> CHEF uses its explanation of why a failure has occurred to build links that will allow it to predict the failure later, in similar circumstances.

Once a plan is debugged and the sources of any problem are marked as predictive of that problem, CHEF stores the plan using two types of features. The first is the standard vocabulary of goals met by the plan, such as what foods and tastes are included in it, as well as what type of dish it is. These features are generalized so that plans which only partially satisfy a set of goal requests can be accessed in the absence of exact matches.

The second is a different sort of vocabulary that relates more to the failures encountered in building the plan than the goals that the finished plan now directly satisfies. This means that the plan is indexed by the possible problems between substeps that it avoids. By storing plans this way, it is possible for the planner to use the prediction of a previously encountered problem to find a plan that solves that problem. CHEF can avoid past errors by predicting them and then finding a plan that deals with them. In the case of the BEEF-AND-BROCCOLI plan, the plan is indexed by the fact that it deals with the interaction between the meat sweating and the need to have a dry pan while cooking crisp vegetables.

Before searching for a plan at all, CHEF tries to anticipate any failures that will result from the goals it has been given, using the links formed between goal features and the failures that they have caused in past episodes. By doing this before searching for a plan, the anticipation of a problem can tell CHEF to find a plan to avoid it.

The program uses its new knowledge of what went wrong in the making the BEEF-AND-BROCCOLI recipe to anticipate and avoid the same problem in making a later one. Because the past failure is indexed by the features that originally caused it, CHEF is able to recall the past failure when those features arise again.

While planning for a stir-fried dish with chicken and snow peas it predicts the possibility of the snow peas getting soggy if cooked with the chicken. It will later use this prediction to find the beef and broccoli plan which deals with this problem. This plan, rather than one having to do with either chicken or snow peas, is then modified to account for the specific goals.

```
Searching for plan that satisfies -
   Include chicken in the dish.
   Include snow pea in the dish.
   Make a stir-fry dish.

   Collecting and activating tests.

  Fired: Is the dish STYLE-STIR-FRY.

  Fired: Is the item a MEAT.

  Fired: Is the item a VEGETABLE.
         Is the TEXTURE of item CRISP.
```

```
 Chicken + Snow Pea + Stir frying = Failure
   "Meat sweats when it is stir-fried."
   "Stir-frying in too much liquid makes vegetables soggy."
    Reminded of BEEF-AND-BROCCOLI.
    Fired demon: DEMONO

Based on features found in items: snow pea, chicken and stir fry
adding goal: Avoid failure of type
SIDE-EFFECT:DISABLED-CONDITION:CONCURRENT exemplified by
the failure 'The broccoli is now soggy' in recipe
BEEF-AND-BROCCOLI.
```

> CHEF uses its understanding of past failures to anticipate problems that will arise in new situations.

Once a problem has been anticipated, CHEF can use the prediction of the problem to find a plan that avoids it. It does this by adding a goal to explicitly avoid the problem to the list of goals it is using to search for a plan. The BEEF-AND-BROCCOLI plan is indexed in memory by the fact that it avoids the same problem of the interaction between meat and vegetable that has been predicted. So CHEF is able to use the anticipation of a problem to find the plan that avoids it.

```
Searching for plan that satisfies -
   Include chicken in the dish.
   Include snow pea in the dish.
   Make a stir-fry dish.
   Avoid failure of type SIDE-EFFECT:DISABLED-CONDITION:CONCURRENT
 exemplified by the failure 'The broccoli is now soggy' in recipe
 BEEF-AND-BROCCOLI.

Found recipe -> REC9 BEEF-AND-BROCCOLI

Recipe exactly satisfies goals ->
    Avoid failure of type SIDE-EFFECT:DISABLED-CONDITION:CONCURRENT
exemplified by the failure 'The broccoli is now soggy' in recipe
BEEF-AND-BROCCOLI.
    Make a stir-fry dish.
```

```
Recipe partially matches ->
    Include chicken in the dish.
          in that the recipe satisfies: Include meat in the dish.

Recipe partially matches ->
    Include snow pea in the dish.
          in that the snow pea can be substituted for the broccoli
```

When CHEF decides to use the BEEF-AND-BROCCOLI recipe as its starting point it is passing up other recipes in memory that have similarities to the current goal situation. It has, in fact, a recipe with chicken and green beans that, in the absence of the beef and broccoli experience, it would have been happy to modify to account for the chicken and snow peas. But because it has encountered a failure stemming from a similar situation in the past, it anticipates the problem and prefers a plan for a situation that was built to deal with that problem. It favors this plan, although it has fewer surface features in common with the current situation than another plan in memory, because it knows that this plan deals with an interaction between goals that is not addressed by the other. This interaction between plan steps, because it has so great an effect on the final structure of the plan, is more important to CHEF than the details of the surface goals in choosing its initial plan.

> CHEF uses its anticipation of a problem to find a plan that avoids it.

Once this plan is retrieved, CHEF then makes the changes needed to fit it to the current goals,

```
Building new name for copy of BEEF-AND-BROCCOLI based on its goals.
Calling recipe CHICKEN-STIR-FRIED

Modifying recipe: CHICKEN-STIR-FRIED
to satisfy: Include chicken in the dish.
  Placing some chicken in recipe CHICKEN-STIR-FRIED

Modifying recipe: CHICKEN-STIR-FRIED
to satisfy: Include snow pea in the dish.
  Placing some snow pea in recipe CHICKEN-STIR-FRIED
```

and thus produces the required recipe.

```
Created recipe CHICKEN-STIR-FRIED

               CHICKEN-STIR-FRIED

          A half pound of chicken
          Two tablespoons of soy sauce
          One teaspoon of rice wine
          A half tablespoon of corn starch
          One teaspoon of sugar
          A half pound of snow pea
          One teaspoon of salt
          One chunk of garlic

Bone the chicken.
Chop the garlic into pieces the size of matchheads.
Shred the chicken.
Marinate the chicken in the garlic, sugar, corn starch,
rice wine and soy sauce.
Chop the snow pea into pieces the size of chunks.
Stir fry the snow pea for three minutes.
Remove the snow pea from the pan.
Stir fry the spices, rice wine and chicken for three minutes.
Add the snow pea to the spices, rice wine and chicken.
Stir fry the spices, snow pea, rice wine and chicken
for a half minute.
Add the salt to the spices, snow pea, rice wine and chicken.
```

Surface features of a situation in which a failure has been anticipated are important, however. If CHEF were given the goals to make a stir-fry dish with chicken and bean sprouts after storing its new CHICKEN-STIR-FRIED plan in memory, it would anticipate the problem with the bean sprouts getting soggy, but would not use the BEEF-AND-BROCCOLI plan as its baseline. Instead it would use the CHICKEN-STIR-FRIED plan that deals with the problem of stir-frying meats and crisp vegetables together *and* has more surface features in common with the current situation than the other plan that also deal with this problem, the BEEF-AND-BROCCOLI recipe. Once a failure is anticipated, it becomes one of the features that is used to find a plan, but not the only one.

CHEF is a model of memory-intensive planning. CHEF designs new plans out of its memories of old ones. It uses memories of successful plans as the basis for new ones. It uses memories of its own failures to warn itself of possible problems. And it uses memories of past repairs to fix those problems when they arise.

As CHEF plans it learns. It learns new plans by creating successful recipes and storing them in memory. It learns to predict problems by experiencing and explaining failures. It also learns new ways to avoid the problems it predicts by repairing failed plans and storing the repairs for later use. The essential idea of CHEF is that planning is interaction with the world and that interaction can lead to learning.

2.3 Learning plans

A case-based planner learns plans in the sense that it stores the new plans it creates in its plan memory. Learning, in this context, means figuring out the features that should be used index the plan in memory and then storing the plan using them. The task is to organize experience such that it can be retrieved and reused at the appropriate time.

> A case-based planner stores the most obvious result of planning, the plan itself, in a plan memory.

The object that a case-based planner stores in memory is the plan itself. The plan is a series of steps and list of ingredients that has been built to satisfy some particular set of goals. This plan is not generalized in any way. To do so would be to lose information that could be used again, without gaining anything in terms of more general applicability.

For example, in the CHEF program, altering a specific plan such as STRAWBERRY-SOUFFLE to satisfy a slightly different set of goals, such as including kirsch, is no more difficult than altering a generalized version of the same plan. But in a situation where the planner has to plan for goals that are identical to those in the original situation, a generalized plan would be more difficult to adapt, because the specifics of the original plan would be lost.

While a case-based planner need not generalize the plans it stores, it does need to generalize the features that are used to index them. Because of this, the plan can be suggested for use in a wide range of situations and can still retain the specific information that makes it more useful when applied to situations in which the goals that are being planned for are completely satisfied by the plan itself. By generalizing the indices rather than the plan, a case-based planner is able to avoid much of the trade-off between generality and power of application. The general indices makes it applicable in many situations and the specificity of the plan makes it a powerful tool in those situations in which the match between the current goals and those satisfied by the plan is a good one.

Because all indices are generalized (*e.g.,* broccoli to vegetable, beef to meat) the task of retrieval replaces that of matching. These are used to place the plan in a discrimination net that is later searched by the RETRIEVER. When a feature used in retrieval has to be abstracted (can't find broccoli, look for vegetable), a further drive down is done using subfeatures of the original (once down vegetable, drive down on texture=crisp). Because we assume a strict hierarchy of goals (corresponding to features) search of the discrimination net is always downwards-driven with no backup.

> In storing a plan in memory, a case-based planner does not generalize the plan itself. It instead generalizes the features that are used to index the plan in memory.

A case-based planner has to index the plans it stores by two different sorts of features. First, it indexes them by the goals that they satisfy. Second, it indexes them by the problems they avoid. In actually placing a plan in memory, these features are used in exactly the same way, but they come from somewhat different sources.

By the time a planner stores a plan in memory, the plan has been run and has been repaired if necessary. This means that the planner knows what goals the plan satisfies and what problems it has had to deal with in doing so. The goals that a plan satisfies form state descriptions that have to be true once the plan has been run. The problems that a plan avoids should take the form of a causal description of the problems, so that the prediction of similar problems can be used to access the plan in memory.

In the CHEF program, the goals include the taste and texture of the different items in a plan and the ingredients that are included in it. These goals, along with the goal to make the type of dish that the plan builds, are the initial features that are used in indexing the plan. Problems that a plan avoids are represented by the TOP that describes the abstract causal situation linked to the specific failure state. For example, the BEEF-AND-BROCCOLI plan that was repaired to avoid the problem of soggy vegetables is marked as dealing with this problem. In CHEF, a plan can have many problems due to goal interactions that it solves, just as it can satisfy many goals directly. These two sets of items are combined into a single list of features that will be used to index the plan in memory.

The fact that a plan avoids a particular problem can be treated by a case-based planner as a *goal* to avoid that failure that the plan associated with it satisfies. These goals to avoid failures can be treated as any other goal for use in indexing of plans in memory. They may be considered to be more important than most other goals, however, because it is often easier to alter a plan to satisfy a new goal than to make the changes required to deal with an interaction between goals.

A plan is indexed in memory by the goals that it satisfies and the problems that it avoids. It also has to be indexed by the features of a situation that are independent of the goals but do direct the planner to one plan or another. As mentioned before, the plan to call the front desk for a wake-up call is a good plan to get the planner up in the morning, but only in certain circumstances. These circumstances, which can be reduced to states that describe the world, also have to be used to index plans in memory.

In the CHEF program, the actual implementation of its memory of plans is via a discrimination net in which plans are indexed by the goals that they satisfy and the problems that they avoid. These goals and problems are ordered by their importance, with the higher-priority features used at the higher levels of discrimination. Once the features are ordered, a plan is placed in the discrimination net, using the features as indices. The ordering of features allows CHEF to somewhat limit the branching in this net by allowing discrimination from any one node to be made only on the basis of features of less importance than the last one used to index to it.

As each goal is used to place a plan in memory, more general versions of the goals are also used. BEEF-AND-BROCCOLI is indexed by the fact that it includes beef and broccoli, but it is also indexed by the fact that it includes meat and vegetables in general. The level of generality of the goals used to index plans is preset and corresponds to the level of generality that is used in defining the modification rules used in substituting one ingredient for another in a plan. As a result, the goal to include one type of ingredient can be used to find a plan for a similar ingredient.

```
Created recipe STRAWBERRY-SOUFFLE

If this plan is successful, the following should be true:

        The batter is now baked.
        The batter is now risen.
        The dish now tastes like berries.
        The dish now tastes sweet.

The plan satisfies -
        Include strawberry in the dish.
        Make a souffle.
```

Figure 2.1: Goals satisfied by STRAWBERRY-SOUFFLE

> CHEF stores new plans indexed by the goals that they satisfy and the problems that they avoid.

Once a plan is placed in memory this way it can be accessed by the planner when it is searching for a plan that satisfies similar goals and for a plan that avoids failures that it predicts may appear.

For example, in building the STRAWBERRY-SOUFFLE recipe CHEF has to deal with the fact that the liquid from the fruit disables the conditions required for the soufflé to rise. It deals with this by adding more egg white to the recipe, thus re-establishing the relationship between liquid and leavening that the fruit put out of balance. The final recipe satisfies a set of goals having to do with making a soufflé, including strawberries, making the soufflé taste sweet and like berries and having a fluffy texture. These goals come from the input request and some are generated by the planner out of its understanding of what this type of plan should be like in general (figure 2.1). The plan also has a token associated with it that indicates that it deals with the problem of the added liquid from the fruit interfering with the baking (figure 2.2).

These goals are collected and used to index the plan in memory, the goal to make a soufflé and the goal to avoid the failure taking priority over all others. These are then used to insert the plan into CHEF's plan memory. The only generalization that goes on is with the goal to include the strawberries, which is generalized up to the level of FRUIT. There are

```
Created recipe STRAWBERRY-SOUFFLE

   The plan avoids the failure of type
   SIDE-EFFECT:DISABLED-CONDITION:BALANCE
   exemplified by the failure 'The batter is now flat'
   in recipe STRAWBERRY-SOUFFLE.

   Token = SIDE-EFFECT:DISABLED-CONDITION:BALANCE0
```

Figure 2.2: Avoidance goal under STRAWBERRY-SOUFFLE

no other goals that can be further generalized.

Once stored, this plan can be found whenever the planner is trying to plan for any subset of the goals that it satisfies and can be found in any situation in which the problem of an imbalance between liquid and leavening is predicted. Even without the prediction of the failure having to do with the liquid from the fruit giving the plan problems, it could be found when the planner is given the goals to make a soufflé with fruit. Because it is also indexed by the fact that it does avoid this particular problem with added liquid, it can also be accessed when the planner is given the goals to make a kirsch soufflé, which activates the prediction of the problem and then allows CHEF to find the plan. So, this additional index allows the planner to find the plan in situations that do not match the individual goals but do have problems occurring in them that the plan solves.

2.4 Learning to predict failures

A case-based planner can use its own memories of past failures to anticipate new ones by associating failures with the surface features that predict them. This association can be made at the time of a failure by forming links between features of goals and the failures that they have caused. These links can then be used to activate the memory of the failure when the goals arise again, thus giving the planner the warning that it should find a plan that avoids the problem. The problem of learning to predict failures so as to anticipate and avoid them is a problem of figuring out which features of an existing situation have caused a current failure, so that these links can be created.

> A case-based planner saves memories of failures, indexed by the features that predict them. It uses these memories to anticipate problems when these features arise again in new situations.

When reminded of a failure, the planner needs to recall the token that has been built to represent the failure and to index the plan that avoids it in memory. By having the planner be reminded of the same representation of the failure that was used to index the plan which avoids it in memory, it can use the reminding of the failure directly in searching for the appropriate plan.

For example, CHEF's STRAWBERRY-SOUFFLE plan is indexed by the fact that it avoided a particular problem. The token used to index the plan was then associated with the planner's memory of the failure. Because of this the activation of the memory of the failure could be used directly to index to the plan that deals with it.

> In saving a memory of a failure, CHEF saves the token that was used to index the plan that avoids that failure in CHEF's plan memory.

A case-based planner that does any sort of causal analysis of a problem in order to repair it has a powerful tool for figuring out which features in a situation have to take the blame for causing a problem. The explanation created to fix a faulty plan can also be used to identify the features of a situation that will later predict that fault. As in learning new plans, the planner does most of the work and the learner's task is to form the links that will recall that work. The planning task is to repair the plan by figuring out what went wrong and then changing the circumstances that caused the problem. The learning task is to just recall these circumstances so the planner can recognize when a failure is imminent and search for a plan to avoid it.

CHEF, for example, uses the explanation of *why* a failure has occurred to point out which features are responsible in a current situation for the problem and then uses it again to find the features that will be predictive of the problem in later situations. These are the same features, but the learner in CHEF wants to know not only the exact features that caused the problem but also the more general versions of them that might cause it again. It gets these more general features by doing what I call *generalizing to the level of the rules*. This means generalizing an object in an explanation up to the highest level of generality is possible while still staying within the confines of the rules that explain the failure.

The difference between this notion of explanation and that suggested by other theories of explanation-driven learning (*E.g.*, [DeJong 83] and [Mitchell 83]) lies in what is learned. Within case-based planning, the explanation of why a plan has failed is used to figure out the features that will later predict similar failures. In other theories of explanation-driven learning, explanations of why a plan has been successful are used to weed out the steps that are irrelevant and generalize those that are too specific. Explanation of failures is far more constrained a task in that only a single anomalous state has to be accounted for and the planner is not trying to generalize the plan it is building at all. It is only trying to generalize its understanding of the circumstances in which that plan can be used.

A case-based planner uses the explanation of a failure to identify the features that will predict it. It generalizes these features to the highest level of description allowed by the rules in the explanation.

In an example of the CHEF program dealing with the problem of the a failed strawberry soufflé, in which the liquid from chopped strawberries causes the soufflé to fall, one of the links in the chain of the explanation is provided by a rule that states that the extra liquid in the batter was a product of the chopping of the strawberries. A simple way to avoid this failure in the future would be for the planner to mark strawberries as predictive of it and be reminded of the failure and the repaired plan whenever it is asked to make a strawberry soufflé. But it turns out that the rule that explains the added liquid as a side-effect of chopping the strawberries does not require that the object of the chop be strawberries at all. It actually explains that chopping *any* fruit will produce this side-effect. Instead of marking STRAWBERRY as predictive of the problem CHEF can mark FRUIT as predictive (figure 2.3).

In some cases, the rule that explains a link in the causal chain leading to a failure does have specific requirements. For example, in explaining the soggy broccoli in the BEEF-AND-BROCCOLI plan, CHEF uses a rule that explains that stir-frying any crisp vegetable in liquid will make it soggy. In this case, BROCCOLI is too specific a feature to hang the prediction off of and VEGETABLE is too general. To deal with this, CHEF uses the tests on the rule itself to control the activation of the failure prediction. These tests are associated with the general ingredient type that the rule tests for, VEGETABLE, and tests for the features that are required for the rule to

```
Building demons to anticipate failure.

Building demon: DEMON2 to anticipate interaction between rules:
"Chopping fruits produces liquid."
"Without a balance between liquids and leavening the batter
 will fall."

 Indexing demon: DEMON2 under item: FRUIT
 by test: Is the item a FRUIT.

 Indexing demon: DEMON2 under style: SOUFFLE

 Goal to be activated = Avoid failure of type
 SIDE-EFFECT:DISABLED-CONDITION:BALANCE
 exemplified by the failure 'The batter is now flat'
 in recipe STRAWBERRY-SOUFFLE.
```

Figure 2.3: Marking FRUIT and SOUFFLE as predictive of problems

apply, (TEXTURE = CRISP). This means that each time the planner has to deal with stir-frying vegetables it will test their texture and partially activate the memory of the failure if they are crisp. These tests are always checks for existing semantic features. As a result, they can take the form of a network through which markers can be passed without the need for explicit inference. This means that anticipating known failures is a low-cost task.

In most situations, it is not a single feature but a set of features that combine to cause a failure. The BEEF-AND-BROCCOLI situation is one of these because the failure is not the result of either stir-frying the beef or stir-frying the broccoli, but is the result of stir-frying them together. In these situations, a single feature alone should not activate the prediction of the failure. It is only when all of the features are together (The style of the dish is STIR-FRY, one ingedient is MEAT and another ingredient is a CRISP VEGETABLE), that the prediction should be made. To deal with this, the activation of a single feature that is linked to a failure only partially activates the memory. It is only when all features send a signal that they are present that the memory of the failure is itself activated and the planner is warned of the impending problem. CHEF does not anticipate a problem when it plans for crisp vegetables alone. it only does so when it is asked to plan for stir-frying crisp vegetables along with other goals that will combine with the first to cause the problem again.

> When multiple features are required to predict a failure, all of them are linked to the memory of the failure. This memory is not activated unless all of the linked features are present.

In tracing back through the explanation of a failure to the initial causes, a planner passes through states that those original causes have created. These states are the ones that are the more proximate causes of the problems but not the first causes in terms of the recipe. The liquid from chopping the strawberries is the actual cause of the problem with the strawberry soufflé but it is not the initial cause, the goal to include strawberries itself.

Although these states are not the initial causes of the problems that the planner has to deal with, they can still be used to predict the problems in later situations. A planner has to handle these intermediate states in the same way as it handles the ingredients it has to mark as predictive of problems. It generalizes them up to the level of the rules that explain the failure and link them to the token representing the failure. If other conditions are also required for the failure to occur, they are also linked to the memory of the failure so that the one feature alone will not predict the failure when it is inappropriate.

The CHEF program responds to the failure of the strawberry soufflé by marking the goal to include any liquid spice in a soufflé as predictive of that soufflé falling (figure 2.4). This is implemented by placing a test on the concept SPICE that checks for the texture and partially activates the memory of the failure when the test is true.

> Intermediate states that serve as links in the causal chain that led to a failure are also linked to the memory of the failure and thus can be used to predict it if they arise in a later situation.

When a set of features that combine to predict a failure is present, a case-based planner is reminded of the memory of the failure itself. In CHEF, the request for a soufflé with raspberries in it reminds the planner of the problem of extra liquid in a soufflé and allows it to find and modify the STRAWBERRY-SOUFFLE plan that deals with it. It also allows CHEF to be reminded of it when planning for a kirsch soufflé, in which the added liqueur would have the same effect as the liquid from the chopped fruit. This is a plan that the planner would not have used had it not been for

```
Building demons to anticipate failure.

Building demon: DEMON3 to anticipate interaction between rules:
"Liquids make things wet."
"Without a balance between liquids and leavening the batter
 will fall."

Indexing demon: DEMON3 under item: SPICE
by test: Is the TEXTURE of item LIQUID.

Indexing demon: DEMON3 under style: SOUFFLE

Goal to be activated = Avoid failure of type
SIDE-EFFECT:DISABLED-CONDITION:BALANCE
exemplified by the failure 'The batter is now flat'
in recipe STRAWBERRY-SOUFFLE.
```

Figure 2.4: Marking LIQUID and SOUFFLE as predictive of problems

the prediction of the failure. The fact that the ASSIGNER has earlier established these links between features and failures allows it to find and make use of plans that otherwise would have not interesting features in common.

Before closing the discussion of learning to predict failures, there is one point that has to be made about indexing in a case-based planner. A case-based planner indexes its plans by the fact that they avoid particular problems. It also indexes memories of these problems by the features that predict them. Given this fact, the question that arises is: Why not just index the plans by the features that predict the problem that they solve directly?

There are two answers to this question. First, because a single class of problems can have many specific causes, it is just more efficient to index the plan under a single characterization of the problem and have the problem be predicted independently instead of indexing the plan by all possible circumstances that might cause the problem. Problems can be predicted with only a few features. There is little interaction between them that would lead to the need for a complex indexing system. But adding these features to the those already used to index plans would increase the complexity of plan indexing dramatically.

But efficiency is not the only argument. A more compelling argument is that indexing the plans that solve problems by the features that predict them, without marking those features in any way, doesn't work. As was pointed out earlier in this chapter, it is often the case that the best plan for a situation is not the one that has the closest match in terms of low-level features.

In CHEF, for example, the prediction of the "soggy vegetable" failure allowed the program to find the BEEF-AND-BROCCOLI plan that avoided it. Without this prediction, however, the planner would have to rely on finding a plan using only the features of the initial goals. Because the planner does have a plan for CHICKEN-AND-PEANUTS in memory, this would be taken as the base-line plan. But this plan, when modified for the current goals, will lead to soggy snow peas while a modified BEEF-AND-BROCCOLI will not.

The fact that a case-based planner indexes plans by the problems they solve and then predicts these problems for use in search allows it to recover them in situations where the low level features of the current goals would lead it to less appropriate plans.

2.5 Learning critics

Aside from storing plans and failures, a case-based planner also stores some of the repairs that it makes to plans so that they can be used again. These repairs, stored in the form of critics, allow a planner to repair plans it knows to be faulty *before* it runs them. A planner would run into this situation when it predicts a problem, but cannot find a plan of the proper type to deal with that problem. When this occurs, it has to use a plan that it knows to be faulty and then change it with the same patch it used to repair another faulty plan in the past.

> A case-based planner stores some of the repairs that it makes, indexed by the problems that they solve.

As with learning plans, the task of the learner is not to build the repair that is going to be stored, but only to decide how it is going to be indexed so that it can be accessed at the right time. There is a difference, however, in that not all repairs can be saved. Some repairs, because they involve interactions between many parts of a plan, are too complex to transfer to new problems. Others are also linked to the type of plan that is being built, so there is never a possibility that the problem is predicted but no plan of the dish type needed can be found. Aside from deciding where to store the repair, the learner also has to decide which repairs can be saved at all.

The decision to save a repair as a critic is based on the repair strategy that is used to build the specific repair and on the cause of the failure in the first place. Some failures are the product of multiple ingredients interacting so no one ingredient can be blamed for the problem and thus no one ingredient be given a critic that will repair. The first test for turning a repair into a critic is whether it relates to a single ingredient. The second test depends on the complexity of the repair itself. Some strategies, such as ALTER-PLAN:PRECONDITION, ALTER-PLAN:SIDE-EFFECT, and SPLIT-AND-REFORM depend on specific steps being present in a plan and their changes cannot reliably be reused. On the other hand, strategies such as REORDER and REMOVE-FEATURE create simple changes that can be added to most plans. For example, the addition of a step to remove the fat from duck created by REMOVE-FEATURE, can be added to any plan involving duck. Likewise, the ordering change suggested by REORDER when the marinating of shrimp blocked shelling it later can be applied to any case of the two steps being misordered.

> A case-based planner can only save those repairs that can be transferred to any plan in which the problem that they repair arises.

In turning a repair into critic, a case-based planner has to store the specific change suggested by the strategy under the ingredient that it relates to. This is again so the prediction of a problem can lead to finding the repair that will fix it. By doing this, the past repair can be suggested when and only when the problem it relates to is noticed or predicted.

In CHEF, for example, a repair that the planner creates that adds the step of removing the fat from the duck is stored under the concept duck itself. Unlike other repairs that take the form of critics, however, these new critics are indexed by the problem that they solve. To activate them CHEF has to anticipate the problem and then fail to find a plan that solves it. This restriction prevents CHEF from applying a repair to a plan that has already been fixed. It only applies the new critic when the features predicting the problem are anticipated and the plan that is used by the planner fails to deal with it.

Building a critic out of a repair requires that the planner only put together the pieces that have already been built or identified. The explanation

```
Applying TOP -> SIDE-FEATURE:GOAL-VIOLATION
to failure The bunch of dumplings is now greasy.
in recipe BAD-DUCK-DUMPLINGS

Implementing plan -> After doing step: Bone the duck
                  do: Clean the fat from the duck.
Suggested by strategy REMOVE-FEATURE
```

Figure 2.5: Repairing DUCK-DUMPLINGS with REMOVE-FEATURE

that is used to repair the plan in the first place identifies where the critics should be stored. The critic itself is the actual repair that was built by the strategy to patch the plan in the first place.

> CHEF builds new critics out of current repairs and then indexes them by the description of the problem being repaired.

An example of this notion arises when the CHEF program has to confront the problem of the grease from the duck fat. In dealing with the fat from the duck making the dish greasy, CHEF repairs the plan using the strategy REMOVE-FEATURE (figure 2.5). Because the repair is a simple one having to do with only one ingredient, it can then go on to store it as a critic under DUCK, indexed so that the prediction of the problem will

```
Building critic to avoid failure: The bunch of
dumplings is now greasy.
caused by condition: The duck is now fatty.

Critic =
After doing step: Bone the duck
              do: Clean the fat from the duck
         because: The duck is now fatty.
Storing critic under DUCK
Indexing by SIDE-FEATURE:GOAL-VIOLATIONO
```

Figure 2.6: Storing new critic under DUCK

```
Problem predicted - SIDE-FEATURE:GOAL-VIOLATIONO

Considering critic:
After doing step: Bone the duck
              do: Clean the fat from the duck
         because: The duck is now fatty. - Critic applied.
```

Figure 2.7: Using a new DUCK critic.

activate the critic for use in a different plan (figure 2.6). When it later has to make a duck pasta dish and cannot use its DUCK-DUMPLINGS, it is in the position of predicting a problem that it does not solve with a complete plan. During modification, it activates the critics and adds the step that removes the fat from the duck (figure 2.7). Even though it could not find a complete plan to deal with the problem then it is able to avoid it before running its new plan by using its earlier repair.

As with the other aspects of a case-based planner's learning, the stress in learning new critics is not on the construction of the critics themselves. The stress is on how they are to be stored so that they can be accessed at the appropriate time. By indexing the patches to a plan under the prediction that it will fail, a case-based planner can activate those patches only when the features that predict the failure are present and thus avoid them before the plan is run.

2.6 How learning from planning is different

Learning for a case-based planner is a by-product of planning, so the needs of the planner determine what is going to be learned, when it is going to be learned and how it is going to be learned. Other learners that learn categories or plans in the absence of a use for what they learn are concerned with creating new structures but have little interest in how they are stored and managed for use in an active memory. A learner associated with a planner, on the other hand, does not do any building on its own. It is instead concerned with how to organize the results, both positive and negative, of its planner in a dynamic memory of experience that the planner can use.

Learning is the organization of experience. As a result, the core issues of learning are memory organization and indexing. The most important problem in learning is deciding how to describe and store an experience so that it can be used again. In a planner that learns, this means finding a way to organize the planner's results so they can be used again in the appropriate situations.

Because a case-based planner makes use of existing plans to create new ones, the most natural thing for it to be learning is new plans so that it can adapt them for later use. A case-based planner plans by finding the "best match" between new goals and old plans that satisfy them so it also makes sense that the most important issue in learning plans is indexing them so that they can be found at the appropriate time. A case-based planner must predict problems so that it can find plans that avoid them, so it makes sense for it to learn the features that predict the problems it encounters. Because it is possible to predict a problem that cannot be handled with an existing plan, it also makes sense for a planner to learn specific fixes that can be applied to repair the plan it has to use. The needs of the planner decide what is going to be learned: plans, problems and repairs.

Planning is a test of the planner's knowledge. When that knowledge fails, the planner can see through its own experience that it needs to learn some new way to discriminate between the situation it thought it was in and the one it is actually in.

Because a planner is able to test its knowledge of the world by building new plans, its planning experiences can tell it when it has to learn something from those experiences. When a case-based planner builds a successful plan, it knows to store it for later use. Because it knows in what sense the plan is successful, in that it knows the goals it satisfies and the problems it avoids, it also knows how to index it in memory. When a case-based planner fails, it knows to mark the features that caused the failure as predictive of it so that it can anticipate it in the future. The failure itself tells the planner that its knowledge has a gap, and that the gap has to be filled with the prediction of a problem that the planner was not able to anticipate before. And when a case-based planner repairs a plan, it knows that this repair is a patch that fixes a failure created by its own modification process. In response, the planner adds this patch to the knowledge used by that process. The planner determines when the learner is turned on: when the planner succeeds, fails and repairs.

Finally, the planner itself provides the learner with the content of what is learned. It builds the plans that are stored in memory. It builds the explanation that is used to assign blame for a failure. It even builds the patch that is stored as a new ingredient critic. The learner does not create what is learned, the planner does. In every case, the task of the learner is the task of collecting the features that should be used to index the planner's work and then store that work away for later use.

The planner does the reasoning. The learner examines that reasoning and decides how it should be stored in memory such that it can be recalled again when needed. Unlike systems that do nothing but learn and as a result do nothing with what they learn, a case-based planner that learns is managing a dynamic memory of experience in service of planning.

Learning means storing the different results of the planner's activity indexed by the features that determine their usefulness.

2.7 How learning from planning is better

A case-based planner must build functional categories that allow it to anticipate problems and then react to them. This is opposed to programs that build definitional categories that are no more than lists of necessary and sufficient features. The notion of learning not only a plan, but the features that it should be indexed by, is an improvement over other learners that are aimed at plan learning. A planner is concerned with the reuse of its plans while other systems are not. It is not satisfied with just having the plan in hand, it has to understand when it should be used and thus where it should be stored.

A case-based planner can use its knowledge as a planner to guide the credit assignment decisions it makes in marking features as predictive of problems so it does not run into the difficulties associated with inductive learning algorithms. It only has to see one instance of a problem to learn the features that predict it. It ignores extraneous features. It uses the explanation of a situation to determine the level of generality that those features will be pushed to. And it does not have to rely on a tutor to hand it the correct set of examples for generalization. By using the knowledge of what it is learning to guide it, a case-based planner can replace credit assignment through repetition with a more powerful credit assignment through causal relevance.

A planner knows when to learn. Unlike learning systems that do nothing but learn, a planner actually has a motivation for learning: the improvement of its planning abilities. Because it learns in response to the needs of the planner, it learns when and only when the planner requires it to. Because it learns in order to improve the planner, its learning is constrained to be only that which will help the planner with later efforts. The stress of the learning is on the use of what is learned instead of on the moment of learning itself.

> Learning from planning is an improvement over other types of learning in that it uses the knowledge of the planner to determine what it learns, how to index it and when to learn it at all.

All of these improvements come for the basic idea that learning is not separate from planning. Learning is the management of the planner's memory of its own experience so that it can plan more effectively and avoid the problems that it has encountered before. Learning does not just involve memory, learning is memory.

Chapter 3

Planning from Memory

3.1 Our view of memory

Popular culture has created quite a few myths about computers and Artificial Intelligence. One of the oddest of these is the notion that computer intelligences will have memories that are vastly superior to those of human beings. They will be able to recall details with greater clarity, access huge libraries of knowledge and be reminded of situations from the past that exactly fit the needs of the present. Science fiction is filled with annoying super memory computers and robots who are always reminding their users about events they have neglected and details they have wanted to forget.

The popular culture view of robot and machine memory is built, however, on a faulty model of how memory works in the first place. It is built on the view that, somehow, we never search for anything in memory. Instead, we just name a memory and out it pops. When a person does this, the memory that comes out is something faulty, because human memory is implemented on hardware that slowly decays with time. However when a machine does this, the memory is crisp and clear, because the memory of a machine resides in the cold, clean, and unchanging world of digital circuitry.

The problem with this view is that it ignores the fact that memory requires two elements: the objects being stored and the organization that makes it possible to find them. The science fiction view that depicts robots and thinking computers includes only the first requirement of raw material and has ignored the need for organization. A memory with no organization

- no notion of how to find the objects stored there - is as useless as a library without a card catalog. It contains information, but it is inaccessible. Even if each memory is named or each book titled, finding a desired one without some sort of organization would be a tedious task at best and practically impossible at worst. The best strategy for such a situation would be to just grab memories or books at random and check them against some description of what is wanted, discarding them until the right one is found. This method fails at the leisurely level of libraries, and does worse than fail at handling the real time needs of a working memory.

Defining a memory requires more than a description of what will be stored there. It also requires a description of how those stored items are going to be organized, how they are going to be indexed and searched for, so they can be found again at a later time.

> Memory is defined by the objects it stores, the vocabulary used to store them and the search that is used to rediscover them.

3.2 The function of memory

Libraries are organized in a straightforward way. Books are all indexed by author, title and subject matter. A user can look for a book on the basis of who wrote it, what its name is or what subject he is interested in. Books are indexed this way because they are used this way, because these are the features that determine their function. Books are indexed by the features that the librarians of the world have decided are the most functional, given the needs of library users. The indexing reflects the needs of the search. The features used to organize books reflect the use to which they will be put.

Given another set of needs, another set of features would be used to index books. In a world where books were just ornamental items used to support works of art, they might be indexed by size, color and cover design. These would be the features that would most affect their functionality, their usefulness, and thus they would be the features most useful in indexing them.

Unfortunately, in trying to describe human memory and prescribe machine memory, some researchers have given people far less credit for intelligent organization of knowledge than they give their local libraries. They don't seem to think of memory as a resource that serves the needs of understanding and planning. They don't seem to think of memory as something organized and indexed to best fulfil its own function. Instead they have opted for the view that the features used to organize memory, the features that control what a person is reminded of from one situation to the next, are almost random in nature.

For example, both Gentner [Gentner and Landers 85] and Holyoak [Gick and Holyoak 83] have argued that features used to control analogical remindings, that is remindings from one situation to another, are primarily based on the surface similarities between the two situations. Holyoak has also gone on to propose a computer model of memory for planning that makes use of spreading activation through a random set of features that link episodes together [Thagard and Holyoak 85].

The problem with this work, as with much of the work on human memory organization, is that it is an attempt to look at memory abstracted away from the function it serves. Gentner and Holyoak have spent much of their time looking at the features that they feel are used to access memories. But they have done so while ignoring the tasks that are being performed by their subjects when these memories are accessed. As a result their theories do not take into account the needs of the task being performed or even the information that their subjects would actually have in hand as a result of the partial completion of these tasks. This second omission is particularly troublesome in that they are ignoring information that is more than likely used by their subjects in accessing memories.

There are a set of problems that rise out the lack of attention to questions of function in examining memory. Because they are interested only in the details of the similarity between individual episodes involved in the reminding from one situation to another, both Gentner and Holyoak seem to ignore the fact that a reminding of one episode from another is a reminding out of all of memory. They forget that their task is not to just explain why one episode was found but also explain why others weren't. They are satisfied to explain a reminding from a current episode to one in the past by simply listing the features that they have in common. But the major problem with this work is that it avoids the fact that memory is used for something. They have failed to ask what purpose the reminding they have studied might have, and thus have failed to ask why and how it was retrieved in the first place.

The point here is simple: memory exists to serve a function and any study of memory has to be in terms of that function. If memory does not serve a function, then what is the point of studying it at all?

No matter what the situation, the features used to index something should have a functional relationship to its use. The vocabulary used to index episodes and the choice of the particular features of a situation used to find those episodes should be decided by the needs of the program that makes use of the memory they define. This gives a user the ability to describe an item in terms of his needs and then use that description to find the object that fits it. Without this ability, what would be the point of indexing at all?

> The organization of a memory should reflect its function. The content of the objects stored in memory, the vocabulary used to index those objects and the features used to search for them should rise out of the needs of the process that ultimately uses them.

3.3 A planner's memory

The memory organization of a case-based planner can be seen as four separate organizations that are defined by the planner's different needs. These are:

A plan memory that provides initial plans for a set of goals to be satisfied and problems to be avoided.

A failure memory that predicts failures on the basis of the similarity between past and current situations.

A modifier memory that provides the alterations that have to be made to an old plan to account for new goals.

A repair memory of strategies and their implementations that suggests the strategies that will be useful in repairing particular plan failures.

These four memories exist for different reasons as they serve different processes and different functions. As a result, they make use of four very different indexing schemes. They are not different in that they are implemented with different processes or data structures. They are different in that the vocabulary that is used to describe the objects they store reflect the different needs of the function to which those objects will are put.

For example, a case-based planner's memory of plans has to be indexed by at least two kinds of descriptors: the goals that the plans satisfy and the problems that they avoid. The strategies that it uses to repair faulty plans, however, have to be stored in a very different way. They have to be stored by a description of the failures that they repair. While they make use of different vocabularies and even store different types of knowledge, both make use of the same principle in indexing that knowledge: index objects by the features that determine their usefulness. For a plan memory, this means the goals that the plans satisfy. For a memory of plan repairs, this means the different situations for which the particular repairs are useful.

Memories that serve different functions should have different organizations. Each organization, however, should reflect the needs of that function.

Even if the many memories used by a case-based planner are implemented as a single network, a single collection of connected concepts, the needs of the different processes using that memory will have to be reflected in different vocabularies that can be used to access the memory objects themselves. The argument is not that different processes that use memory define different memories that are physically distinct, but that they define different vocabularies as a result of their different indexing needs.

To store and access plans for example, CHEF uses a vocabulary of goals, problems to be avoided and initial states. To access modifications, it uses a vocabulary of plans to be modified and relationships between those plans and the goals that they should satisfy. The point is, the contents of these memories serve different functions and thus the indexing of them should reflect those functions.

In the CHEF program these different memories are implemented as independent structures. Its memory of successful plans is implemented as a discrimination net indexed by the goals that the plans satisfy and the problems that they avoid. Its memory of failures is implemented as a network of nodes through which markers are passed to connect the surface features of a new planning situation to the failures that they predict. Its memory of modifications is a table, indexed by the general plan to be altered and the new goal that is being added. Its memory of repair strategies is stored under TOPs, which themselves are indexed in a discrimination network by causal descriptions of planning problems.

The first three of these memories, plan, failure and modifier, are *dynamic*. That is, they change in response to CHEF's experiences. It is through alterations of these memories that CHEF learns.

The memories of a case-based planner change in response to the experiences it has. A plan memory grows with each new plan that is built. But the features that are used to access this memory also changes reacting to the information about their relative importance that a planner gets through experiencing failures that they cause. A memory of failures begins empty and expands as a planner encounters difficulty in building plans on its own. But as its memory of failures expands, so does its ability to predict and avoid the failures that it can recall. By remembering its own failures a planner can avoid their reoccurrence. Finally, a planner's knowledge of the modifications to plans it has to make to account for the idiosyncrasies of the objects in its domain also changes in response to its failure to anticipate those idiosyncrasies. The more a case-based planner fails, the more it learns about the world and thus the better a planner it becomes.

> A case-based planner's dynamic memories all respond to its failures, storing the information as to why and when it failed and how it recovered so that it can recognize and avoid the problems it has already encountered.

I'd like to pause for a moment to look at an issue relevant to this chapter as well as the rest of the book. The most important issue in any system that makes use of "memory" is that of indexing. By indexing however, I do not mean the *process* that accesses memory. I mean instead the ***vocabulary*** that is used to describe what is needed from memory or how a new item should be stored. While each of CHEF's memories is implemented the theoretical thrust of this work is not centered around these implementations. It is instead centered around the representations that these processes use.

3.3.1 Memory of plans

A case-based planner's most important resource is its memory of past successes. This memory is used to find the past plan that it will adapt to its current goals and is also used to file away successful plans for later use. Without this memory of plans, a case-based planner would have nowhere to start its planning from and nowhere to place the results of its planning once it was done.

There are two issues that are essential in building a plan memory: the form of the objects that are stored and the vocabulary that is used to store them. In a case-based planner, the objects that are stored are specific plans rather than abstractions of plans. the vocabulary that is used to index these plans in memory is a vocabulary of the goals that the plans satisfy and the problems that they avoid.

Rather than storing generalized versions of plans in memory, a case-based planner stores specific plans for specific circumstances. But this does not mean there is no generalization going in a case-based planner. The generalization is just at the level of the features used to index plans rather than at the level of the plans themselves. By indexing plans by general descriptions of the goals that they satisfy as well as the specific goals, the plans can be retrieved for use in situations where they partially satisfy the planner's current goals. This means that the planner can use the plans, after modification, in a wide range of situations in which they partially match the current goals while still retaining the specificity required to be used directly in those situations where they exactly match the current goals.

The first component of a case-based planner's memory of plans is the plans themselves. These plans are represented as a fully ordered set of steps at the level of the planner's primitive actions. Along with the steps is an explicit description of the specific objects that the steps are run on.

In CHEF, these plans are the recipes that the planner either knows about or has created on its own. The representation for the initial plans that CHEF begins with and the plans that it creates on its own are identical. Each has a set of ingredients and a set of steps that make use of those ingredients. The steps all refer back to the ingredients themselves, to the results of previous steps, or to size and time restrictions. Each plan is also defined as being a particular type of plan, a plan for a certain type of object. In the CHEF domain this means that each plan is something like a STIR-FRY plan or a SOUFFLE. This information does not limit the types of steps that can be included in the plan, it only defines the class of results, the class of goals that the plan is expected to satisfy. The definition of a plan basically includes its ingredients, its steps and the type of plan it is (figure 3.1).

The planner's knowledge of ingredients is defined in a semantic net that includes information such as the taste, size and texture of each ingredient as well as functional information such as the role that the ingredient plays in different dishes.

Every plan that a case-based planner has in memory has a set of goals associated with it that is generated from general role information on the plan type and the specific ingredients in the current plan. These goals are inferred from the knowledge about the requirements of the general dish type of the plan, (in CHEF this would mean plan types such as STIR-FRY, SOUFFLE and PASTA-DISH) combined with the information associated

```
(def:rec broccoli-with-tofu
  (ingredients
     ingr1 (tofu lb .5)
     ingr2 (soy-sauce tablespoon 2)
     ingr3 (rice-wine spoon 1)
     ingr4 (corn-starch tablespoon .5)
     ingr5 (sugar spoon 1)
     ingr6 (broccoli lb 1)
     ingr7 (r-pepper piece 6))
  (actions
     act1 (chop object (ingr1) size (chunk))
     act2 (marinade object (result act1)
                  in (& (ingr2) (ingr3) (ingr4) (ingr5))
                   time (20))
     act3 (chop object (ingr6) size (chunk))
     act4 (stir-fry object (& (result act2)  (ingr7)) time (1))
     act5 (add object (result act3) to (result act4))
     act6 (stir-fry object (result act5) time (2)))
  (style style-stir-fry))
```

Figure 3.1: The definition of BROCCOLI-WITH-TOFU.

with the items that are included in the plan itself (broccoli, beef, shrimp). In CHEF for example, a STIR-FRY plan that includes broccoli generates the goal to have the broccoli crisp while a SOUFFLE plan that includes broccoli includes the goal to have the broccoli be soft. Going back to the example from architecture in which windows were added to different designs, a window in a two story house would have to open and close while a window in a climate control high-rise would have to be sealed shut. The general nature of the overall plan effects the specifics of individual goals. So, from the basic definition that includes the general plan type and the objects that are included in it, a case-based planner can infer the goals that a plan should satisfy.

CHEF's knowledge about stir-fry plans, for example, includes the fact that all vegetables should end up crisp, each piece should be no larger than a certain size and that the dish in general should take on the taste of the major spices. This default information allows the planner to infer the presense of goals that may not have been specified in the original request.

In an plan for a stir fry dish of broccoli and tofu that CHEF builds, it combines this general knowledge stir frying with the specifics of the particular plan to generate the following goals:

```
BROCCOLI-WITH-TOFU

If this plan is successful, the following should be true:

The dish now tastes savory.        The dish now tastes sweet.
The dish now tastes salty.         The broccoli is now crisp.
The dish now tastes hot.           The tofu is now soft.
```

Plans also have links to any failures that occurred while they were being built. These links are attached to plans that have failed and have been repaired to now avoid those failures. Every plan has knowledge of the goals it satisfies and the problems it avoids. This, of course, is only the case with plans that a planner experiences problems with. Plans that run smoothly the first time will have no failures associated with them. But plans that are the result of repaired failures are also linked to the failures that they avoid.

In CHEF, the BEEF-AND-BROCCOLI plan discussed in the first chapter that was repaired after having had a failure resulting from the interaction between the stir frying of the beef and the stir frying of the broccoli records the fact that it does so.

```
BEEF-AND-BROCCOLI

If this plan is successful, the following should be true:

The beef is now tender.            The dish now tastes salty.
The dish now tastes savory.        The dish now tastes sweet.
The broccoli is now crisp.         The dish now tastes like garlic.

The plan avoids failure of type
SIDE-EFFECT:DISABLED-CONDITION:CONCURRENT
exemplified by the failure 'the broccoli is now soggy'
in recipe BEEF-AND-BROCCOLI.
```

> Each of the plans in CHEF's memory of plans knows the ingredients it requires, the steps it defines and the general type of plan that it is. Each plan also knows the goals it is supposed to achieve and the problems that it is designed to avoid.

Recipes make up the content of CHEF's plan memory. It begins with only 10 recipes for different types of dishes and expands this to a final set of 40 recipes that it uses as the basis for later planning. As CHEF makes modified versions of the recipes it has on hand, the task of planning becomes easier as it stores the results of that planning away for future use.

A set of plans is useless however, if they are not organized so that they can be accessed at the appropriate times. So we need more than plans, we need plans and a memory organization. But the question of memory organization is actually a question of function, a question of use. So what function is this memory of plans going to have? To what use are the individual plans going to be put? In answering this, we will start with the basic needs of a simple plan retriever and expand the memory it uses as those needs are expanded.

Given that we are discussing a planner with the primary task of building plans that achieve its goals, it seems straightforward enough to think that the plans in its memory of plans should be stored by the goals that they satisfy. Each goal that a case-based planner has to plan for should be able to find some plan, if it exists, that satisfies it.

In CHEF, the goal to have a stir fry dish should point to one or more stir fry plans. The goal to have a dish that is hot should point to a set of hot dishes and so on for goals such as including beef in a dish or having a shrimp in the dish. In general there should be a link between the planner's different goals and the plans that satisfy them (figure 3.2). Such a link would allow CHEF to find plans that satisfy individual goals and also allow it easily to place plans in memory by associating them with the particular goals they satisfy.

But it is often the case that a case-based planner has to plan for many goals at once and has to find a single plan that satisfies a set of goals rather than just one. In order to deal with this, it needs a memory of plans that is organized by more than just simple links between goals and plans. It needs to be able to hand a set of goals to its memory and have it return a plan that satisfies all of them, if one exists. The memory of a case-based planner has to be designed so that multiple keys can be used in combination to find plans in memory.

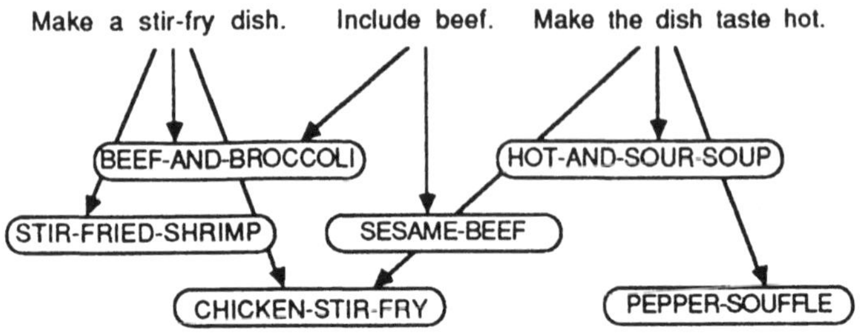

Figure 3.2: Goals point to plans.

> A case-based planner's memory has to be organized such that multiple features can be used in combination to search for plans.

One way to implement a memory that uses a set of features to index to the objects it stores is through a discrimination net. To organize and access plans by the multiple goals that they satisfy, CHEF's plan memory is implemented as a discrimination net of plans in which the discriminators are the goals that each plan satisfies. Given a set of goals such as having a hot stir fry dish with shrimp, CHEF can drive down through the discrimination network of its plan memory and find a plan that satisfies all of these goals, if one exists (figure 3.3). If CHEF cannot drive down any further, it picks between the plans lower down in the net at random.

As with any descrimination net implementation, there was a trade-off made in CHEF between space and flexibility. In CHEF we made the trade-off in the direction of saving space by strictly ordering the features used in building the net in a value hierarchy. Traversal of the net is always done using the most valuable (*e.g.*, hardest to plan for) goals first.

> The basic organization of CHEF's plan memory is a discrimination net of plans indexed by the goals they achieve.

Often there are times when there isn't a plan in memory that satisfies all of the goals that the planner is interested in. At these times, the "best match" will be a plan that only satisfies some if its goals that it will have

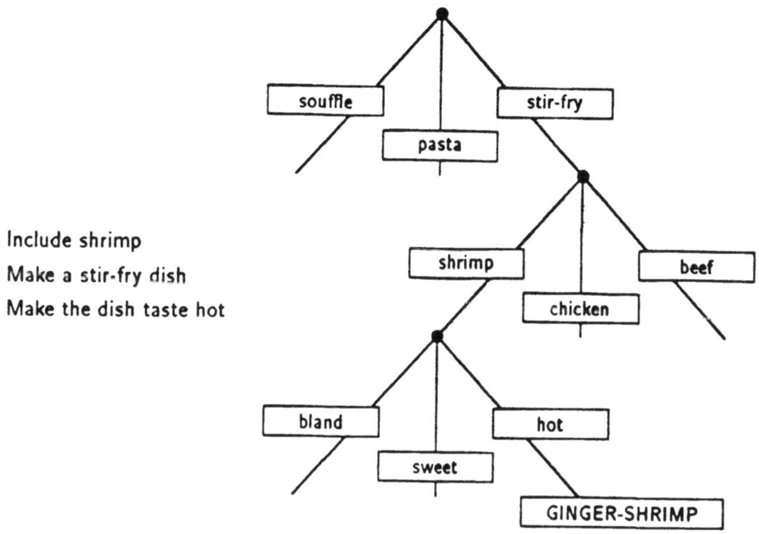

Figure 3.3: Discrimination network of plans indexed by goals.

to modify to satisfy others. In these situations it would be helpful if the planner could find a plan that accounted for at least some of the features of the goals that it does not completely satisfy. This partial satisfaction of goals would mean less work later on for the process that has to add the steps for the unsatisfied goals to the plan. It would be helpful to have some sort of notion of a partial match between goals so plans that satisfy goals similar to the current ones could be identified. A plan that partially satisfied a goal has to be altered less than a plan that did not satisfy the goal in any respect whatsoever.

Imagine that CHEF is trying to find a plan that satisfies the goal of having a hot stir fry dish that includes shrimp. Imagine that it does not have such a plan, that it only has a hot beef dish and a hot fish dish. Now, because the fish has a lighter taste than the beef, the amount of seasoning used in it is slightly lower than for the beef dish. If the beef dish is chosen as the initial plan, its seasoning will have to be altered along with its main ingredient. If the fish dish is taken, however, the shrimp can be added directly in place of the fish along with a step for shelling the shrimp. There is an advantage to choosing a plan that satisfies goals similar to the planner's own goals, even if one cannot be found that satisfies the goals directly. So a case-based planner needs some idea of which goals are similar to each other. It can then use this similarity metric to find plans that at least partially satisfy a goal if it cannot find one that exactly satisfies it.

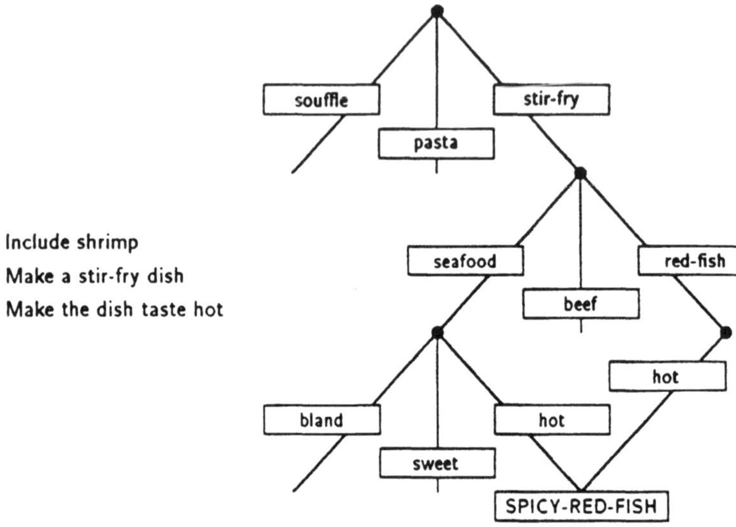

Figure 3.4: Finding plans that satisfy partially matching goals.

CHEF implements its similarity metric using a hierarchy that links similar goals to one another. The more alike two goals are, the closer they are in this hierarchy. The information in this hierarchy is used when plans are searched for and when they are placed in the plan memory. When a new plan is stored in memory, each goal that it satisfies is used in placing it deeper into the network and, at each level of discrimination, more general versions of these goals are also used to index it, in anticipation of the later need to find partial matches. So a plan that includes fish will be indexed by the fact that it includes fish and by the fact that it includes a seafood. If a specific goal cannot be used to drive deeper down into the network, more general versions of it are tried. In looking for a plan that includes shrimp, the RETRIEVER will first use "shrimp" and then will back off and use the more general "seafood". Doing this it finds the plan that includes fish (figure 3.4). So partial matches on particular goals are only searched for after exact matches fail to be found.

If a plan to satisfy a particular goal cannot be found, CHEF searches for a plan that satisfies a similar goal.

In cases where there are many plans that partially match the goal that is currently determining a planner's search, it must be able to use other features to decide which of the plans that partially satisfy the goal does so in the best possible way. For example, if there were two seafood plans in memory, one for red fish and one for crawfish, a planner would have to choose between them when looking for a plan that partially satisfies the goal to include shrimp. While both have similar seasoning, the plan that includes the crawfish also has provisions for shelling the fish, making it the better plan for adaptation to shrimp. The fact that both shrimp and crawfish have shells, represented in the TEXTURE slot of both items, should be used to choose the crawfish plan over the red fish plan. A case-based planner needs to be able to notice the similarity between the features within individual goals as well as noticing that two goals are specialized versions of same abstraction.

In order to allow this sort of discrimination on individual features of the goals in a plan rather than features of the plan itself, CHEF's plan memory has a level of feature discrimination that immediately follows any discrimination on the basis of general versions of the goals that a plan satisfies. While both the red fish and the crawfish plans are discriminated by the fact that they both include seafood, there is a further level of discrimination under that which uses the features of each of the goals themselves rather then the features of the overall plan. The TASTE, TEXTURE, SIZE and COLOR of each item included in the goal is used at this level. After discriminating down to the two plans that include seafood, because shrimp is a seafood, the plan retriever uses the individual features of shrimp to further discriminate down to a plan that is not only for an item of the same general type but also for an item that shares features in common with the goal currently being planned for (figure 3.5).

In deciding which of the individual features of a particular goal to use in further discriminating between possible partial matches, CHEF uses a static ordering of the features that determines which should be discriminated off of first. This ordering for goals involving the inclusion of particular foods, the only goals for which partial matching is really useful, is TASTE, TEXTURE, SIZE and COLOR. To decide between possible partial matches, the planner checks the features of the current search goal against the features of the goals satisfied by the plans in memory in this order. If all or none match on TASTE, it goes on to TEXTURE, then on to SIZE and COLOR. Any ties, in which one feature determines a set of plans rather than just a single plan is decided by the next significant feature.

The features that are important to a match, however, often change in response to context. In choosing between the plan which includes red fish

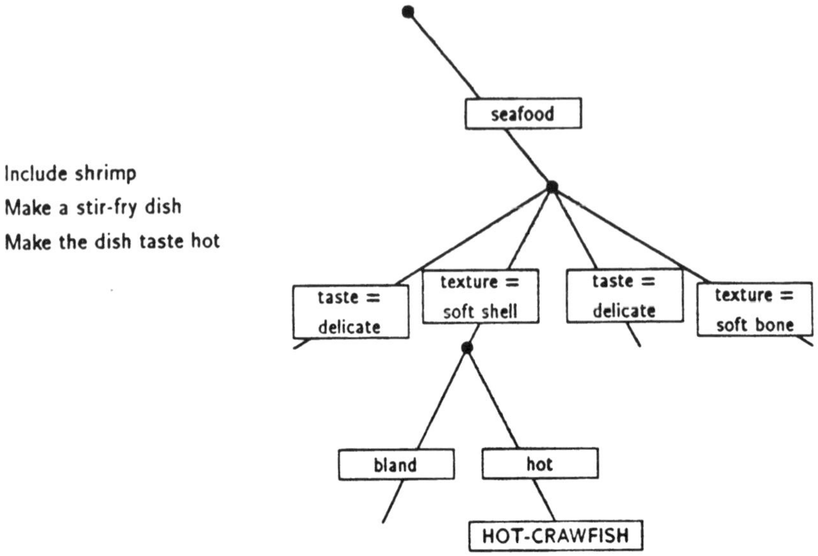

Figure 3.5: Discriminating on the features of partially matching goals.

and the one which includes crawfish for use as the baseline plan for the shrimp, the important factor is actually the TEXTURE of the items not the TASTE. It would be desirable to be able to choose the features of a partial match that are most relevant to the current situation to use in further discrimination down to a particular plan. Further, this choice of features should be made on the basis of the experiences that the planner has had with the particular features it is looking at.

CHEF deals with this issue by associating each feature of an item to be included in a dish with the failures that it has participated in. For example, CHEF knows that the fact that crawfish have a shell has caused a failure because of the ordering constraint that the removal of the shell places on a plan. It knows that the shell has to be removed before any other steps are performed on the crawfish, but learned this only after a plan was tried in which the crawfish were going to be shelled after being marinated. This resulted in a failed precondition on the SHELL that the crawfish be manageable before shelling. Besides repairing the plan, CHEF also marks TEXTURE = soft/shell as problematic. Later, when the plan retriever is deciding which feature to use to discriminate between partial matches, it sees that shrimp has TEXTURE = soft/shell and uses this feature to discriminate between possible plans rather than the first feature on its static ordering, TASTE. The fact that a feature has been problematic in the past gives the planner the idea that it may be problematic in the present. If it turns out that more than one feature has a failure associated with it, the one with the greatest number of associations is used first. Failures alone are used to mark features because a failure associated with a feature is an indication of the fact that it is problematic.

This method of choosing relevant features allows CHEF to find the plan that is best suited for adaptation to a particular goal, because it makes use of its past experiences to identify problematic features that should be planned for even if the entire goal cannot be.

> In making similarity judgments between goals, a case-based planner tries to find goals of the same type that have similar features. In matching goals, it first looks at those features which it has experienced as being problematic.

It is important to point out that this use of experience to select relevant features is not the indexing by problems that plans avoid which has been mentioned in earlier sections. That sort of indexing will be discussed later and relates to interactions between the plans for multiple goals. The method that has just been described here relates only to the use of experience to select the features of goals that are most important in putting together a partial match between a new goal and the goals that an existing plan already satisfies.

There is another sort of problem that arises when a case-based planner is using its plan memory. It is the problem of deciding between plans that satisfy the same number of different goals. For example, in trying to find a plan for a stir fry dish that includes both beef and broccoli, the CHEF planner is faced with two possibilities: a plan for broccoli with tofu and a plan for beef with green beans. Each of these plans satisfies two of the three goals that the planner has. The first satisfies the goal of making a stir fry dish and the goal of including broccoli. The second satisfies the goal of making a stir fry dish and the goal of including beef. Each satisfies two of the three goals held by the planner, but one could be more useful to its needs. The question is, which of these plans does the planner actually want, and what kind of knowledge can it use to assure that it will choose or find the right one.

The choice of the right plan here is not altogether obvious. But because the meat in a stir fry dish usually determines the seasoning the right choice in this situation is the plan that already includes the beef. If the other plan were taken, more changes would have to be made to it giving the planner more work to do. One of the considerations in choosing between two plans then, has to be the amount of work that the planner at large is going to have to do to alter them to account for the goals that they do not satisfy. Just as the plan retrieval mechanism needs a similarity metric to decide how well a plan partially satisfies a goal, it also needs some way to determine the relative utility of the goals that it fully satisfies. If CHEF had to use the tofu dish as a starting point, it would have to go through the process of removing the tofu and any special steps or ingredients that it required before adding the beef. This would require more work on the part of the planner than just replacing the vegetables.

CHEF implements this utility metric through a static ordering of the general goal types that reflects the difficulty of altering an existing plan to satisfy a member of that type. For example, it is trivial to add spices to a dish, but it is very difficult to modify a dish of one type to be a dish of another type. Because of this, the general goal to have a certain type of dish ranks higher on the priority list used to order goal types than does the general goal to include the tastes associated with spices. So in searching for a plan to satisfy the two goals of having a stir fry dish and having the dish be hot, the planner uses the fact that the first is a high priority goal and the second a very low priority goal to choose a stir fry plan that isn't hot rather than a stew plan that is. It is just easier to add red pepper to a stir fry plan than it is to modify a plan for a stew to be a stir fry dish.

> CHEF decides between competing plans that satisfy the same number of different goals using a notion of the relative value of each goal. This value metric is based on how hard CHEF will have to work later to incorporate a new goal into a plan it has found. It uses goals that are less difficult to incorporate into existing plans only after the more problematic goals have been exhausted.

The memory that has been defined thus far is able to react to a set of goals and provide a plan that satisfies or partially satisfies as many of the high priority goals as possible. A case-based planner first uses its knowledge of the relative difficulty of modifying plans to prioritize the goals it is handed. This difficulty is represented by an ordered list of the general goal types. It then uses the highest priority goal to drive into memory and abandons the search on the basis of that goal only after it has failed to find a plan that even partially satisfies it.

The effectiveness of this is seen the first time CHEF builds a plan for fish when it only has access to stir fry plans for chicken, beef and tofu and a plan for fish stew. It never even sees the plan for fish stew, because it first discriminates on the goal of having a stir fry dish. While it misses the specifics of the fish plan it gains the information that it has to have to make the stir fry plan in general. Unfortunately, it cannot find a fish stir fry plan. Because of this, it has to back off on the goal for fish itself and be satisfied with the partial match with chicken. The chicken plan is chosen because the TASTE of the chicken is a closer match to the fish than either the tofu or the beef. Once it make this discrimination, it is able to continue to drive down in memory and find a stir fry chicken plan that also tastes hot.

```
Searching for plan that satisfies -
   Include fish in the dish.
   Have the dish taste hot.
   Make a stir-fry dish.

Placing goals in order of difficulty -
   Make a stir-fry dish.
   Include fish in the dish.
   Have the dish taste hot.

   Driving down on: Make a stir-fry dish.
 Succeeded -
Driving down on: Include fish in the dish.
  Failed - Trying more general goal.
    Driving down on: Include sea food in the dish.
      Failed - Trying more general goal.
        Driving down on: Include any animal in the dish.
         Succeeded -
        Driving down on: TASTE
         Succeeded -
Driving down on: Have the dish taste hot.
 Succeeded -

 Found recipe -> REC6 HOT-CHICKEN

Recipe exactly satisfies goals ->
     Make a stir-fry dish.
     Have the dish taste hot.
```

```
Recipe partially matches ->
    Include fish in the dish.
      in that the fish can be substituted for the chicken.
```

While this type of organization satisfies many of the requirements that a case-based planner has for its plan memory, we have not yet discussed the one feature that makes the plan indexing of a case-based planner that learns from failure so different from the plan storage of other planners: indexing plans by the problems that they avoid. This indexing allows a planner that learns from failure to *anticipate and avoid* problems that it has encountered before.

When an *anticipate and avoid* planner is planning for a set of goals, it is often the case that it is able to predict that the normal plans for some of the goals will interact to cause a problem. That is, it predicts that its normal indexing methods and its normal modification procedures will result in a failed plan. The next section will discuss how a case-based planner makes this type of prediction, but for now, this is not as important as the fact that it is able to do it at all.

When the CHEF program looks at the goals to make a stir fry dish with chicken and snow peas, it can predict that the snow peas are going to end up soggy as a result of stir frying them with the chicken. When it looks at the goals to make a pasta dish that includes duck, it predicts that the fat from the duck is going to make the dish too greasy. When it looks at the goals to make a soufflé with Kirsch, it can predict that the liquid is going to make the batter too wet to rise. In many different situations, it can predict that some sort of failure is going to occur if the normal planning procedures are followed.

But what can a case-based planner do with this sort of prediction? How can it change its regular approach of finding a plan that satisfies as many goals as possible and then modifying it?

One thing it can do is take the prediction and use it to find a plan that explicitly avoids the problem that has been predicted. It can search for a plans that avoid soggy vegetables, do something to take care of the grease or deal with the problem of too much liquid. It can use the fact that it predicts a problem to find a plan that avoids it. This is exactly what the CHEF planner does.

When CHEF generates the prediction of a failure from a set of goals it generates a goal to avoid that failure. This goal is then added to the initial set of goals that is handed to the plan retriever. which then uses this goal to search for a plan that avoids the problem in exactly the same way it searches for plans that directly achieve other goals.

A planner, however, can only use the fact that a plan avoids a particular problem if it is stored in memory indexed by that fact. This turns out not to be a problem, in that each plan that is altered in response to a failure, and now avoids that failure, carries the information that it does so. This information can be associated with the plan when it is repaired and later used to index it in memory. So each plan that avoids a particular problem is indexed by the fact that it does so. Thus the a case-based planner can later find the plan when it predicts the need to avoid that problem.

One example of this rises out of the beef and broccoli plan built by CHEF. The BEEF-AND-BROCCOLI plan mentioned in the last chapter initially was a failure. The broccoli, because it was stir-fried with the beef, ended up being soggy. But it was repaired so it now avoided the problem that rises out of stir frying a crisp vegetable with meat. To make it possible to find that plan again it was then indexed under the fact that it does avoid that problem along with the other goals that it satisfies. This means that the goal to avoid this problem can now be used to find this plan, independent of any other goals in the current situation that the BEEF-AND-BROCCOLI plan might satisfy.

> If a case-based planner predicts that a problem will occur while planning for a set of goals, it will search for a plan that avoids that problem while also satisfying or partially satisfying its current goals.

In terms of which goal should be used initially to search memory, the priority on goals to avoid problems should rank higher than most other goals. In CHEF for example, when the program searches for a plan for a set of goals that includes a goal to avoid a problem, the only goal that will have more priority and thus be used in the search before the avoidance goal is the goal to make the particular kind of dish that has been specified. In the example where CHEF anticipates that the snow peas are going to end up soggy if stir fried with the chicken, the goal to avoid that situation has higher priority than either the goal to include chicken or the goal to include snow peas. It has lower priority, however, than the goal to make a stir fry dish.

Goals to avoid problems must have high priority. This chicken and snow pea example shows why.

Imagine a memory that has only three plans in it. The first is a plan for beef and broccoli that avoids the problem of the vegetable getting soggy because of being stir fried with the meat. The second is a plan for chicken and green beans. The third is a plan for snow peas and shrimp.

The first plan deals with the problem of the interaction between the meat and vegetable by first stir frying the vegetable, removing it from the pan, stir frying the meat and then adding the vegetable back in before serving. The other two plans, because green beans do not get soggy if stir fried in liquid and shrimp does not put off the liquid that other meats do, just have the meat and vegetables stir fried together (figure 3.6).

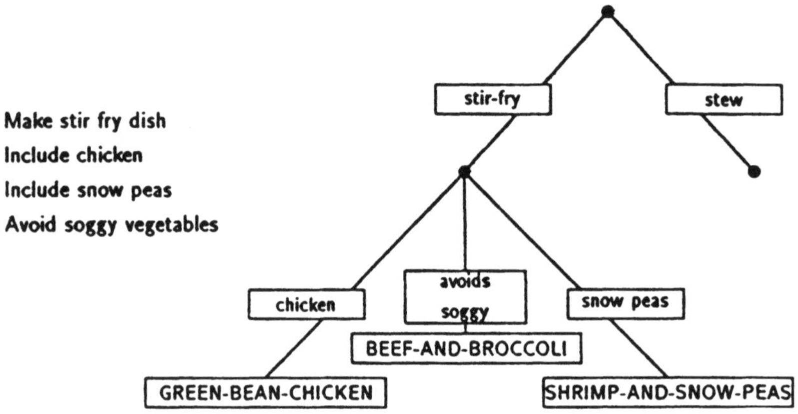

Figure 3.6: Three plans that could be used.

In trying to find a baseline plan to modify, the planner has four goals that it has to satisfy: make a stir fry dish, include snow peas, include chicken, and avoid the problem of the snow peas getting soggy because of the liquid from the chicken. The first three goals were handed directly to the planner and the final avoidance goal was generated by the plan as a result of anticipating the problem.

Now it seems clear that the first plan, the plan for beef and broccoli, is the best match for the goals that CHEF currently has. For it to completely satisfy CHEF's goals, it only has to have the chicken substituted for the beef and the snow peas substituted for the broccoli. The chicken will also have to be boned, but this step is added automatically. The other two plans, even though each will require only one ingredient substitution, will require major alterations of their steps to accommodate the interaction between the stir frying of the chicken and the stir frying of the snow peas. Because it is a plan to deal with the interaction between a set of goals, it is a plan for the overall situation rather than a plan for any of the individual goals alone.

But if the goal to avoid the failure is given lower priority than either the goal to include the chicken or the goal to include the snow peas, then the beef and broccoli plan will not be used. Instead the chicken and green bean plan, which requires alteration that CHEF is really not up to, will be chosen. While it can make the changes to add or delete new ingredients, the modification mechanisms are not designed to make changes to avoid predicted failures. But this plan, if the normal modifications to add a new goal are taken, will result in exactly the failure that CHEF has anticipated. If the other plan, to stir fry shrimp and snow peas, is used, the same sort of failure will occur as a result of the normal plan modification process.

Goals to avoid problems have to have a higher priority in search than the goals to include particular items and tastes. They must have lower priority than the goals to make the plan a certain type of dish, (such as STIR-FRY or SOUFFLE) because there is a qualitative difference between changing the specifics of a particular plan and changing the general type of plan that it is.

> Goals to avoid the problems have higher priority in search than goals for individual additions. This allows CHEF to find plans for the overall situation in preference to plans that only attend to the details.

As with other goals, however, it is possible that no plan in memory exists that satisfies both the goal to avoid a particular problem and the goal to make a particular kind of dish. In these cases, the planner has to prefer the plan that satisfies the goal for the dish type. This means that the planner has to make the changes that the plan requires to avoid the problem which has been predicted. In one example from CHEF, the planner anticipates a problem due to the grease from a fatty duck when requested to build a dish with duck and pasta but is unable to find a plan that avoids the problem. The program is able to anticipate the problem of grease from the duck because of its experience in making Duck Dumplings, but has no PASTA plan that deals with it. In this case, the planner has to select a pasta dish for pork and deal with the problem of the extra fat (figure 3.7) by modifying the plan that is being built.

Adding goals to avoid problems to the set of achievement goals used to retrieve plan does not change the process of plan retrieval. It only

```
Found recipe -> REC9 ANTS-CLIMB-A-TREE

Recipe fails to match ->
    Avoid failure of type SIDE-FEATURE:GOAL-VIOLATIONO
    exemplified by the failure 'The dumplings are now greasy'
    in recipe DUCK-DUMPLINGS.

Problem predicted - SIDE-FEATURE:GOAL-VIOLATIONO

Considering critic:
After doing step: Bone the duck
              do: Clean the fat from the duck
         because: The duck is now fatty. - Critic applied.
```

Figure 3.7: Using new DUCK critic.

changes the attributes of a plan that can be used to store and search for it. The avoidance goals are treated just like any other goal, and are used to discriminate down into memory in the same way.

```
Searching for plan that satisfies -
   Include chicken in the dish.
   Include snow pea in the dish.
   Make a stir-fry dish.
   Avoid failure of type SIDE-EFFECT:DISABLED-CONDITION:CONCURRENT
    exemplified by the failure 'The broccoli is now soggy'
    in recipe BEEF-AND-BROCCOLI.

Placing goals in order of difficulty -
 Make a stir-fry dish.
 Avoid failure of type SIDE-EFFECT:DISABLED-CONDITION:CONCURRENT
  exemplified by the failure 'The broccoli is now soggy'
  in recipe BEEF-AND-BROCCOLI.
 Include chicken in the dish.
 Include snow pea in the dish.

Driving down on: Make a stir-fry dish.
 Succeeded -
Driving down on:
  Avoid failure of type SIDE-EFFECT:DISABLED-CONDITION:CONCURRENT
  exemplified by the failure 'The broccoli is now soggy' in recipe
  BEEF-AND-BROCCOLI.
```

```
  Succeeded -
 Driving down on: Include chicken in the dish.
  Failed - Trying more general goal.
   Driving down on: Include meat in the dish.
    Succeeded -
 Driving down on: Include snow pea in the dish.
  Failed - Trying more general goal.
   Driving down on: Include vegetable in the dish.
    Succeeded -
  Found recipe -> REC9 BEEF-AND-BROCCOLI

 Recipe exactly satisfies goals ->
     Avoid failure of type
     SIDE-EFFECT:DISABLED-CONDITION:CONCURRENT
     exemplified by the failure 'The broccoli is now soggy'
     in recipe BEEF-AND-BROCCOLI.
     Make a stir-fry dish.
   Recipe partially matches ->
     Include chicken in the dish.
       in that the recipe satisfies: Include meat in the dish.

 Recipe partially matches ->
     Include snow pea in the dish.
       in that the snow pea can be substituted for the broccoli.
```

In CHEF, aside from the form of one of the goals the planner treats the task of finding a baseline plan for the goals of including chicken and snow peas in a stir fry dish in the same way it treated the task when confronted with the goals of including fish in a hot stir fry dish.

With the addition of indexing plans by the problems they solve, a case-based planner's memory of plans is complete. The planner can use its memory to find the plans that fit its needs. Plans that best achieve the goals that it is given and avoid the problems that it can anticipate. Plans that partially satisfy goals can be found along with those that completely satisfy them. The features that a case-based planner uses to discriminate between plans that partially satisfy a particular goal change with the planner's experiences, reflecting the problems it has had and the features it has seen cause them. The plans that the planner finds satisfy the goals that are most difficult for it to deal with, meaning that the work that the planner has to do after finding a plan is reduced to the minimum. A case-based planner's plan memory is designed to meet the needs of the planner at large and the features that are used to access it are those that best describe the problems that the plans searched for have to solve.

> A case-based planner's plan memory organizes plans by the goals they satisfy and the problems they avoid. It searches through this memory using its current goals and predictions of problems. It uses a notion of similarity between goals and the idea of their relative value to find a "best match" even in those situations where a plan that satisfies all of its goals cannot be found.

3.3.2 Memory of failures

To avoid failures, a case-based planner has to be able to anticipate them, to notice that they are going to occur in order to give the planner the goal to avoid them. The process that predicts the occurrence of failures anticipates them on the basis of goal features that predict them and the knowledge base it uses to do this is the planner's memory of failures.

The idea behind problem anticipation is to predict failures on the basis of the surface features of a situation that have caused similar failures in the past. This is what happens when a surgeon predicts the possibility of cardiac arrest when putting a patient with low blood pressure under general anesthetic or when an engineer predicts heat build up problems when clustering a power supply next to a communications bus. The reoccurrence of features that participated in past failures brings the memory of the failures to mind, warning the planner of the problems that have to be attended to in building the current plan.

In CHEF, this means predicting that the plan for the goals of including a meat and a crisp vegetable in a stir fry dish will lead to the vegetable becoming soggy after being stir fried with the meat. Once this prediction has been made, a plan that avoids this problem can be found by adding the goal to avoid the problem to the other goals that are used to search for a plan. But before the problem can be solved, it must be anticipated. And to anticipate these failures, a case-based planner's memory of them has to be organized so as to link its memory of past failures to the features of the goals that predict them.

Before the question of what the organization of a case-based planner's memory of failures looks like can be answered, the question of what a single memory of a failure looks like has to be addressed.

Planner's in general judge failures using the goals associated with each of their plans and their knowledge of undesirable states that it wants to avoid. A failure can be a goal that is unsatisfied or an undesired state that has resulted from a plan. In either case, however, a failure is a particular state in the world that has come about or failed to come about as a result of the running of the current plan. This notion of failure is at the level of the plan as it is run, not at the level of the construction of the plan. These are not failures in plan *building*. These are failures in the results of the plan that has been built.

In most domains failures are straightforward: a patient dies, a wall fails to stay in place or a car fails to start.

In the CHEF domain they are equally straightforward. In the example of the beef and broccoli recipe, the failure is that the broccoli is soggy. In the case of the strawberry soufflé, the failure is that the soufflé is flat. In the case of the duck dumplings, the failure is that the dumplings are greasy. Even in those situations where the failure is the lack of a certain state, as in the case of the soufflé where the failure is actually that the soufflé didn't rise, the failure that CHEF recalls and reasons about is identified with the state that actually occurred.

But the failure state itself is not all that CHEF stores when it places the recollection of a failure in memory. It also stores three other aspects of the situation: the general causal configuration of the situation that led to the failure, the plan in which the failure occurred, and the features which are predictive of the failure. Of these, the most important is the set of features that are predictive of the failure, because these are used to organize the failure in memory.

> A case-based planner's memory of a failure includes the failure state itself, the plan in which it failed, the causal situation that led to the failure and the features that can be used to predict it.

The organization of a memory of failures is less complex than its organization of plans. It is simpler because its function and the requirements of the process that uses it are simpler. The task that uses this memory is to infer the possibility of a failure from a set of surface features. The memory of failures that it uses has to be organized in a way that connects those features to the failures they predict.

A case-based planner's memory of failures can be thought of as a simple network of nodes, in which particular failures are connected to the goal features that predict them. In case-based planning, the surface features of a situation all stem from the goals that it is asked to plan for. The goals that the planner is planning for define its situation, so it makes no sense to link memories of failures to anything but these goals. In CHEF, for example, the failure in the beef and broccoli situation is linked to the goal to include meat, the goal to include any crisp vegetable and the goal to have a stir fry dish. These features then predict the failure.

When a particular feature of a goal can be identified as participating in a failure, a test is built for that feature and is associated with the most specific version of the goal that allows the most general use. If all members of a class of items is associated with the failure, a link is made directly from that class to the memory of the failure itself. If only specific members of a class predict a certain failure, a link can be made to the class which passes through a test for the specific, predictive features before going on to link up with the memory of the failure itself.

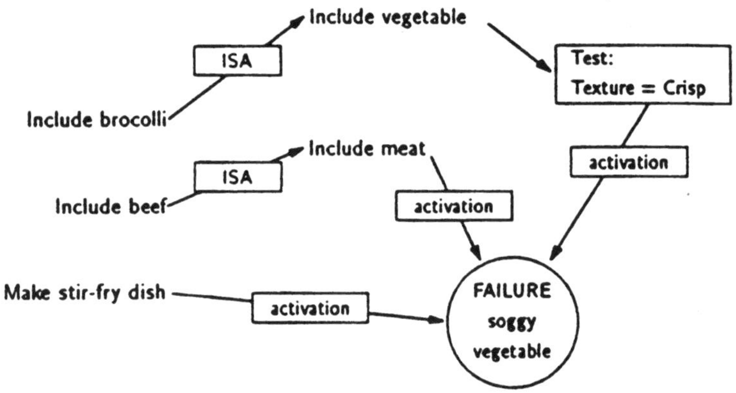

Figure 3.8: Features linked to the memory of a failure.

There is a simple example of this from CHEF. As a result of the beef and broccoli failure, a test on the texture of vegetables, is built and associated with the concept VEGETABLE because a goal for a crisp vegetable predicts this failure while goals for other vegetables do not. It is associated with VEGETABLE rather than BROCCOLI because the prediction is valid for all crisp vegetables not just broccoli. Because any meat will put off the liquid like that which participated in the failure no test is needed and a link is built directly from the presence of the goal to the memory of the failure. The same holds true for the goal to make a stir fry dish (figure 3.8). These links and tests are constructed after a failure has occurred to enable the planner to predict their occurrence again in the appropriate situation.

There are various ways to choose which features in a situation should be linked to a failure that has arisen. CHEF chooses which features of a failure to mark as predictive of it on the basis of a causal explanation it builds of why the failure occurred. The rules that explain the individual causal links are used to create tests that are associated with each goal.

> The features that predict a failure are linked to the memory of the failure itself. This allows the presence of those features to activate the memory of the failure at a later time.

```
Building demon: DEMON0 to anticipate interaction between rules:
"Meat sweats when it is stir-fried."
"Stir-frying in too much liquid makes crisp vegetables soggy."

Indexing marker passing demon under item: MEAT
by test: Is the item a MEAT.

Indexing marker passing demon under item: VEGETABLE
by test: Is the item a VEGETABLE.
     and Is the TEXTURE of item CRISP.

Goal to be activated = Avoid failure of type
SIDE-EFFECT:DISABLED-CONDITION:CONCURRENT
exemplified by the failure 'The broccoli is now soggy'
in recipe BEEF-AND-BROCCOLI.
```

When a new set of goals is handed to a case-based planner, its first step is to collect all of the tests associated with the goals and fire them. The true firing of a test activates the associated feature, which, in turn, sends a marker to a node related to the failure the feature predicts. If all of the features that are required to predict any failure send markers to its node, it activates itself and the planner builds a goal to avoid that failure and adds it to the planner's goal list.

When CHEF looks at the goals to have a stir fry dish that includes chicken and snow peas, for example, the fact that the chicken is a meat and the snow peas are a crisp vegetable activates the memory of a past stir fry failure stemming from these features.

```
Searching for plan that satisfies -
   Include chicken in the dish.
   Include snow pea in the dish.
   Make a stir-fry dish.

 Collecting and activating tests.

  Fired: Is the dish STYLE-STIR-FRY.
  Fired: Is the item a MEAT.
  Fired: Is the item a VEGETABLE.
         Is the TEXTURE of item CRISP.

     Chicken + Snow Pea + Stir frying = Failure
    "Meat sweats when it is stir-fried."
    "Stir-frying in too much liquid makes vegetables soggy."
     Reminded of BEEF-AND-BROCCOLI.
     Fired demon: DEMON0

Based on features found in items: snow pea, chicken and stir fry
Adding goal: Avoid failure of type
SIDE-EFFECT:DISABLED-CONDITION:CONCURRENT exemplified by
the failure 'The broccoli is now soggy' in recipe
BEEF-AND-BROCCOLI.
```

> A case-based planner uses the features of its current goals to activate the memories of any failures that they predict. If a failure is recalled, a goal to avoid it in the current situation is added to the planner's list of active goals.

Sometimes the surface features that led to a failure and are predictive of a problem were not the immediate cause of the problem. The failure in the example of the strawberry soufflé that didn't rise is a case in point. The failure of the soufflé to rise was a result of too much liquid as opposed to just the result of adding fruit. In cases like this, links are made to the memory of the failure from both the features that predict the failure, such as the goal of including high moisture fruit, and from the actual cause, in this case added liquid. This even happens in the case of the soggy broccoli, because the planner understands that the true problem is the liquid in the wok and will predict this failure if it is asked to increase any liquid while stir-frying broccoli.

```
Building demon: DEMON3 to anticipate interaction between rules:
"Liquids make things wet."
"Without a balance between liquids and leavening
 the batter will fall."

Indexing marker passing demon under item: SPICE
by test: Is the item a SPICE.
         Is the TEXTURE of item LIQUID.

Goal to be activated = Avoid failure of type
SIDE-EFFECT:DISABLED-CONDITION:BALANCE
exemplified by the failure 'The batter is now flat' in recipe
STRAWBERRY-SOUFFLE.
```

> A case-based planner also has to link features that were not part of the initial planning situation, but did participate in the failure, to its memory of the failure.

If a new situation arises which has goals that are different from those in the original situation that led to the failure, but are related to the states that actually caused it, these states will be activated thus activating the failure. This, in turn, will cause the creation of a goal to avoid the failure to be added to the planner's goal list. For example, if the planner is asked to build a recipe for a soufflé dish that includes the liqueur kirsch the passing of activations is made through the memory of failures and the goal to avoid the problem of liquid causing the soufflé to fall is added to the goal list. This means that even situations that are different than those which led to a past failure can be used to activate the memory of that failure and give the plan retrieval mechanism the information it needs to find a plan that avoids the problem.

```
Searching for plan that satisfies -
   Include kirsch in the dish.
   Make a souffle.

Collecting and activating tests.
```

```
Fired: Is the dish STYLE-SOUFFLE.
Fired: Is the item a SPICE.
       Is the TEXTURE of item LIQUID.

     Kirsch + Souffle = Failure
    "Liquids make things wet."
    "Without a balance between liquids and leavening
     the batter will fall."
     Reminded of STRAWBERRY-SOUFFLE.
     Fired demon: DEMON3

Based on features found in items: kirsch and souffle.
Adding goal: Avoid failure of type
SIDE-EFFECT:DISABLED-CONDITION:BALANCE exemplified by
the failure 'The batter is now flat' in recipe
STRAWBERRY-SOUFFLE.
```

> A case-based planner uses all connections between the features of a situation and its memories of failures to predict failures even in situations that are for very different goals than those that first caused them.

A case-based planner's memory of failures is organized around the features of the goals and states that predict them. This lets the planner go directly from a set of goals to be planned for to a memory of those failures that it should be trying to avoid. By also associating the failures with the actual features that caused them, features that may not have been directly attached to a goal that the planner was working on when the failure occurred, it is also able to be reminded of failures in situations that have surface features different from those of the original situation. So the planner's memory of failures can provide appropriate predictions of problems in situations that are similar to those it has seen before at the level of initial goals and at the level of the actual causes of particular problems.

The CHEF program had to deal with and learn from a range of problems. It had to be able to deal with plans that had objectionable side-effects, those that did not satisfy their own goals and those that were not able to run to completion. These included:

- The problem in a BEEF-AND-BROCCOLI plan rising out of the interaction between the meat and vegetables being stir fried together.

- The problem in a FISH-STIR-FRY plan of the iodine taste of the fish ruining the dish.
- The problem in CHEF's first shrimp dish of ordering the SHELL step after the MARINATE.
- The problem of stir frying beef with salt, a step which dries the meat out, in the dish HOT-BEEF.
- The problem on maintaining a balance between liquid and leavening encountered by CHEF in two different forms in making soufflés.
- The problem encountered in building duck dishes of the dish becoming too greasy.

Other problems had to do with misordered steps and problems rising out of the side-effects of different approaches to satisfying the same goals.

3.3.3 Memory of modifiers

A case-based planner's memory of plan modifiers is designed to give the planner the alterations it needs to make to an old plan so as to make it satisfy new goals. In order to do this, the memory of modifiers has to be sensitive to the plan that is being changed and the new goal that is being added. It also has to be aware of any failures that have been predicted but are not avoided by the plan that the plan retrieval mechanisms have found. The memory needed to do this actually combines two storage systems. The first is a static table of standard modifications, indexed by the plan being altered and the goal being added. The second is a dynamic set of ingredient critics that are stored under particular ingredients, indexed by the failures that they repair.

As was argued in the first chapter, the goal to add a window to a wall will be implemented in different ways given different initial designs. A window in a house will be different than one in a high-rise. So the mechanisms that add new features to a design or goals to a plan have to be sensitive to both the goal being added and the plan that is being altered.

> A case-based planner's memory of plan modification has to be sensitive to both the goal being added and the plan being modified.

The rules that the CHEF program uses to alter plans to accommodate new goals are indexed by both the goal and the general plan type. Its memory of standard modifiers is a table, indexed by the general plan type, (*e.g.*, STIR-FRY, SOUFFLE, PASTA) and general versions of each of the planner's goals (*e.g.*, Include meat, Include vegetable, Make dish taste hot). Searching for a set of steps to add a new goal is a matter of looking up the entry in the table and adding the steps listed there. If an entry is empty, a more general version of the goal is used, until a set of steps is found.

> CHEF stores rules for modifying plans in a table of steps that is indexed by the plan to be modified and the general type of the goals to be added.

In adding broccoli to a stir fry dish CHEF searches its memory of standard modifications for steps indexed under BROCCOLI and STIR-FRY. As it is, no such modification exists, forcing the MODIFIER to look for the steps indexed under VEGETABLE and STIR-FRY. Here it finds the steps that tell it to CLEAN, CHOP and STIR-FRY the broccoli (figure 3.9).

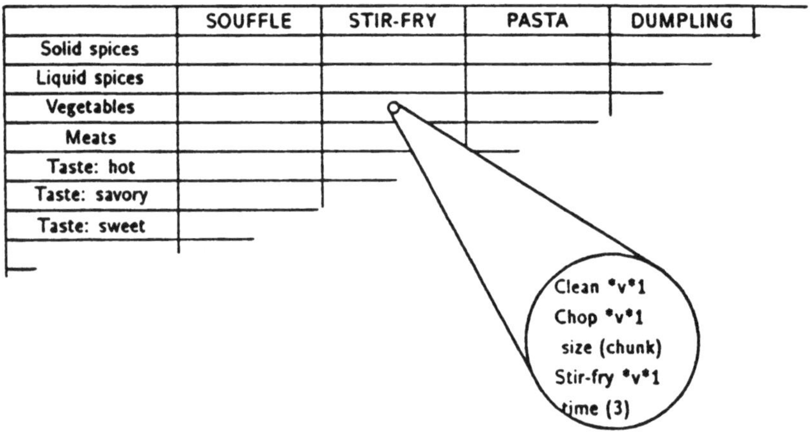

Figure 3.9: Table of standard modification rules.

There are some steps that are specific to particular objects that the planner knows about. In the CHEF domain, for example, shrimp has to be shelled in every plan and chicken has to be boned before chopping. To deal with these idiosyncratic problems, the planner has access to a set of *critics*, which are stored under the ingredients that they deal with. Each of these critics has a test that it applies to the current plan, and a modification it makes if the test is true. These critics deal with the specific problems not covered by the more general modification rules.

> *Critics* are rules that add steps which compensate for the idiosyncrasies of particular ingredients. They are stored under the ingredient that they handle.

In adding chicken to a recipe that once used beef, CHEF applies a critic associated with chicken that says the chicken must be boned before chopping:

```
Modifying recipe: CHICKEN-STIR-FRIED
to satisfy: Include chicken in the dish.

Role substitution of chicken for beef in CHICKEN-STIR-FRIED.

Placing some chicken in recipe CHICKEN-STIR-FRIED

Considering critic:
 Before doing step: Chop the chicken
  do: Bone the chicken. - Critic applied.
```

While a case-based planner can start out with a set of critics that are useful, its initial set can never be exhaustive. A planner often encounters objects or items that have features it has never had to deal with before, features that lead to planning failures. When a planner has an encounter like this, and is able to assign blame for the resulting failure to an individual object rather than to an interaction between many objects, it can builds a new critic that describes the same alteration to a plan that was originally done to correct the plan in which the failure occurred. This new critic can then be stored under the problematic item, indexed by the problem that it solves. If, in a later planning situation, the planner predicts that this failure is going to occur again, but cannot find a plan that avoids it, the planner will still be able to access the new critic because it has the prediction of the problem to use as an index.

One example of this occurs when the CHEF program is building a plan for Duck Dumplings. After running a basic plan that just replaces duck for pork in an existing recipe, it finds that the fat from the duck makes the recipe too greasy. It repairs this problem in its new plan by removing the fat from the duck before grinding it. It also creates an ingredient critic that suggests the same step. Later, when it is planning for a pasta dish with duck, it predicts that the same problem will occur but cannot find a pasta dish that avoids it. The best it can find is the recipe for Ants Climb a Tree, a pasta dish with pork, that it puts the duck into. Because it has predicted a problem with grease, however, it has access to the ingredient critic that deals with it and can apply the repair before the failure occurs again.

```
Modifying recipe: DUCK-PASTA
to satisfy: Include duck in the dish.

Role substitution of duck for pork in recipe DUCK-PASTA.

Placing some duck in recipe DUCK-PASTA

Considering critic:
Before doing step: Grind the duck
 do: Bone the duck.  - Critic applied.

Considering critic:
 After doing step: Bone the duck
 do: Clean the fat from the duck
 because: The duck is now fatty
 avoiding: SIDE-FEATURE:GOAL-VIOLATION
 - Critic applied.
```

> A case-based planner learns new critics when it repairs faulty plans. These are stored under the item they relate to, indexed by the problems they solve.

This two part system makes up a case-based planner's memory of modifiers, used to store information about how to add new plans to existing goals while avoiding the failure that the initial plan was not able to. It consists of a static table of standard modification steps, indexed by the type of plan being altered and the goal being added. This is augmented by a set of critics that make changes to a plan to deal with problematic features of particular objects. These critics are stored under the objects that they provide for, indexed by the particular failure that they repair. This system then, allows the planner to access changes that have to be made to add new goals to a plan and to avoid problems that will rise out of the modifications it has just made.

There is a point to be made about the three that have been mentioned thus far.

All three of these memories are *dynamic* organizations that are altered in response to failures on the part of the planner. When a case-based planner has a failure it makes three changes to its view of the world:

- First, it changes its plan memory by adding a new repaired plan that now avoids a particular problem. This plan is indexed by the fact that it avoids the problem the planner first encountered.
- Second, it changes its memory of failures, adding links between the features that predict the problem to its memory of the problem itself. With these links it can now predict the failures it has encountered and use that prediction to find plans that avoid them in its memory of plans.
- Third, it also stores the changes that it had to make to the original plan in repairing it, indexed so that they will be accessed when those repairs have to be made again.

When a case-based planner learns from a failure, it learns more than just a new plan. It also learns the features which predict failures, which are used to find plans that avoid them, and it learns new ingredient critics which are used to repair existing plans that do not avoid the problems its has predicted.

When a case-based planner encounters and repairs a failure it saves the plan that now avoids it, saves a description of the situation that predicts it and saves the changes that had to be made to repair it.

3.3.4 Memory of repairs

CHEF has a set of strategies that suggest repairs to the failures it encounters. Its memory of these repair strategies is completely static. It does not add new strategies and does not alter their organization. It begins with a set of strategies for repairing failed plans and ends with exactly the same set. While it is not at all dynamic, this organization has the same functional motivation as the organization of the planner's other memories. The details of this organization and the specific strategies that it stores will be discussed later. Right now, however, an "in principle" argument about the type of indexing used to organize these strategies will make some clarifying points about the nature and the use of memory in general.

> While it is not dynamic, CHEF's memory of repairs is organized to best serve the function of plan repair.

When a plan that a case-based planner has built does not function correctly, it must repair the plan on the spot. To do this, the planner needs a set of *repair strategies* that tell it how to fix a plan. It is important to contrast these with the modification rule which are designed to add a new goals to existing plans. These repair strategies are not designed to add new goals. They are designed to alter a plan to achieve the goals that it was supposed to achieve but did not, because of an unforeseen feature of some ingredient or an interaction between many ingredients.

> Each repair strategy suggests a plan alteration that will fix a particular kind of problem.

CHEF has 17 of these strategies. These are repair strategies that any planner, case-based or otherwise, needs to deal with to fix plans that fail. They reorder steps that interfere with each other, replace steps that have bad side-effects, recover from bad states and add steps that will allow bad states to stand without destroying the overall plan. In most situations only a few of these strategies will be of any help at all in repairing the plan.

These strategies are specific, in that they suggest repairs for particular classes of problems, but they are not *domain* specific:

- ALTER-PLAN:SIDE-EFFECT
- ALTER-PLAN:PRECONDITION
- RECOVER
- REORDER
- ADJUST-BALANCE:UP
- ADJUST-BALANCE:DOWN
- ADJUNCT-PLAN:REMOVE
- ADJUNCT-PLAN:PROTECT
- ALTER-TIME:UP
- ALTER-TIME:DOWN
- ALTER-ITEM
- ALTER-TOOL
- SPLIT-AND-REFORM
- ALTER-PLACEMENT:BEFORE
- REMOVE-FEATURE
- ALTER-PLACEMENT:AFTER
- ALTER-FEATURE

The task is to find a way to link the problem that the planner is faced with to the strategies that will solve that problem. But what are the features of a planning problem that are most closely linked to the kind of repairs that will fix it?

The features that best describe a problem for the purposes of finding a way to solve it are the features of the causal situation that actually defines it.

Organizing the strategies used to repair different problems are a set of structures that correspond to different causal configurations defining the circumstances leading up to a problem. These are planning TOPs. Each of these structures organizes a small set of repair strategies, with each repair strategy being associated only with the TOP or TOPs for which it is appropriate. Any one strategy can be associated with many TOPs, because each strategy suggests an alteration of one aspect of the causal situation that led to the failure and that one aspect can be part of many different configurations.

> Repair strategies are stored under planning TOPs. Each TOP corresponds to a planning problem and the strategies it stores are all designed to fix with that problem.

When a case-based planner is confronted with a failure it builds up a causal explanation of why that failure has occurred. The explanation describes the steps and states that have caused the failure and the goals that were being served by each of those steps and states. This explanation of the causes of the failure indexes to a TOP and the strategies that will repair the failure.

The causal description of a failure provides an explanation as to why the failure occurred. This explanation takes the form of answers to a series of questions that the planner asks about the failure.

> Each TOP is indexed in memory by a causal description of the type of problem it corresponds to. So the strategies stored under each TOP are only recalled when the problems that they fix arise.

Going to CHEF for an example, in the case of the fallen strawberry soufflé built by the program, the explanation that the planner builds for why the failure occurred is that a side-effect of chopping the strawberries, (liquid in the bowl), has caused an imbalance in the relationship between the liquid and the leavening in the soufflé, which has disabled a precondition of the bake step. It also includes the fact that the goal of chopping the strawberries was to enable adding them to the batter, that the precondition on the bake step was that the liquid and leavening be in a particular balance and that the goal of baking the batter was to make it rise.

The general version of this explanation, (the side effect of a step violates a balance condition on a later step) accesses SIDE-EFFECT:DISABLED-CONDITION:BALANCE, a TOP which has 5 repair strategies indexed under it. Each of these strategies describes a change in the causal structure of the situation that will break the chain of events that led up to the failure without interfering with the goals being planned for:

- ALTER-PLAN:SIDE-EFFECT suggests finding a step that satisfies the initial goal that does not have the offending side-effect.
- ALTER-PLAN:PRECONDITION suggests finding a step that satisfies the later goal but does not have the precondition that is violated by that side-effect.
- RECOVER suggests recovering from the side effect before running the second step.
- ADJUNCT-PLAN suggests adding an adjunct plan that allows the later step to succeed even in the presence of the side-effect.
- ADJUST-BALANCE:UP suggests adjusting the relationship that the side-effect has put out of balance.

```
Searching for top using following indices:

Failure = It is not the case that: The batter is now risen.
Initial plan = Bake the batter for twenty five minutes.
Condition enabling failure = There is an imbalance between
  the whipped stuff and the thin liquid.
Cause of condition = Pulp the strawberry.
The goals enabled by the condition = NIL
The goals that the step causing the condition enables =
 The dish now tastes like berries.
```

```
Found TOP TOP3 -> SIDE-EFFECT:DISABLED-CONDITION:BALANCE
TOP -> SIDE-EFFECT:DISABLED-CONDITION:BALANCE has 5
       strategies associated with it:

       ALTER-PLAN:SIDE-EFFECT       ADJUNCT-PLAN
       ALTER-PLAN:PRECONDITION      RECOVER
       ADJUST-BALANCE:UP
```

> Each repair strategy suggests a repair that breaks a link in the causal chain that leads to the failure.

These strategies are used to find the actual alterations that have to be made to the steps in the plan, but this is not the issue right now. At this point the issue is the relationship between the features in the initial situation, the TOP that those features allow access to and the strategies that are stored under that TOP.

At the surface level, the situation defined by the failed strawberry soufflé plan has a multitude of features. Any of these could be used to find either a memory of past plans that might be helpful in dealing with the problem or a set of strategies aimed at correcting it. Any of the ingredients, the steps or the states that the ingredients passed through while the plan was being run, could be used to index to some memory that might be applied to the situation. But what would be the point of using any feature except those that actually participate in the problem. What would be the point of looking for a past plan that was linked to the current one by the fact that they both include salt? In general, what would be the point of indexing to a past episode or more abstract structure on the basis of any feature outside of the problem description?

If indexing is to be of any use at all, the *needs* of the search have to be reflected in the *means* of the search. The indexing has to reflect the function of the items being indexed. If strategies for dealing with particular planning failures are going to be organized at all, they should be indexed by a description of the problems that they deal with. Likewise, if a planner is trying to find the strategies it needs to deal with a problem, it should use only those features of the situation that participate in that problem. To search for a solution to a planning problem using features other than those involved with the problem is like looking for a ballerina in a football locker room. You may find what you are looking for, but there is no reason whatsoever to believe that you will. And there are far better places to look.

> The needs of plan repair define the organization of the planner's memory of possible repairs.

This argument for storing and retrieving general strategies can be applied to episodic memory. In storing an episode that solves a problem, it make sense that among the features that are used to index it will be those that actually define the problem. It may be stored by other features as well, because it could have uses besides those of solving that one problem alone, but it makes sense to store it by the features that will allow it to be found again if a similar problem arises. Further, when new problems arise, it makes no sense whatsoever to search for past solutions using any features other than those that define the problem itself. This would be like searching for general strategies for dealing with a problem using features that have nothing to do with the problem. It could be done, but what would be the point?

Any discussion of indexing and memory has to attend to the ultimate function of the items in memory and to the needs of the process doing the searching. Because the point of a memory organization is to allow outer processes to effectively find what they need, so an organization that does not reflect that need is useless. The fact that humans have a memory organization at all argues that it must be one that has grown out of the needs of the processes that use it, otherwise why would it be there at all?

The memory of repair strategies that CHEF uses to deal with plan failures is static. But its organization has much to say about the organization of a dynamic memory where processes are actively deciding how to store new items in memory and how to access them at a later date. Any memory organization should be centered around the function of the object that it organizes. Processes that store new items in memory should index them by the features that determine their usefulness. Later processes that have to access those items should search for them on the basis of the features of its present situation, whether it be an understanding or planning situation, that best describes the problem it is trying to solve. The organization of repair strategies is based on this idea, with repairs indexed in memory by the descriptions of the very problems they solve.

> A case-based planner's memory of plan repairs is indexed by the features that determine the use of the items it stores. Each repair is indexed by a description of the problems it deals with.

There has to be a relationship between the function to which a memory is put, whether it be a memory of a past episode or a memory of a set of strategies, and the features that are used to find it. In the case of a memory of repairs, this means that the memory of repair strategies is indexed by causal descriptions of the problems that they solve. In choosing the indices to use in finding these strategies the planner has to identify the causal chain that leads to the failure it is repairing and use the description of that chain of events to access the appropriate strategies.

Chapter 4

Planning TOPs and Strategies

Any planner, case-based or otherwise, should repair plans by explaining the circumstances behind a failure and then using this explanation to find the TOP and the repair rules stored under it that will deal with the problem. As the last chapter argued, without these repair rules and the TOPs that house them, the planner would have to backtrack and replan entirely, losing work that has already been done. The ability to identify when a set of repairs is applicable and which of them can be instantiated is crucial to planning in that it allows the planner to intelligently recover from its own errors.

4.1 TOPs in understanding and planning

In *Dynamic Memory* [Schank 82] Schank suggested the idea that structures relating to the *interaction* of goals and plans could be used to organize narrative episodes in memory. He called these structures *Thematic Organization Packets*, or TOPs. The idea behind these structures was simple: just as the concept underlying a primitive action such as ATRANS [Schank and Abelson 77] could be used to store inferences relating to that action, structures relating to the interactions between these actions and the goals that they serve could also be used to store inferences that relate to the interaction. He also suggested that these structures could be used to organize episodes that they describe to as well as the inferences that they relate to.

Schank suggested that these structures could be used for understanding in two ways: to supply expectations about a situation and to provide remindings of past situations that are similar to a current one that could be used in generalization.

In one of Schank's examples, he discussed the similarity between the stories *Romeo and Juliet* and *West Side Story*. The similarity, he argued, could be described at an abstract level of the goals interactions in both stories. Both stories had young lovers, but more importantly, both stories were cases of **Mutual Goal Pursuit; With Outside Opposition** which corresponds to the TOP MG;OO. This is simply saying that both stories were cases of two individuals joining together to plan for the same goal in the context of opposing forces. What is interesting about this characterization is that it gives the understander some expectations. One possible expectation is that the opposing forces will try to divide the partners, thus reducing their chances of success. Another is that there may be conflicts that rise out of each of the partners using a different plan to achieve the mutual goal.

But there are also specific expectations that can be made because of the further similarities between the two stories. The details of *Romeo and Juliet* can actually provide specific expectations that can be used in understanding *West Side Story*. We can predict the problems due to the false account of Maria's death because we have seen them before in the false account of Juliet's death. We can tell what will happen in *West Side Story* because we are reminded of what happened before in *Romeo and Juliet*.

Having expectations and memories stored under TOPs like MG;OO allows an understander to make predictions on the basis of the interactions between story elements along with those that can be made from the individual story elements themselves. But the fact that these structures store actual memories allows the understander to also learn more about these interactions by comparing repeated instances of them and then generalizing. In the *Romeo and Juliet/West Side Story* example, the understander is able to learn that in case of MG;OO, lack of communication between partners can lead to problems of misunderstanding and cross-planning. This is a piece of information that can be associated with MG;OO, itself, not only those cases of MG;OO that relate to star-crossed lovers.

By having structures in memory that correspond to goal interactions rather than individual goals or actions, an understander can have access to expectations that relate to those interactions and can learn more about them by generalizing across similar instances that they describe.

Planning TOPs are quite similar to understanding TOPs in that they are memory structures that correspond to the interactions between the steps and states of a plan. Each planning TOP describes a planning problem in terms of a causal vocabulary of effects and preconditions. Instead of storing inferences about the situation described, however, each planning TOP stores possible repairs to the planning problem it corresponds to. Once a problem is recognized, the planner can use the repairs stored under the TOP that describes it to alter the faulty plan and thus fix the failure.

For example, the TOP SIDE-EFFECT:BLOCKED-PRECONDITION describes situations in which the side effect of one step violates the preconditions for a later one. One case of this would be Sussman's example of a planner painting a ladder [Sussman 75] before painting a ceiling and then finding the precondition for painting the ceiling, having a useable ladder, has been violated by an earlier step in the plan that has left the ladder wet. This TOP is recognized because the planner can see that a step is actually blocked, the state that blocks it is the product of an earlier step, and the state itself does not satisfy any goals. Once the planner has the TOP it is then able to apply the different general strategies for repairing the faulty plan that are stored under the structure. In this case, the strategies are:

- ALTER-PLAN:PRECONDITION - Find a way to paint the ceiling that does not require a ladder.
- ALTER-PLAN:SIDE-EFFECT - Find a way to paint the ladder that does not leave it wet.
- REORDER - Paint the ceiling before painting the ladder.
- RECOVER - Do something to dry the ladder.

Each of these strategies is designed to break a single link in the causal chain that leads to a failure.

Like understanding TOPs, planning TOPs correspond to situations involving the interactions between goals and plans. Unlike understanding TOPs that organize inferences, however, planning TOPs organize the steps that a planner can make in response to the problems that the TOPs describe.

The planning TOPs discussed in this chapter were developed for the CHEF program and are built out of a general vocabulary of causal interactions (see Appendix A). The problems that they describe include many of those discussed by both Sussman [Sussman 75] and Sacerdoti [Sacerdoti 75] but the descriptive detail of TOPs allows a richer description than was possible using the vocabulary of critics suggested by them. As a result, a planner that uses TOPs to diagnose and repair planning problems is able to describe problems in greater detail and thus suggest a wider variety of repairs for each problem encountered.

4.2 TOPs and strategies

CHEF's approach to plan repair is based on the idea that the strategies for repairing a problem should be stored in terms of that problem. In much the same way that it makes sense to organize plans in terms of the goal that they satisfy so that they can be found when the goals arise, it makes sense to store plan repair strategies in terms of the situations to which they apply, so that too they can be found when those problems arise.

CHEF implements this idea of storing repairs in terms of the problems that they solve using a set of planning TOPs that correspond to different planning problems. Each TOP organizes a set of repair strategies, which in turn suggest abstract alterations of the circumstances of the problem defined by the TOP. For CHEF, part of the definition of a problem includes the positive goals that were being attempted by the steps that participate in it. A TOP is defined not only by the series of steps that define the failure, it is also defined by the goals that those steps were originally designed to satisfy. Only those strategies that will fix the problem defined by a TOP while at the same time maintaining the goals that are already satisfied by the existing steps are found under that TOP. Any strategy that can be applied will repair the current problem without interfering with the goals that the steps involved with that problem still achieve.

> A planning TOP consists of the description of a planning problem and the set of repair strategies that can be applied to solve the problem.

A TOP stores those, and only those, strategies that will solve the problem corresponding to the TOP without interfering with the goals that are satisfied by the steps included in the problem. This is an important point that deserves an example.

In a failure encountered by CHEF while creating its strawberry soufflé plan, the problem is diagnosed as a case of SIDE-EFFECT:DISABLED-CONDITION:BALANCE. This TOP is distinguished by the fact that the condition that is disabled is a balance condition and the state that disables it is a side-effect. That the state that undermines the plan is a side-effect is important in that it allows the strategies RECOVER and ALTER-PLAN:SIDE-EFFECT to be associated with the TOP. The first of these strategies suggests finding a step that will remove the side-effect state before it interferes with a later step. The second strategy suggests finding a replacement for the step that caused the side-effect with a step that accomplishes the goal of the original action without producing the undesired effect. Both of these strategies depend on the fact that the state in question is a side-effect, that is, a state that does not satisfy any goals that the planner is trying to achieve.

If the situation were different (*e.g.*, if the liquid produced by chopping the strawberries satisfied one of the planner's goals), these two strategies would no longer apply. Adding a step that would remove the added liquid would violate the goal that it achieved. Replacing the step that causes the liquid with one that does not would likewise violate the goal. Changing the goals changes the strategies that can be applied to the problem because some strategies will now interfere with those goals while fixing the problem. Such differences between situations are reflected in the TOPs that are found to deal with them. If the liquid served some goal but violated a balance condition, the TOP found would be DESIRED-EFFECT:DISABLED-CONDITION:BALANCE. Unlike the TOP SIDE-EFFECT:DISABLED-CONDITION:BALANCE, this structure does not suggest the strategies ALTER-PLAN:SIDE-EFFECT and RECOVER, because they would fix the initial problem only at the expense of other goals.

Another important point about the relationship between planning TOPs and the strategies they store is the problem of applicability. Every strategy that is stored under a TOP will, if it can be applied, repair the problem that originally accessed the TOP. There is no guarantee, however, that a strategy can be applied in every situation. In the case of the problem when CHEF stir fries beef and broccoli together, one strategy, ADJUNCT-PLAN, suggests finding a step that can be run concurrent with the STIR-FRY step that will absorb the liquid produced by the beef. Unfortunately, no such step exists in CHEF's knowledge of steps. So ADJUNCT-PLAN, while it would have repaired the plan, can not be implemented in this situation because the steps required to turn it into an actual change of plan do not exist. Each strategy describes what a change that would fix a failed plan looks like but no strategy can be implemented if the steps that would make that change do not exist.

Every TOP describes a specific causal configuration that defines a problem. In turn, each of the strategies under a TOP describe one way to alter the configuration that will solve the problem described by the TOP. The individual strategies suggest changes to one part of the overall configuration. Because the different causal configurations are built out of a vocabulary of interactions that is common to all of them, some share many features. For example, one TOP corresponds to the situation in which the side-effect of a step alters the conditions required for the running of a later step while another corresponds to the problem of the side-effect of a step itself being an undesired state. These two TOPs share the feature that a side-effect of a step is interfering with the planner's goals, although in different ways. Because of this, they share the strategy ALTER-PLAN:SIDE-EFFECT which suggests finding a step to replace the original step in the plan that causes the side-effect with one that achieves the same goals but does not cause the side-effect. Each of these TOPs also organizes other strategies, but because some aspects of the problems that they describe are shared, they also share the strategy that suggests changes to that aspect of the problem.

> The repair strategies stored under a TOP are those, and only those that will repair the problem described by the TOP. Because each strategy alters one aspect of the problem it may be associated with many TOPs that share that aspect.

4.3 TOPs

Each of CHEF's TOPs has two components: the features of the problem used to index to it and the strategies that it suggests to deal with that problem. CHEF stores its TOPs in a discrimination network, indexed by the features that describe the problem that they correspond to. In searching for a TOP, CHEF extracts these same features from its explanation of the current problem and then the TOP suggests the strategies it stores to solve that problem.

It is important to note that there are two ideas here. The first is that repair strategies should be organized by the problems that they solve. This is the idea that goal interactions should be used to organize plan repairs at all. This is the structural part of the notion of using TOPs in planning. The second idea is composed of the actual content of the different TOPs and strategies that are presented here. The suggestion that a TOP such as SIDE-EFFECT:DISABLED-CONDITION:CONCURRENT exists as a particular structure is different than the idea that these structures exist at all.

CHEF uses sixteen TOPs in organizing its repairs. Each is defined and indexed by the features of a particular planning problem and organizes the two to six strategies that can be applied to the problem it corresponds to. While there are clearly more TOPs that can be used in plan repair than CHEF knows about, those it has describe the planning problems that it is forced to deal with. An expanded domain with a different set of problems, and possible reactions to them, would require an equally expanded set of TOPs and strategies.

4.4 CHEF's TOPs

CHEF's TOPs fall into five categories or families of problems. Some have to do with side-effects of a step interfering with later steps, some with the features of objects enabling bad effects, and some with the problems of blocked preconditions. The TOPs within each family share features with one another. The fact that they describe similar problem situations means they must share those strategies that are designed to repair the aspects of the problem that they have in common.

- SIDE-EFFECT, or SE, TOPs that describe problems that are generated by the side-effects of STEPs.
- DESIRED-EFFECT, or DE, TOPs that describe problems that are generated by the desired effects of STEPs.
- SIDE-FEATURE, or SF, TOPs that describe problems generated by the features of OBJECTs that do not satisfy any goals.
- DESIRED-FEATURE, or DF, TOPs that describe problems generated by the goal satisfying features of OBJECTs.
- STEP-PARAMETER, or SP, TOPs that describe problems generated by improperly set STEP parameters.

CHEF's TOPs fall into families of configurations whose members correspond to similar causal situations and organize similar repair strategies.

4.4.1 SIDE-EFFECT (SE)

The most commonly used TOPs in CHEF are from the family of TOPs that describe problems with the side-effects of one step interfering with the overall plan in one way or another. There are five TOPs that belong to the general family of SIDE-EFFECT TOPs (SE):

- SE:DISABLED-CONDITION:CONCURRENT - The side-effect of a step disables its own success requirements or the requirements of a concurrently run step.
- SE:DISABLED-CONDITION:SERIAL - The side-effect of a step disables the success requirements of a later step.
- SE:DISABLED-CONDITION:BALANCE - The side-effect of a step disables a success requirement of a later step by causing an imbalance in a required relationship.
- SE:BLOCKED-PRECONDITION - The side-effects of a step violate the preconditions of a later step that are required for it to run at all.
- SE:GOAL-VIOLATION - The side-effects of a step are in themselves an undesired state.

> SE TOPs describe situations in which the side-effects of a step interfere with the successful running of a plan.

SE:DISABLED-CONDITION:CONCURRENT (SE:DC:C)

This TOP describes situations in which a side-effect of a step interferes with the satisfaction conditions of the step itself or of another step that is being run concurrent with it. Here the side-effect has to occur as the step is being run, not just at the end. Likewise, the condition that is violated is not just a precondition, it is a condition that has to be true for the entire duration of the step. In CHEF these are referred to as *developing side-effects* and *maintenance conditions.* One example of this situation is in the case of the BEEF-AND-BROCCOLI plan in which the liquid generated by stir frying the beef violates the maintenance condition on the step to stir fry the broccoli that the pan remain dry. As a result, the plan fails because the broccoli becomes soggy.

The indices for SE:DC:C are:

- There is a failure.
- The failure is caused by a violated condition.
- The step that caused the state violating the condition is concurrent with the step which has resulted in the failure.
- The condition satisfies no goals.
- The step that causes the condition satisfies at least one goal directly or indirectly.

The strategies that are stored under SE:DC:C are: SPLIT-AND-REFORM, ALTER-PLAN:SIDE-EFFECT, ADJUNCT-PLAN:REMOVE, ADJUNCT-PLAN:PROTECT and ALTER-PLAN:PRECONDITION.

Each of these strategies aims its attack at one part of the causal chain that led to the failure. For example, SPLIT-AND-REFORM suggests breaking the self defeating single step into a series, ALTER-PLAN:SIDE-EFFECT suggests that a different step be used that does not produce the violating condition and ADJUNCT-PLAN:REMOVE suggests that a new step be added that removes the effects altogether.

SE:DISABLED-CONDITION:SERIAL (SE:DC:S)

The complement to the TOP SE:DC:C is SE:DC:S, which differs from its sibling in that the step that causes the problem side-effect occurs before the step which the side-effect interferes with. The problem condition is still a side-effect, but the steps involved are separate so there are more options than in the case of SE:DC:C.

The indices to this TOP differ from those of SE:DC:D only by the fact that the two steps involved are not the same:

- There is a failure.
- It is caused by a violated condition.
- The step that would have achieved the desired state follows the step that caused the violating conditions.
- The condition satisfies no goals.

- The step that causes the condition satisfies at least one goal directly or indirectly.

The fact that two steps are separated in time gives the planner more options than if they had been the same. The strategies indexed under the TOP reflect this added flexibility: REORDER, ALTER-PLAN:SIDE-EFFECT, ALTER-PLAN:PRECONDITION, RECOVER, ADJUNCT-PLAN:REMOVE and ADJUNCT-PLAN:PROTECT.

SE:DISABLED-CONDITION:BALANCE (SE:DC:B)

A slightly different situation in which a side-effect causes problems is defined by SE:DC:B. This is the situation in which the side-effect of a step produces the effect of changing an existing state so as to increase an amount, in turn causing an imbalance in a relationship required for a later step. Unlike SE:DC:S, the condition caused by the earlier step is already accounted for by the plan but not to the extent that the new version of the plan causes. The fallen soufflé in the STRAWBERRY-SOUFFLE plan is an example of this problem. The added liquid from the chopped berries causes an imbalance between liquid and leavening in the batter which leads to a fallen soufflé.

The difference between the features that access this TOP and those that access SE:DC:S is clear. SE:DC:B is found when the condition that is violated is a balance relationship that has to hold for a step to succeed.

- There is a failure.
- There is a violated balance condition on the step that caused it.
- The step that would have achieved the desired state follows the step that caused the violating conditions.
- The condition satisfies no goals.
- The step that causes the condition satisfies at least one goal directly or indirectly.

The strategies organized by the TOP are also the same, with the exception of two new strategies, ADJUST-BALANCE:UP and ADJUST-BALANCE:DOWN.

SE:BLOCKED-PRECONDITION (SE:BP)

SE:BP describes the situation in which the side-effect of a step actually halts the running of the plan. This occurs in the case of the first stir fried shrimp dish CHEF creates in which the MARINADE step that is run before the SHELL step blocks the precondition on SHELL that the shrimp be handleable.

The features used to access this TOP are:

- There is a blocked precondition.
- The condition that caused the block was caused by an earlier step.
- The condition satisfies no goals.
- The step that causes the condition satisfies at least one goal directly or indirectly.

The four strategies associated with this TOP are: RECOVER and REORDER as well as ALTER-PLAN:PRECONDITION and ALTER-PLAN:SIDE-EFFECT.

SE:GOAL-VIOLATION (SE:GV)

The TOP SE:GV describes the situation in which the side-effect of a step itself is an undesired state in the present circumstances. The state generated by the step does not interfere with other steps, it is just objectionable in its own right.

The features used to index to this TOP are:

- There is a failure.
- The step that caused it has no violated conditions that the planner can identify.

The strategies stored under this TOP are: RECOVER, ALTER-PLAN:SIDE-EFFECT and ADJUNCT-PLAN:REMOVE.

4.4.2 DESIRED-EFFECT (DE)

A somewhat different class of TOPs are those that describe situations in which the desired effect of a step, that is a state that either directly satisfies a goal or enables the satisfaction of a goal, causes problems later in the plan. The main difference between DESIRED-EFFECT and SIDE-EFFECT TOPs is that DE TOPs do not suggest strategies designed to remove or avoid the effects that are interfering with the plan. To do so would be to undercut the goals satisfied by the interfering state.

There are four DE TOPs. They are parallel to the first four SE TOPs that were discussed in the last section. But because these correspond to situations in which the interfering state satisfies a goal, the strategies that they store are aimed at altering the aspects of the problem that are not related to the desired effect itself. The DE TOPs are:

- DESIRED-EFFECT:DISABLED-CONDITION:CONCURRENT - A desired effect of a step disables its own success requirements.
- DESIRED-EFFECT:DISABLED-CONDITION:SERIAL - A desired effect of a step disables the success requirements of a later step.
- DESIRED-EFFECT:DISABLED-CONDITION:BALANCE - A desired effect of a step disables a success requirement of a later step by causing an imbalance in a required relationship.
- DESIRED-EFFECT:BLOCKED-PRECONDITION - The desired effects of a step violate the preconditions of a later step that are required for it to run at all.

CHEF does not use the TOP DESIRED-EFFECT:GOAL-VIOLATION because it defines a situation that it never has to encounter. DE:GV describes a situation in which the goal satisfying effect of a step is itself a state the planner wants to avoid. While this can happen in some planning situations, it is never the case that CHEF has to deal with states that both meet and violate its goals.

DE TOPs describe situations in which the desired effects of a step interfere with the successful running of a plan.

DE:DISABLED-CONDITION:CONCURRENT (DE:DC:C)

This TOP describes the ultimate self-defeating plan. The desired effects of a step infer with the conditions that it itself requires to succeed. Because the violating state is also serving the planner's goals, strategies such as ADJUNCT-PLAN:REMOVE and ALTER-PLAN:SIDE-EFFECT cannot be applied because they would negate a state that the planner wants to maintain. Only those strategies that are aimed at correcting the situation without altering the part of the causal chain leading to the failure that includes the violating state are included under this TOP.

The features that are used to find this TOP are:

- There is a failure.
- There is a violated condition on the step that caused it.
- The plan to achieve the desired state itself caused the violating conditions.
- The condition satisfies at least one goal directly or indirectly.

The strategies stored under this TOP are: ALTER-PLAN:PRECONDITION, SPLIT-AND-REFORM and ADJUNCT-PLAN:PROTECT.

DE:DISABLED-CONDITION:SERIAL (DE:DC:S)

Like its brother DE:DC:C, the TOP DE:DC:S is aimed at situations in which the desired effect of a step interferes with the plan rather than a side-effect that can be removed or avoided altogether. This TOP describes the situation in which the desired effect of a step violates the satisfaction conditions of a later step.

The features that index to it are:

- There is a failure.
- There is a violated condition on the step that caused it.
- The step that would have achieved the desired state is different from the step that caused the violating conditions.
- The condition satisfies at least one goal directly or indirectly.

The fact that two steps are separate in time give the planner more freedom than if they took place in parallel. The strategies under the TOP reflect this: REORDER, ALTER-PLAN:PRECONDITION, RECOVER and ADJUNCT-PLAN:PROTECT.

DE:DISABLED-CONDITION:BALANCE (DE:DC:B)

A variant of the situation in which a relationship between two states is put out of balance is DE:DC:B, which describes the situation in which the desired effect of a step is the culprit rather than a side-effect.

DE:DC:B is indexed by the following features:

- There is a failure.
- There is a violated balance condition on the step that caused it.
- The step that would have achieved the desired state is different from the step that caused the violating conditions.
- The condition satisfies at least one goal directly or indirectly.

The strategies organized by the TOP reflect the fact that the state causing the problems is a desired one by including only those that deal with the problem without interfering with that state. They are: ALTER-PLAN:PRECONDITION, ADJUNCT-PLAN:PROTECT and ADJUST-BALANCE:UP.

DE:BLOCKED-PRECONDITION (DE:BP)

The TOP DE:BP describes the situation of one of the classic problems in machine planning: the problem of ordering the steps required to build a three block tower [Sussman 75]. In this problem, the planner has the dual goals of having block A on block B, (ON A B), and block B on block C (ON B C). Unfortunately, if it starts the tower by putting A on B, (MOVE A B), before putting B on C, (MOVE B C), it is unable to continue because of the precondition on the MOVE step that the block being moved must have a clear top (figure 4.1). Because A is on B, B cannot be moved but having A on B is also one of the planner's goals. The effects of the first step violate the preconditions for the later one. This is the situation described by DE:BP. The desired effect of one step blocks the preconditions required to

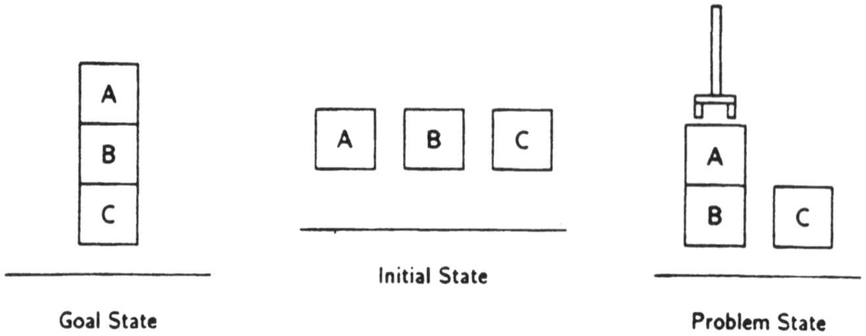

Figure 4.1: The Three Blocks Problem.

perform another step, where both steps satisfy one or more of the planner's goals. The problem is how to change the situation so that both parts of the plan can be run.

The solution that has been suggested in the past ([Sacerdoti 75] and [Sussman 75]) is to repair the plan by reordering the steps, putting B on C before putting A on B. This solution is the same as one of the two suggested by the TOP DE:BP. But DE:BP also suggests the strategy of finding some way to move the B block that does not require that it has a clear top. At the very least the approach of splitting the process of plan repair into diagnostic and prescriptive stages has allowed a gain of one new solution to this classic problem. But, quite truthfully, this is not a particularly exciting gain.

A more exciting gain lies in the vocabulary used to describe this problem at all. The vocabulary suggested by Sussman in building HACKER describes this situation as one of **Brother-goal-clobbers-brother-goal.** While this description covers cases of DE:BP, it also covers cases of SE:BP where the state blocking the goal is not a protected one. Because of this, HACKER would suggest the limited solution of *REORDER* in cases described by SE:BP where CHEF would be able to suggest the strategies of RECOVER, ALTER-PLAN:SIDE-EFFECT, ALTER-PLAN:PRECONDITION, ADJUNCT-PLAN:REMOVE as well as REORDER. Because CHEF is able to distinguish between situations in which an interfering state serves some goals and those in which it does not, it is able to know when it can apply more powerful strategies than those planner's that could not describe problems in these terms.

This is less a point about TOPs and more a point about the level of detail used to define them and describe different causal situations. Because the description of the situations leading to failures include distinctions between side-effects and desired effects, CHEF is able to distinguish between cases where different strategies apply where earlier planners could not. Because it has knowledge of exactly what steps and states in the problem have to be protected, it is able to make alterations that other planners would not have the assurance to make.

The features that are used to index to DE:BP are almost identical to those used to access SE:BP but the single difference between them has a great affect on the strategies that CHEF can apply to deal with the different situations. The features the access DE:BP are:

- There is a blocked precondition.
- The condition that caused the block was caused by an earlier step.
- The condition satisfies at least one goal directly or indirectly.

Because the planner has to protect the goals satisfied by the blocking condition it only has two strategies that it can apply to repair the situation: REORDER and ALTER-PLAN:PRECONDITION.

4.4.3 SIDE-FEATURE (SF)

In many situations, a failure will rise out of a problem having to do with a particular feature of an item in a plan rather than having to do with the effects of one step relating to the effects of another. This is the type of situation described by TOPs in the SIDE-FEATURE family of structures. These SF TOPs relate to situations in which the features of new items that have been added to plans interfere with the goals that the plans are trying to achieve. This family of TOPs is called "SIDE-FEATURE" because the TOPs in it all describe situations where a feature of an object that does not satisfy a goal interferes with the plan. This is opposed to the DESIRED-FEATURE TOPs that describe situations in which the desired feature of an object disrupts a plan.

There are three TOPs in this family that are actually used by CHEF:

- SIDE-FEATURE:ENABLES-BAD-CONDITION - An object's feature enables a step to have a faulty result.
- SIDE-FEATURE:BLOCKED-PRECONDITION - An object's feature disables a required precondition on a step.

- SIDE-FEATURE:GOAL-VIOLATION - An object's feature is itself an objectionable state.

SF TOPs describe situations in which a non-goal satisfying feature of an item interferes with the successful running of a plan.

SF:ENABLES-BAD-CONDITION (SF:EBC)

The TOP SF:EBC describes situations in which some feature of an object enables a step to have a bad result. The failure CHEF encounters in building FISH-STIR-FRY is an example of this sort of situation. The taste of the fish interacts with the stir fry step to create an iodine taste. The failure is caused by a feature of the fish itself rather than by the side-effect of a step leading into a later one.

The features of the situation that lead to recognizing this TOP are as follows:

- There is a failure.
- There is a violated condition on the step that caused it.
- The plan to achieve the desired state has a violated satisfaction condition.
- The violating state satisfies no goals.
- The condition is an inherent feature of an object.

Because there is only one step involved in this type of situation, the strategies to deal with the failure are centered around it. But because there is an identifiable state that is related to an object feature, there is also a strategy that is aimed at removing that feature: ALTER-PLAN:PRECONDITION, ADJUNCT-PLAN:PROTECT and REMOVE-FEATURE.

SF:BLOCKED-PRECONDITION (SF:BP)

Sometimes a new object is added to a plan that the steps of the plan are not designed to deal with at all. If the MODIFIER allows this to happen, it is possible that certain steps will be blocked altogether by some feature of the new object. This is the situation described by SF:BP. One example of this is the problem adding lobster to a fish dish, replacing it for the existing fish. In this situation, the planner has to deal with the problem of the shell, either when building the plan or later when a failure points to the problem. Because the texture of the lobster does not meet the preconditions for a CHOP step, the plan cannot be run without alteration. The problem is not that one step is interfering with another. It is that one of the items in the plan does not meet the requirements for running one of its steps.

The features that make it possible to recognize this situation are:

- There is a blocked precondition.
- The condition that caused the block is a feature of an object.
- The feature satisfies no goals.

The strategies that this TOP organizes are again aimed at changing the violated step itself and altering the feature of the object involved: ALTER-FEATURE and ALTER-PLAN:PRECONDITION.

SF:GOAL-VIOLATION (SF:GV)

Sometimes the problem with an item is not in that it leads to difficulties, but instead that it has a feature that by itself is a problem. This is the situation described by SF:GV. One example of this situation that CHEF deals with is the problem it encounters while trying to create Duck Dumplings. In this case, the fat from the duck itself is an objectionable feature that violates one of the planner's goals. This TOP has only those strategies that are aimed at removing the features from an item that are themselves objectionable and has no suggestions about changing the existing steps in the plan.

This situation is easy to recognize:

- There is a failure.
- The failure is an inherent feature of an object.

The strategies suggested in this situation are aimed only at changing the object itself: ALTER-ITEM and REMOVE-FEATURE.

4.4.4 DESIRED-FEATURE (DF)

Another family of TOPs related to the features of items rather than the interactions of steps is DESIRED-FEATURE (DF). DF TOPs all describe situations in which a feature of an object that actually satisfies a goal causes trouble. Unlike SIDE-FEATURE TOPs, DF TOPs store strategies that only alter the steps affected by the problem feature.

There are only two TOPs in this family that CHEF uses:

- DESIRED-FEATURE:DISABLED-CONDITION - A goal satisfying feature of an object enables a faulty result from a step.
- DESIRED-FEATURE:BLOCKED-PRECONDITION - A goal satisfying feature of an object actually blocks a required precondition of a step.

> DF TOPs describe situations in which a goal satisfying feature of an item interferes with the successful running of a plan.

DF:DISABLED-CONDITION (DF:DC)

DF:DC describes situations in which a desired feature of an object causes a step to have a bad result.

The features used to recognize this situation are:

- There is a failure.
- There is a violated condition on the step that caused it.
- The plan to achieve the desired state has a violated satisfaction condition.
- The violating state satisfies at least one goal directly or indirectly.
- The condition is an inherent feature of an object.

The strategies suggested to deal with this problem are limited to three: ADJUNCT-PLAN:PROTECT ALTER-PLAN:PRECONDITION as well as ALTER-FEATURE.

DF:BLOCKED-PRECONDITION (DF:BP)

This TOP describes a situation in which an object's feature blocks a step but the feature itself is a desired one. Because the step is actually blocked by the feature, thus removing the possibility of running an adjunct plan as in DF:DC, the strategies associated with this TOP are very limited.

The features used to recognize this situation are:

- There is a blocked precondition.
- The condition that caused the block is a feature of an object.
- The condition satisfies at least one goal directly or indirectly.

The strategies that this TOP organizes are again aimed at changing the violated step itself and altering the feature of the object involved: ALTER-FEATURE and ALTER-PLAN:PRECONDITION.

4.4.5 STEP-PARAMETER (SP)

The last family of TOPs relates to problems involving the amount of time a step takes and the tools it uses. Problems involving objects are described the SF: and DF: TOPs.

The STEP-PARAMETER family has two TOPs:

- STEP-PARAMETER:TIME - A failure is blamed on the amount of time step has run.
- STEP-PARAMETER:TOOL - A failure is blamed on the tool used in a step.

SF: TOPs describe situations in which the bad parameter of a step interferes with the successful running of a plan.

SP:TIME (SP:T)

SP:T is actually two TOPs, one for steps that have run too long and one for steps that have not run long enough. These are particularly useful TOPs in the CHEF domain where cooking times have a great effect on the results of a step. While significant, however, the features used to index to the TOPs and strategies used to repair the problems described by those TOPs are trivial.

The indices for SP:T:LONG, which describes situations in which steps have been run too long, are:

- There is a failure.
- The plan to achieve the desired state has a violated satisfaction condition.
- The violated condition is a time that is greater than the time constraint on the objects of the step.

There are two strategies to deal with this problem: SPLIT-AND-REFORM and ALTER-TIME:DOWN.

The indices for SP:T:SHORT, which describes the reverse situation in which situations in which step have not been run long enough, are:

- There is a failure.
- The plan to achieve the desired state has a violated satisfaction condition.
- The violated condition is that the time on the step is less than time required by the objects of the step.

Again there are two strategies to deal with this problem: ALTER-TIME:UP and SPLIT-AND-REFORM.

SP:TOOL (SP:TL)

Sometimes the instruments used in a step lead to problems of their own. Baking a soufflé in the wrong size pan, for example, will lead to the outside cooking too fast or too slowly. SP:TL describes situations in which a step fails because of an inappropriate instrument.

The indices for SP:T are:

- There is a failure.
- The instrument used causes the failure.

There is only one strategy associated with this TOP: ALTER-TOOL.

4.5 Why TOPs?

In CHEF, TOPs are used to organize the repair strategies that can be applied to the problems that they describe. But strictly speaking, this is not necessary. The different strategies could each be indexed under the particular causal connection that they deal with. Instead of using a causal description of a situation to index to a TOP and then accessing the strategies that are housed under it, a planner could use the pieces of the same causal description to index directly to each of the strategies independently. Given this, what function do CHEF's TOPs really serve?

The answer to this has three parts: two within the CHEF implementation and one outside of it.

The first part of this answer is that CHEF uses its TOPs for something other than organizing repair strategies. It also uses them to guide it in learning from its failures. Along with the strategies it organizes, each TOP also indicates which features in the situation it describes should be marked as predictors of the current problem. Because each TOP corresponds to a particular causal configuration, it can store the information as to which aspects of the overall situation are important for CHEF to notice in future planning.

For example, CHEF had to repair the problem of the iodine taste of fish ruining a dish. In doing so, it diagnosed the situation as one of SIDE-FEATURE:ENABLES-BAD-CONDITION. This TOP organizes a set of strategies that can be applied to the problem, but because the TOP describes a situation in which a feature of an item interacts with a step (the taste of sea food and the stir-fry step), it is able to direct the planner to mark both of them as predictive of the failure. Once this is done, the co-occurrence of the two features, the goal to include sea-food and the goal to make a stir fry dish, will cause the planner to anticipate and try to avoid the failure. Neither feature alone, however, predicts this problem.

The TOP SIDE-FEATURE:GOAL-VIOLATION, which describes situations in which a feature of an item directly violates a goal, directs the learning in a slightly different direction. Like SF:EBC, SF:GV states that the feature of the object should be marked, but it does not suggest that any particular step be marked, because the feature violates one of the planner's goals independent of any step that has acted on it. CHEF diagnoses the greasy texture in the Duck Dumplings it builds as a case of SF:GV, because duck will have fat in any situation. As a result, CHEF marks the duck itself as predictive of a greasy texture in all circumstances.

CHEF uses its TOPs to indicate which aspect of a situation should be marked as predictive of a problem in later planning. Because the TOP corresponds to the causal circumstances of the situation it can indicate which features are important to a current problem and which will be important to later ones. Unlike organizing repair strategies, this is a function that requires the knowledge of all aspects of a planning problem. The entire description of the problem is needed to choose the features that will be marked. Even if the individual aspects of the problem could be used independently to point out individual features that were important, they would have to be combined at some point to form the proper conjunction of features that would predict a particular problem. One way or another, the configurations that correspond to the TOPs would have to be recognized.

The second answer to the question of the functionality of TOPs has to do with the prediction of failures and the indexing of plans. When CHEF anticipates a problem it has to have some way of describing that problem to its RETRIEVER so it can search for a plan that solves it. Instead of using a description that stays at the level of a specific failure, (*e.g.*, soggy broccoli), CHEF uses its TOPs to describe what it predicts and what it is looking for. CHEF also indexes the plans that deal with problems by the TOPs that described them. The prediction of a problem described by a TOP is used to find a plan that solves that problem. The TOPs allow the planner to access plans that solve problems that are analogous to current ones.

The different plans that are indexed by a single TOP are similar in that the causal configuration of the problems they solve are the same. Each TOP is used to index to the plans that deal with different instances of the single causal situation it describes. So each TOP acts as the access mechanism that links problems to the analogous plans in memory that will solve them.

One possibility that CHEF does not explore in dealing with plan failures is searching for another plan to replace its current one altogether. This would be a process similar to the initial retrieval of a plan to deal with a problem that CHEF does when it predicts one. In this case, however, it would happen after CHEF actually encounters a failure and has to recover from it. In this sort of situation, the TOPs themselves could be used to store past episodes that deal with the problems they describe. This situation demands that the plan being searched for deals with the causality of the current problem, which is described by the TOP, and so it makes sense to store these plans under the TOP itself. TOPs could carry greater weight by directly storing complete replacement plans to deal with failures as well as strategies.

Beyond this, TOPs could also be used to help deal with the problems that would rise out of a more realistic implementation of repair strategies. In a more ambitious implementation of strategies, one in which the table look-up of steps that meet certain requirements is replaced with a planner that can deal with simple state changes, the current approach to the competition between strategies would have to change. Generating all possible alterations and then choosing between them is too costly. A better approach would be to associate the successful and unsuccessful applications of a strategy to problems described by a TOP with the TOP itself. These episodes could then *focus* the planner's attention on the strategies that have been most helpful in this situation, *suggest* implementations of different strategies, and *warn* if certain strategies have had problematic results in this type of situation [Hammond 84]. These functions have to be linked to the TOPs in that the competition between strategies has to be between them as they apply to the current problem, not as they apply globally to all problems.

In CHEF, TOPs organize strategies, indicate the features that will predict a failure, and link predictions of problems to the plans that solve them. They also have the potential to organize plans so that they can be suggested as replacements for failed plans and to better manage the choice between strategies that can be applied to a problem. While many of these functions could be implemented without the use of TOPs, others require TOPs because they correspond to entire causal situations and can be used to organize inferences that have to be made about those situations. The functional gains from the use of TOPs more than justifies their presence as organizing structures for planning.

4.6 CHEF's repair strategies

The repair strategies used by CHEF owe a great deal to the work on plan repair that has preceded it ([Sacerdoti 75], [Sussman 75], [Wilensky 80] and [Wilensky 83]). CHEF's repair rules, however, are somewhat more detailed than those that have gone before and make greater use of an organization that links the description of a problem to the solutions that can be applied to it. Because many planning projects have been developed in somewhat impoverished domains many repair strategies have been overlooked because they had no application within the these domains. Sussman's blocks world and Sacerdoti's pump world limited the actions of any planner working within them and thus limited the kinds of repairs that a planner could make. The failures encountered by HACKER and NOAH were usually the product of scheduling errors and were repaired by one or another variation of REORDER. They did not, in general, have to deal with questions such as the difference between a side-effect and a desired effect of an action. Wilensky suggested a wider range of plan repair strategies in PANDORA, but did not provide the organization that would have made them useful or give a method for actually implementing the general strategies to for use when solving specific problems.

> CHEF's repair strategies differ from those of past planner's in that they are more specific and are organized such that a single situation can have multiple strategies applied to it.

In CHEF the repair rules are all organized under specific TOPs and each TOP is associated with a particular causal configuration. The TOP SIDE-EFFECT:DISABLED-CONDITION:CONCURRENT, for example, is accessed only when a single action has a side-effect that disables states that have to be maintained during the course of that action. CHEF accesses these strategies by accessing the TOP that stores them, and the TOP is indexed by the causal explanation of the problem that corresponds to it.

For CHEF it is always the case that the repair strategies that are applied to a particular problem are those and only those that suggest changes to the causal configuration that will repair the plan. It may be that the change is not possible, because of the specifics of the problem, but if the change can be made then the plan will be repaired. In the beef and broccoli failure, one of the suggested repairs is to run an adjunct plan that will remove the liquid from the pan as the broccoli is cooking. In this case, CHEF does not know of any step to do this, but if such a step were known, such as throwing a sponge in the pan with the food, it would solve the problem. Even though it cannot find such a plan, CHEF is able to describe the kind of action it needs, in terms of the preconditions and effects of different steps.

In order to use this description to find specific plans, CHEF makes use of a library of actions, indexed by their preconditions and effects and by other plans that they are similar to. When a repair strategy is applied, CHEF builds a request into this library using the general description associated with the strategy, filled in with the specifics of the problem. The general strategy is turned into a specific request for a step or set of steps in the domain that have particular preconditions and effects.

Requests to this library of steps can take two forms. They can be requests for steps that have particular results or requests for steps that are similar to given steps but have different preconditions or effects. A strategy such as ALTER-PLAN:SIDE-EFFECT, that suggests replacing an existing step with one that does not produce a particular side-effect builds a request of the second type (figure 4.2). A strategy such as RECOVER, that directs the planner to add a new step to a plan that will remove a particular state, builds a request of the first type (figure 4.3). Each one is defined as a general structure which is filled in with the current answers to CHEF's explanation questions.

```
(def:strat alter-plan:side-effect
 bindings (*condition* expanswer-condition
          *step* expanswer-step
          *sgoal* expanswer-step-goal)
 question (enter-text ("Is there a alternative to " t
                        *step* t
                       "that will enable " t
                        *sgoal* t
                        "that does not cause " t
                        *condition*)
          test (search-alter-memory nil *step* *condition* *sgoal*)
          exit-text ("There is a plan" *answer*)
          fail-text ("No alternate plan found")
 response (text ("Response: Instead of doing step: " *step* t
                "           Do: " *answer*)
          action (replace *step* *answer*))))
```

Figure 4.2: Definition of ALTER-PLAN:SIDE-EFFECT strategy

For example, one problem that CHEF encounters in creating a recipe for FISH-WITH-PEANUTS is that the rice wine marinade it uses to remove the iodine taste of the fish makes the fish crumble during cooking. Because it recognizes that the side-effect of one plan is enabling an undesired condition, CHEF evokes the TOP SIDE-EFFECT:DISABLED-CONDITION:SERIAL, which suggests the strategy ALTER-PLAN:SIDE-EFFECT, as well as many others. ALTER-PLAN:SIDE-EFFECT is a general strategy to use a plan that achieves the initial goal but does not have the undesired side-effect. Because CHEF knows the problematic state, the goal that is to be achieved, and the initial plan that has gone wrong, it is able to build a request for a step described by the general strategy. It builds a request for a plan that removes the iodine taste from fish that does not have the side-effect of adding liquid to the dish. This describes the plan segment in which the fish is marinated in ginger.

```
(def:strat recover
 bindings (*condition* expanswer-condition
          *step* expanswer-step)
 question (enter-text ("Is there a plan to recover from "
                       *condition*)
          test (search-step-memory *condition* nil)
          exit-text ("There is a plan" *answer*)
          fail-text ("No recover plan found"))
 response (text ("Response: After doing step: " *step* t
                "           Do: " *answer*)
          action (after *step* *answer*)))
```

Figure 4.3: Definition of RECOVER strategy

CHEF uses its explanation of what has gone wrong to suggest the TOP, which in turn suggests a set of possible repairs. It then uses it again to provide the specific states and steps that convert the general repair rules into domain specific requests for plans. Having a detailed causal description of the problems it encounters allows it to find very general repair rules and instantiate them as specific repairs.

> To apply an abstract strategy, CHEF fills in the general structure with specific information about the current situation from its explanation of the problem.

CHEF uses seventeen general repair rules in the normal course of its planning. Each one of these is associated with one or more TOPs and suggests a fix to a specific causal problem. Each one of these rules carries with it a general description of a fix to a plan, through reordering of steps, an alteration of the objects involved or a change of actions. These general descriptions are filled in with the specific states that the planner is concerned with at the time when the repair rule is suggested.

It important to realize that these strategies, while they are designed for specific situations, are not *domain* specific. Stated generally, they are:

- ALTER-PLAN:SIDE-EFFECT: Replace the step that causes the violating condition with one that does not have the same side-effect but achieves the same goal.
- ALTER-PLAN:PRECONDITION: Replace the step with the violated precondition with one that does not have the same precondition but achieves the same goal.
- RECOVER: Add a step that will remove the side-effect before the step it interferes with is run.
- REORDER: Reorder the running of two steps with respect to each other.
- ADJUST-BALANCE:UP: Increase the down side of a violated balance relationship.
- ADJUST-BALANCE:DOWN: Decrease the up side of a violated balance relationship.
- ADJUNCT-PLAN:REMOVE: Add a new step to be run along with a step that causes a side-effect that removes the side-effect as it is created.
- ADJUNCT-PLAN:PROTECT: Add a new step to be run along with a step that is affected by an existing condition that allows the initial step to run as usual.
- SPLIT-AND-REFORM: Split the step into two separate steps and run them independently.
- ALTER-TIME:UP: Increase the duration of a step.
- ALTER-TIME:DOWN: Decrease the duration of a step.
- ALTER-ITEM: Replace an existing object with one that have the desired features but not an undesired one.
- ALTER-TOOL: Replace an existing tool with one that has the desired effect but does not cause an undesired one.
- ALTER-PLACEMENT:BEFORE: Move an existing step to run before another one.

- ALTER-PLACEMENT:AFTER: Move an existing step to run after another one.
- ALTER-FEATURE: Add a step that will change an undesired attribute to the desired one.
- REMOVE-FEATURE: Add a step that will remove an inherent feature from an item.

These strategies can be as specific as they are because they are only applied after the planner is able to describe *in detail* the causality of the problem to be repaired. As a result, more powerful changes that would be inappropriate in the case of a less specific problem description can be applied. Just as no knowledge means that only the most general, and thus weakest, repair techniques can be used, more knowledge means that more specific, and thus more powerful techniques can be applied. Because CHEF does have an understanding of why each of its failures has occurred, it is able to choose and apply the most powerful strategies for repairing those failures.

4.7 Strategies not used by CHEF

While CHEF uses quite a few repair strategies to deal with its planning failures, there exists a whole set of these repair rules that it ignores. CHEF excludes these strategies not because they are not useful, but because they deal with problems that CHEF never encounters and suggest changes that make no sense in CHEF's domain. For example, CHEF does not have strategies to deal with planning failures having to do with interactions with other actors. The entire range of *counter-planning* strategies ([Carbonell 79] and [Wilensky 78]) designed to deal with problems that arise when two or more planners interact have been ignored. CHEF also ignores those strategies that require that it alter the initial goals that it is handed as its input. While the changes that CHEF makes to a plan may modify goals that it has generated on its own, it never makes any changes that require modifications of the initial goals it is given as input. This means that subgoals that CHEF is planning for may be changed, but the main goals that CHEF has remain intact.

CHEF is not able to delegate its planning tasks to others, so it does not use strategies such as ALTER-ACTOR, because the problem that this strategy solves never arises for CHEF. Likewise, although the actions controlled by the planner all have durations which can be changed, none of them have alterable rates. For example, it is not possible for CHEF to change the amount of time that it takes to chop vegetables. It can change the duration of cooking steps, but it cannot change the rates of those steps. This means that it cannot use strategies such as SPEED-UP or SLOW-DOWN. They are useful when the amount of time that an action takes to perform can be altered by the planner by changing the rate at which he performs them. These strategies allow a planner to coordinate the times when actions end, to minimize ill effects produced by the performance of an action, or maximize any positive effects produced.

In general, domains with different sorts of actions will allow a planner to use different sorts of strategies. Just as the cooking domain allows CHEF to make use of more interesting and powerful strategies than are possible in a blocks world, a more expansive domain than cooking would suggest a greater set of strategies than CHEF could make use of. The main reason for the expansion of strategies in CHEF, however, has less to do with the domain and more to do with the addition of the vocabulary required to distinguish between goal satisfying and non-goal satisfying actions and states.

Chapter 5

Modifying Plans

Case-based planning is driven by the idea that it is less expensive to find and modify an old plan than to build a new one up from a set of primitive steps. By recalling the results of work that has already been done, a case-based planner can avoid repeating it. Past efforts are recalled in the form of past plans, plans chosen because they satisfy many of the planner's current goals. Because of this, the amount of modification to a plan that has to be done is kept to a minimum. So the MODIFIER that alters them can be a fairly simple process that deals with only the less difficult goals in the domain.

A case-based planner's plan MODIFIER is not designed to be a general-purpose planner. It is designed to alter plans to satisfy new goals. A weak MODIFIER that reasons at a fairly shallow level can be supported by a strong RETRIEVER and REPAIRER. The MODIFIER does not have to reason about past problems that the planner has already encountered because it can depend on the RETRIEVER to find the plans for it to alter that already avoid those problems. It does not have to go on to reason about the possible problems that can result from its modifications because it can depend on the REPAIRER to repair those problems if they arise. Further, any problems that it does create in a plan can be avoided in the future because the REPAIRER incorporates repaired plans into memory.

CHEF's MODIFIER is not concerned with the problems of planning having to do with the interaction between steps that the other modules of CHEF are concerned with. Its only concern is adding the steps to existing plans that will act to achieve new goals.

Both the RETRIEVER and the REPAIRER have far more knowledge about the causality of the CHEF domain than does the MODIFIER. The RETRIEVER has knowledge about the features that predict failures, the similarities between goals and the relative difficulty of adding new goals. The MODIFIER, on the other hand, has only the limited knowledge of how new goals are added to existing plans in general. The REPAIRER analyzes problems in terms of their deep causal structure. The MODIFIER just links new steps into old steps without asking what the real results of those new steps will be. But because the MODIFIER is supported by the ability of the PREDICTOR to find the plans that will be easiest to modify and the power of the REPAIRER to repair and learn from failures, it is able to effectively add new goals to old plans using a only a small amount of knowledge about the causality of its domain.

> A case-based planner's plan MODIFIER is a simple mechanism that is designed to add new goals to plans that it knows are successful. It relies on the greater knowledge of the RETRIEVER to find the plan that is appropriate to its current situation.

Because CHEF plans in what we will call a *design domain*, a domain where a set of goals have to be satisfied by a single plan that results in a coherent object, all of the goals that it is given at any one time have to be satisfied by a single plan. A new goal cannot be planned for on its own. It always has to be dealt with through the addition to an existing plan of the steps to satisfy that goal. In some sense CHEF does not know how to plan directly. It instead knows how to find past plans that satisfy some goals and how to alter those plans to satisfy others.

The work of the MODIFIER is controlled by a set of rules which tell it how to add new goals to existing plans. These modification rules for plan alteration are stored in a table, indexed by two features of the planning situation: the plan being altered and the goal to be added. In most cases, the goal to be added is a goal to include a particular ingredient or taste. CHEF usually has to deal with the problems of adding broccoli to a dish or making that dish hot. Adding goals such as these is done by finding the appropriate rule, indexed by the goal to be added and the plan to be altered, and incorporating the steps and ingredients in the rule with the existing plan.

Sometimes, however, it has to add steps for goals to avoid particular problems, problems that relate to a single ingredient rather than an interaction between ingredients. The fat in duck and the taste of iodine in seafood are example of this kind of problem, in that the features of the ingredients themselves directly cause problems in plans. To deal with the features of problematic ingredients, the MODIFIER has access to plan critics that are stored under individual ingredients. These critics suggest steps that avoid the problems due to special features of particular ingredients. These would be steps such as removing the fat from the duck before using or marinating seafood to cover its iodine taste. After adding a goal to a plan, using the standard modification rule associated with the goal and plan, the ingredient critics associated with the ingredients that have been added are then fired.

In all cases where the MODIFIER adds new steps to a plan, the idea is to integrate the plans into a coherent whole. The rules it has for adding new goals are rules for *adding* goals to a plan, not rules for satisfying the plan on its own.

One note should be made here about the relationship between the MODIFIER and the REPAIRER. While the MODIFIER and the REPAIRER play similar roles, they are separate processes with access to different kinds of knowledge. The REPAIRER has access to a full domain model which it uses to explain and then repair plan failures. While this means that the REPAIRER is able to deal with a wide range of situations, it does so at a fairly high cost—in terms of the computation required as well as the knowledge needed. The MODIFIER, on the other hand, only has access to plan modification rules and domain-level critics. Its breadth comes from the fact that the planner allows for the possibility that the MODIFIER may create a faulty plan.

The trade-off here is one of time versus correctness. The MODIFIER is a fast and simple process that is able to make changes to a plan quickly. The REPAIRER is a far more compute-intensive process that makes use of a richer knowledge base and as a result is less likely to introduce errors into a plan while repairing it.

While the MODIFIER is a weaker process, it can be relied on because it is only used to make relatively small changes to plans accessed by the RETRIEVER. The REPAIRER, on the other hand, is called on to fix plans that are known to be faulty—and beyond the knowledge scope of the MODIFIER. In order to deal with this, the REPAIRER must be, by its nature, a more knowledge-intensive program.

Of course, once a repair has been made and the situation in which it is appropriate has been diagnosed, a critic is built and placed in the knowledge base of the MODIFIER. In this way the causal knowledge that is actually relevant to the planner is compiled and used in the initial planning stages rather than just during repair.

5.1 The MODIFIER's tools

CHEF's MODIFIER has three basic tools or sources of knowledge that guide its alterations. First it has a set of role specifications that define the basic structure of the plans it is altering in general. This is used to guide it in decisions about whether to add a new goal directly or to substitute it for an existing goal in the plan being altered. Second, it has a table of standard modifications that is indexed by the type of plan being altered and the goal that is to be added. This table provides a listing of the steps that have to be taken to add a new goal to an existing plan. Finally, it has its ingredient critics, which correct for the peculiarities of particular ingredients. Some of these are directly associated with the ingredient and some are learned when CHEF repairs failures and are associated with both the ingredient and the prediction that failure is going to arise.

5.1.1 Role specifications on plans

Each of CHEF's general plan types has a set of role specifications associated with it. These specifications amount to general descriptions of the different types of food that could be added to the plan and the effects that should be expected to result from the steps in the plan. These specifications are used after a plan is built, to infer the goals that it should satisfy, but are also used earlier on to tell the MODIFIER whether it should add a new item directly or substitute it for an existing item, thus making the new ingredient play the same role in the plan as the original once did.

These role specifications are not simply lists of the type of ingredients that can be added to a plan. There are three pieces of information associated with each role: the different types of ingredients that can fill the role, the normal and maximum number of ingredients that can fill the role and the purpose, or goals that are associated with the role.

When a new goal is added to a plan role, information is used to decide whether to add the new steps or to substitute for those already in the plan. The substitution has to be done in most cases to avoid the problem of having plans that keep expanding, satisfying not only all of the new goals that they have been asked to achieve but also all of the old goals that they were originally designed for. Role specifications define the limits of a plan, define how much it can be expanded. They limit the type and number of goals that can be added directly to a plan, forcing substitution in order to keep the plan within the confines of the overall specifications of the plan type.

> Role specifications on general plan types tell the MODIFIER when it has to substitute a new item for an old one and when it can just add the new item directly.

The specification for STYLE-STIR-FRY, the plan type of all stir fry plans, has four roles associated with it: The main ingredient (MAIN), the vegetable (VEGE), the liquid spices (LSPICE) and the solid spices (SSPICE). The main ingredient in a stir fry dish can be any meat, seafood, non-spice vegetable or tofu. The specification on the MAIN role assumes one main ingredient but allows two. The main ingredient is expected to provide taste and texture to the dish. The VEGE role of a stir fry dish can be filled with either a major vegetable (*e.g.*, broccoli, carrots, snow peas), a spice vegetable (*e.g.*, scallions, dried mushrooms, lily buds) or tofu. The VEGE specification allows there to be three vegetables in any one dish but favors two. Fillers of the VEGE role are expected to provide taste and texture. LSPICE and SSPICE respectively are filled with liquid and solid spices. Each allows up to four items but favors three. Each of the fillers of these roles is assumed to add taste to the overall dish (figure 5.1).

```
(def:specs style-stir-fry
 main (meat seafood major-vegetable tofu) (1 2) (taste texture)
 vege (major-vegetable spice-vegetable) (2 3) (taste texture)
 lspice ((spice texture (liquid))) (3 4) (taste)
 sspice ((spice texture (solid)) (spice texture (powder)))
       (3 4) (taste))
```

Figure 5.1: Definition of the role specifications of STYLE-STIR-FRY

This notion of role specification is not limited to the CHEF domain. Any design domain in which the goal of a planner is to satisfy a set of goals which are actually specializations of a class of objects has to have this sort of role information associated with those classes of objects. In architecture, for example, the goals are all associated with specialized versions of different general object types. The goals in architecture break down into goals for particular type of objects (*e.g.*, houses, apartment buildings, office buildings, etc.) and specifications on those objects (*e.g.*, umber of rooms, number of stories, material used, etc.). In architecture, a goal for a type of object, such as a house, is equivalent to the CHEF domain goal to make a STIR-FRY or SOUFFLE dish. The goal provides the general outline of the final product, an outline that is filled in by the other goals for including particular features in the object being built.

The choice of the general object type limits the kinds of goals that can be associated with any particular instance of it. Adding a goal to have a bedroom with a southern view to a general plan for a three bedroom house does not mean simply adding another bedroom. It instead means changing the location of a bedroom that is already there. Adding a new bedroom would change the general description of the object, a description that should be considered as important as any particular goal. When chicken is added to an existing stir fry plan, it is not just added, it is used in place of existing items that play a similar role in the original. The idea is to add a new goal while staying within the limits of the general type of object that is being created.

Role specifications on a dish style do nothing to determine the steps that are included in the plan. Instead, they determine the form of the end result. They serve to limit the number of goals, by instructing the MODIFIER to substitute items rather than add them directly. This keeps the overall plans that result within certain guidelines. This avoids the problem of a constant expansion of the number of goals that each new plan satisfies, an expansion that would ultimately lead to a library of plans that are so unwieldy that no new goals can be added to them at all.

> The specifications on a plan type define the expectations for the result of the plan but do not determine the steps to be taken to achieve that result.

5.1.2 Modification rules

To add a new step to an existing plan, CHEF uses a set of modification rules, each of which is indexed by the type of plan that is being altered and the new goal being added. Each of these modification rules lists the set of steps that have to be added to an existing plan in order to achieve the current goal. Each also specifies the amount of the item that should be added. Each of these also includes BEFORE and AFTER information. This information specifies where in an existing plan the new steps have to be placed.

For example, the modification rule for adding any FRUIT to a SOUFFLE is to first chop the fruit into a purée and then mix it into the batter. There is a requirement on the MIX step that it occur before the step of pouring the batter into a pan for baking (figure 5.2). This rule is stored in the MODIFIER's table of standard modifications, indexed by FRUIT and STYLE-SOUFFLE.

```
(add:mod
  index  (fruit style-souffle)
  amount (cup number (1))
  steps  ((do (chop object ?new-item size (pulp)))
          (before (pour object ?object into (nine-inch-baking-dish))
               do (mix object ?new-item with ?object))))
```

Figure 5.2: Rule for adding FRUIT to SOUFFLEs.

> The modification rules tell the MODIFIER the steps it has to take to add a new goal to an existing plan. These rules are indexed by the goal to be added and the plan to be altered.

Because they are related to both the goal being added and the plan that is being changed, these modification rules can know about what is being changed and how to go about changing it. They can detail how to add new steps and how to remove them later. In cases where the plan that is found does not even partially satisfy a goal they can be used to add that goal to the existing plan. While it is not clear that this kind of rule could weather an expansion of the domain, they are useful within the context of the needs of a domain-centered case-based planner.

5.1.3 Critics

While most of the changes that have to be made to add a new goal to a plan can be handled with modification rules, some ingredients have special features that have to be handled by an equally special set of rules. These rules, called *critics*, are designed to augment the table of standard modification rules by tailoring plans to the needs of problematic ingredients.

CHEF has two classes of critics. The first is the set of critics that CHEF starts with. These are directly associated with the ingredients that they compensate for. The second is the set of critics that CHEF learns by experiencing failures in handling particular ingredients. These are associated with the ingredients that they relate to but are also associated with the failure that they protect the planner from making. In theory, however, there is no real difference between these two sets. The first is merely a set of degenerate cases of the second. That is, they are critics that apply to failures that can be predicted by just the presence of a particular item.

> Ingredient critics give the MODIFIER information about special steps it has to add to plans to account for the idiosyncrasies of particular items.

The instructions that are attached to an ingredient critic are somewhat broader in scope than those attached to modification rules. Along with instructions to add steps, the ingredient critics can also instruct the MODIFIER to reorder steps, remove steps, add new ingredients and remove ingredients that are already there. In directing the MODIFIER to add new ingredients, it can also specify what steps the new ingredients should participate in. The MODIFIER does not have to make use of its table of standard modifications in order to add the ingredients that it is instructed to by a critic. This allows the MODIFIER to alter plans to deal with the idiosyncrasies of particular ingredients that could not be dealt with effectively using the modification rules alone.

A single ingredient can have multiple critics. Some ingredients, such as shrimp, start off with multiple critics and have more added as CHEF encounters failures associated with them. These critics are ordered and new critics are added to the end of this ordering. New critics are run after initial ones because they correspond to changes that were made in a plan after the original critics were run and may depend on changes that they make.

One example of an ingredient that has critics associated with it is shrimp. CHEF begins with two critics associated with its knowledge of shrimp. One points out that shrimp, unlike other seafoods, does not need to be chopped because it is already the right size for all dishes that it is included in. CHEF's default is that everything has to be chopped because this is the case for most of the ingredients it has to deal with. The second critic associated with shrimp points out that it has to be shelled before it is cooked. Together these critics define the changes that have to be made to accommodate the fact that shrimp is smaller than and has a different texture from most seafoods (figure 5.3).

```
(add:crit shrimp
 binds (shrimp *new-item*)
 steps ((before (cook-step object *new-item*)
              do (shell object *new-item*))))

(add:crit shrimp
 binds (shrimp *new-item*)
 steps ((delete (chop object (*new-item*)))))
```

Figure 5.3: Two critics for SHRIMP.

> CHEF initially has a set of critics that are stored under the ingredients they relate to and applied whenever those ingredients are added to existing plans.

But CHEF can also build new critics for items when its experience with them demonstrates that it has to add new steps to deal with them. In building its first plans with shrimp, CHEF encounters a problem because the SHELL step that the MODIFIER has added is placed after a MARINATE step, violating a condition on SHELL that the object shelled is handleable. CHEF calls the failure that results SIDE-FEATURE:BLOCKED-PRECONDITION, because there is a precondition on a step blocked by the results of another step, but that other step does not serve any goals before the time of the block takes place. At this point CHEF not only reorders the steps, it also builds an ingredient critic that is associated with the failure. When the failure is predicted, any time a plan has to be altered to include shrimp, this critic is suggested.

> CHEF augments its initial set of ingredient critics with new ones learned while it repairs failures related to unexpected properties of new ingredients.

CHEF's critics take care of planning for the idiosyncrasies of problematic ingredients. They expand in response to new information, information that CHEF discovers as it plans for certain ingredients and finds that the details of those plans are incorrect. By storing and recalling the repairs that it has to make to improve those details it is able to reuse the repairs in the form of new critics that improve its ability to deal with the specifics of non-standard ingredients.

5.2 Different situations for altering plans

Whenever CHEF has to alter a plan, it does so to make the plan achieve a new goal. While the alterations that it makes are determined by the new goal it is adding, they are also affected by the relationship that the new goal has to the initial plan. A goal that is partially satisfied by a plan is added to it in a different way than a goal that is not addressed at all by the steps in the plan. So CHEF's MODIFIER is confronted by different relationships between existing plan and new goals that define different approaches to plan modification.

There are three relationships between plan and goal that CHEF has to deal with that define three somewhat different approaches to plan modification.

The first of these is the situation in which CHEF has to add a goal to a plan that does not include any provisions for that goal, either by satisfying a goal that is similar to it or by satisfying a goal that plays the same role as the new goal to be added. In this situation the MODIFIER has to add the steps to satisfy the goal directly. It doesn't make any substitutions or replacements. It just adds the steps that are dictated by the modification rule that applies.

The second of these is the situation in which CHEF has found a plan that partially matches the goal it is going to add. In this case the MODIFIER can just substitute the new for the old, ignoring the modification rule and relying only on the ingredient critics. It can do this because the new item matches the old, is of the same class of items as the old, and thus will have the same set of standard modification steps as the old.

The final situation that CHEF has to deal with lies between the first two. It is the situation in which the new goal is not of the same type as any goal already satisfied by the existing plan, but will play a role that is the same as some item that is in the plan. In this case CHEF replaces the old with the new, removing the steps and ingredients that satisfied the original goal before placing in the steps and ingredients used to satisfy the new.

5.2.1 Addition

The MODIFIER has to add new steps to a plan when it is confronted with a new goal that has no equivalent in the existing plan. In these situations, it has nothing to remove from the plan. It only has to add new steps and ingredients, using the information stored in its modification rules to guide its actions.

> The MODIFIER has to directly add a new goal to a plan when the role that it plays in the plan is not already filled.

The best example of CHEF's modifier having to add a new goal to an existing plan that does not have a similar goal associated with it is when it is faced with the task of making a strawberry soufflé. In this situation, it begins with a plan for vanilla soufflé, a plan that does not have any goal that fills the FLAVOR role. It does have vanilla, but this plays the BASE role in STYLE-SOUFFLE. Thus the MODIFIER is in the position of having to directly add the steps that it needs to make the plan satisfy its new goals.

Adding a new goal is straightforward: the MODIFIER gets the rule that relates to the goal and the type of the plan from its table of standard modifications, it makes the changes directed by the rule and it then applies any critics that are related to the ingredient being added.

We have already seen the definition for the modification rule associated with FRUIT and SOUFFLE. It directs the MODIFIER to add a CHOP step that purées the fruit and then add a step that MIXes the fruit into the batter. In adding the strawberries the MODIFIER has to also add two new steps, steps that have to be integrated into the plan as a whole.

> Adding a new goal to an existing plan requires running the modification rule associated with the goal and plan and then running the critics associated with the new ingredients.

Because CHEF plans in a design domain, new goals are interpreted as alterations to an existing object. When it is adding a goal to include strawberries, the results of the plan steps it adds have to somehow be merged into the results of the steps in the original. To assure this, there is a restriction on the modification rules used by the MODIFIER. The final step of a plan in a modification rule has to be one of two things: either a step that combines the results of the new steps with the results of the existing plan, such as an ADD or a MIX step, or a step such as STIR-FRY that can be merged with a STIR-FRY step already in the plan. This means that the results of the steps from the modification rule can be merged with the results of the original plan either by explicitly adding them together at one point or by merging a step in the existing plan with a similar one in the modification rule.

In actually putting these steps into place, the MODIFIER starts with the final step in the rule and works back to the first step. This is so any steps that can or must be merged with steps in the existing plan can be recognized. If the MODIFIER starts from the beginning and merges a step in the existing plan with one in the rule, it could turn out that the steps that follow in the plan are not the same as those determined by the rule. But because the steps were merged too early, the results of the merged steps would be linked and this link would have to be broken. For instance, two ingredients that are chopped the same size may not have the same cooking time, so they cannot be merged at the time of the chopping. In working back, the MODIFIER checks each new step that is being put in place to see if it can be merged with steps already in the plan. If it is unable to merge steps at any point it gives up on merger altogether, because the steps have now diverged.

In CHEF's plans, any step that uses the results of a prior step is linked to it by a pointer to those results. A step to ADD the results of one step to the results of another has its OBJECT and TO slots filled with pointers back to those results. Placing a new ADD step or MIX step requires breaking these links and inserting the new step in between the originals. This requires building a link from the original step that follows the new one back to the results of the new step and also building a link from the new step back to the results of the earlier step so that the new step can use it. CHEF adds strawberries to soufflé by adding a new CHOP step and then ADDing its results to the existing batter before it is POURed (figure 5.4). In the three figures that follow, arrows leading away from a step indicate the results of the step feeding into later steps.

In adding the strawberries to the soufflé, the MODIFIER starts from the MIX step and works back. It places the new MIX step in before the POUR step and builds a link between the OBJECT of the POUR and the results of the MIX. This means that the OBJECT of the POUR will be filled with the results of the MIX, the batter with the strawberries added. The new MIX step then uses the filler that was originally in the OBJECT of the POUR, a pointer to an earlier MIX step which resulted in the original batter as the filler of its TO slot. The CHOP step is then added, and the links between it and the MIX step are made as directed by the rule. So the results of the CHOP are used to fill the OBJECT slot of the MIX.

```
Building new name for VANILLA-SOUFFLE based on its goals.

Calling recipe STRAWBERRY-SOUFFLE

Modifying recipe: STRAWBERRY-SOUFFLE
to satisfy: Include strawberry in the dish.

Applying plan
 do: Pulp the strawberry.
 Before doing step: Pour the -Variable- into a nine inch baking-dish
  do: Mix the strawberry with the -Variable-.  - Plan applied.
```

Cooking steps are handled in a somewhat different way. The final cooking step of a modification rule is always merged with the final cooking step of the existing plan. If their times differ, the one with the longest time is broken into two steps, the second of which has a time that meets the requirement that both the step in the existing plan and the step in the rule have the same times. If a rule for adding a vegetable ends with a two minute stir fry step and the plan it is being put into ends with a three minute step, the three minute step is broken into a one minute step followed by a two minute step and the second step is merged with the step from the rule (figure 5.5).

Once a new ingredient is added, its critics are called up to make whatever alterations they have to. The MODIFIER has no critics for strawber-

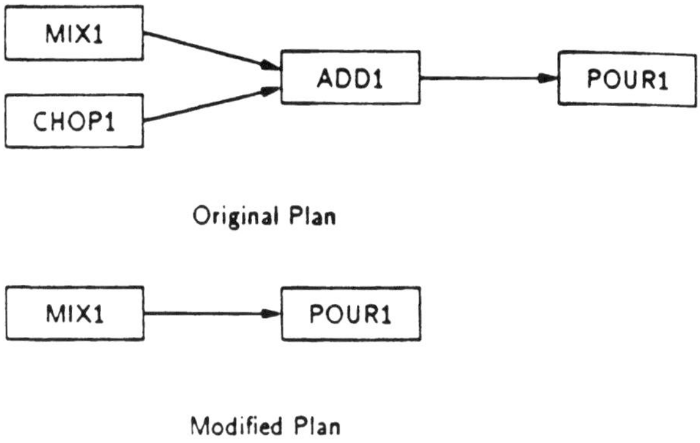

Figure 5.4: Merging ADD and MIX steps.

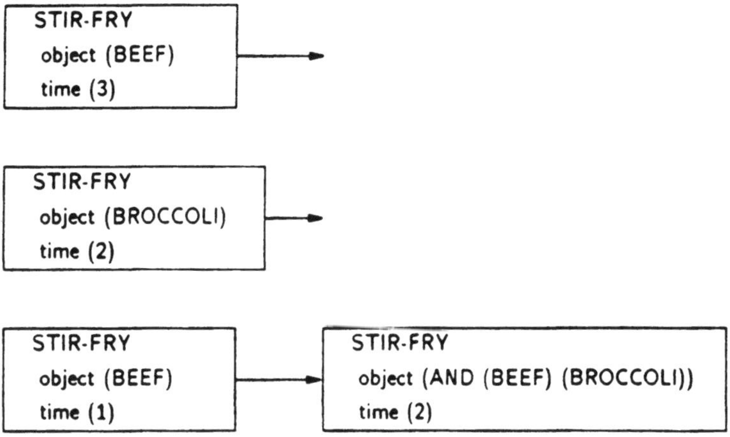

Figure 5.5: Merging cooking steps.

ries, but the idea is the same for every item. If there are steps that are particular to the item, as the SHELL step is to shrimp, then the critic adds those steps.

Adding the steps to satisfy a new goal to an existing plan is a relatively simple task. The new steps are accessed through the appropriate modification rule. They are added in reverse order of their execution, merged with existing steps when they can be and spliced between the results of one step and the later use of those results when they have to be. Any critics associated with the new ingredients that have to be added are then called, and their directions are also spliced into the plan.

5.2.2 Substitution

When the new goal the MODIFIER is adding is a partial match for an existing goal that is already satisfied by that plan, it can do a simple substitution of the new ingredient for the old. A substitution only requires that the MODIFIER put the new ingredient in place of the existing one and then run the critics for the new item. The critics for the item that has been removed also have to be accessed and run in reverse, so as to remove the steps that were added to compensate for its idiosyncrasies. The need to be able to reverse the effects of critics limits them to adding, deleting and reordering steps and adding or deleting ingredients.

The rationale behind this substitution is simple: the old item and the new item are both of the same type, so the steps that would be generated by the standard modification rule for both are the same. The only differences between the two items are accounted for by their ingredient critics. Rather than remove the original item and all of its steps and then add a new item with the same steps, the notation in the ingredients listing of the plan that is being changed can be made directly.

> The MODIFIER substitutes new goals for old goals in the plan when the goals play the same role in the plan *and* are of the same class of items.

A very simple substitution is done when CHEF is building a plan for a raspberry soufflé. Because it anticipates the problem with the liquid from the fruit, it is able to find the strawberry soufflé recipe to use as its base-line plan. It also has a partial match between the raspberry and the strawberry, meaning that it can directly replace the new ingredient for the old. In this case, a partial match means that the two items have the same modification rule for this type of plan.

```
Found recipe -> REC12 STRAWBERRY-SOUFFLE

Recipe exactly satisfies goals ->
    Avoid failure of type SIDE-EFFECT:DISABLED-CONDITION:BALANCE
exemplified by the failure 'The batter is now flat' in recipe
STRAWBERRY-SOUFFLE.
    Make a souffle.

Recipe partially matches ->
    Include raspberry in the dish.
          in that the recipe satisfies: Include fruits in the dish.

Building new name for copy of STRAWBERRY-SOUFFLE based on its goals.
Calling recipe RASPBERRY-SOUFFLE

Modifying recipe: RASPBERRY-SOUFFLE
to satisfy: Include raspberry in the dish.

Placing raspberry in recipe RASPBERRY-SOUFFLE in place of
strawberry.
```

Because no ingredient critics are stored under either RASPBERRY or STRAWBERRY, the MODIFIER can just build a new token for the raspberry and put it in place of the strawberry in the ingredients listing of the new plan it is building. Rather than rebuilding a new set of steps from scratch, the planner is able to do a simple replacement on the existing plan from memory.

Sometimes the new item is of the same basic type as the old, but has special properties. The substitution is followed with the application of the ingredient critics of the new item. If the item that is being removed also has critics, these are applied in reverse, removing rather than adding, adding rather than removing.

We have already seen one example of substitution followed by critics application in the case of altering PEANUT-AND-FISH to be PEANUT-AND-SHRIMP. After the shrimp is substituted for the fish, its critics are applied, removing the CHOP step and adding a SHELL step. Shrimp's new critic then corrects the problem of the order SHELL and MARINATE.

```
Considering critic:
Delete step: Chop the shrimp. - Critic applied.

Considering critic:
Before doing step: Cook the shrimp.
 do: Shell the shrimp. - Critic applied.

Considering critic:
Before doing step: Marinate the shrimp
 do: Shell the shrimp
 because: It is not the case that: The shrimp can be handled.
 avoiding: SIDE-FEATURE:BLOCKED-PRECONDITION
- Critic applied.
```

In short, ingredient substitution is done when a new goal to be added partially matches a goal already satisfied in the plan to be altered. To make a substitution the MODIFIER only has to change the ingredient listing so as to include the new ingredient in place of the old. The only steps that have to be changed are those mentioned by the ingredient critics of the original item, which have to be removed, and those mentioned by the ingredient critics of the new item, which have to be added. Using the fact that similar ingredients are handled in a similar way, the MODIFIER is able to reduce the amount of work it has to do when adding new goals to plans that already satisfy similar ones.

> When a new goal is substituted for an old one in a plan, the new item takes the place of the old one in the plan's ingredient list. Once this is done, the critics related to the old goal are run in reverse and the critics related to the new goal are run in the normal order.

5.2.3 Replacement

There are some situations where the MODIFIER has to put a new item in a plan in place of an existing item because they share the same role in the plan. The need for this replacement is determined by the role specifications on the general plan type. If a plan requires only one item filling a particular role, then the original filler for that role has to be removed to make room for a new one. In the case where the two items are of the same class of items, the MODIFIER has only to do an ingredient substitution. There are other cases, however, where the items fill the same role, but are of different types and thus have different modification rules. When this happens the MODIFIER has to do a role replacement, in which it removes an item from the original plan, unwinding and removing its steps, and then adds the ingredients and steps for the new goal.

> The MODIFIER has to replace one goal for another when they play the same role in the plan *but* are not of the same class of items.

The only difference between the MODIFIER doing a replacement and doing a goal addition is that it has to remove the existing steps and ingredients relating to the original goal before adding those related to the new one. This removal has two phases. First the critics relating to the object being removed are run in reverse. This is exactly the same process that is run when a substitution is done. The second phase, however, is unique to replacement. The modification rule associated with the ingredient being removed is also run in reverse, the steps unwound and removed.

As it turns out, it is easier to remove a set of steps than to put them in place. All of the steps that were not merged with steps in the initial plan

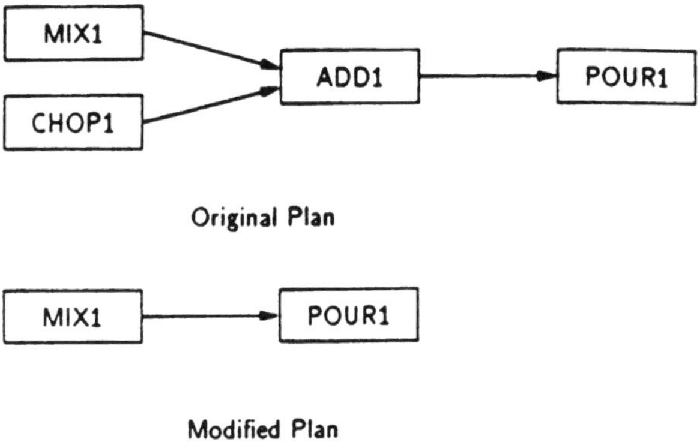

Figure 5.6: Removing steps for an obsolete goal.

are removed completely. The first step that does merge the results of the modification rule steps with the results of the plan itself is then drawn out of the plan and the step that makes use of its results is altered to now make use of the earlier results that the step itself used (figure 5.6). Finally, the ingredient is then removed from the ingredient listing at the head of the plan.

Once the steps for a particular goal have been removed, however, there is the possibility that a cooking step that was split to allow a merger is now unnecessarily divided. If a four minute stir fry step was turned into a three minute step followed by a one minute step to accommodate the one minute cooking time of a new item, and that new item is later removed, the split will remain. After removing the steps for an item the MODIFIER checks for any adjacent cooking steps that have identical objects. If any are found, they are merged back into one step with a longer time.

Once the obsolete goal is removed, the MODIFIER then follows the course directed by the standard modification rule associated with the new goal and by the critics associated with the ingredient.

In the example of replacing strawberries with Kirsch in a soufflé, this is exactly what the MODIFIER does:

```
Calling recipe KIRSCH-SOUFFLE

Modifying recipe: KIRSCH-SOUFFLE
to satisfy: Include kirsch in the dish.
```

```
Removing plan
 do: Pulp the strawberry.
 Before doing step: Pour the -Variable- into a nine inch baking-dish
  do: Mix the strawberry with the -Variable-.  - Plan removed.

Adding plan
 Before doing step: Pour the -Variable- into a nine inch baking-dish
  do: Mix the Kirsch with the -Variable-.  - Plan applied.
```

> The MODIFIER replaces one goal with another by first removing the steps placed in by the modification rules and critics of the old goal and then adding in the steps given by the modification rule and critics of the new goal.

Except for the unwinding of existing steps, the process of role replacement is exactly the same as that of goal addition. The modification rules associated with the goals to be added are applied, and the steps they direct are merged with the existing steps in the plan. After this, the critics associated with each of the ingredients are also run and the changes they direct are made.

5.3 The introduction of failure

The three different type of modifications that the MODIFIER is capable of are designed to keep the amount of work it does to a minimum. This is to reduce the changes that take place in a plan, enforcing a conservativism that strives to maintain the structure of successful plans. The less change that is made to a plan, the less possibility there is of introducing error.

Even within the confines of minimal change however, the MODIFIER often creates plans that have new interactions in them that lead to failures. The very fact that the MODIFIER changes a plan at all, that it alters what could be a balance between factors in the plan it cannot even consider, means that its efforts will sometimes lead to plans that do not satisfy the goals that it has added to them.

Because the MODIFIER does not do any causal reasoning on its own, it cannot anticipate the failures that it may have inserted into a new plan. By using the plans handed to it by the RETRIEVER, it starts with plans that avoid problems that CHEF has encountered before, but it is unable to reason about problems that the planner in general has had no experience with. When failures due to inexperience in the domain are added to a plan, they have to be discovered by executing the plan itself.

For CHEF, plan execution is done through a simulation of the plan, a simulation that is enabled by an extensive set of inference rules that allows the planner to see the results of every action it has built into its plans. This simulation, however, does not correspond to a mental running of the plan. It is the CHEF equivalent of actually running the plan in the real world. A failure that arises when running this simulation is not a failure in CHEF's mind alone. It is a failure in what amounts to CHEF's version of the world.

Just as the MODIFIER depends on the RETRIEVER to give it plans that avoid problems that CHEF has encountered before, it depends on the REPAIRER to handle new problems that the planner has not yet had to deal with. The next chapter will look at the function of the REPAIRER and how it diagnoses and repairs the problems that the MODIFIER has not been able to anticipate and avoid.

Chapter 6

Repairing Plans

The problem of a failed plan presents a case-based planner with the joint tasks of repairing the plan so that it can be used in the present and repairing its own knowledge base so that the failure can be avoided in the future. The result of the first task is a plan that satisfies the planner's current goals. The result of the second task is a set of links that allows the planner to predict the current failure in similar circumstances, a plan in memory that is indexed by that prediction and, if it is appropriate, a new ingredient critic that can change a plan that has a similar fault into one that does not.

The process of failure repair has six phases to it:

- Notice the failure.
- Build a causal explanation of why it happened.
- Use the explanation to find a TOP with repair strategies.
- Apply each of the general repair strategies using the specifics of the problem.
- Choose and implement the best repair.
- Store the repaired plan in the plan memory.

The reason behind most of these steps is straightforward. A planner has to notice a failure before it can react to it at all. It has to try each of its strategies in order to choose the best one. It has to implement one of them to fix the plan. And it has to store the repaired plan in memory if it is going to use it again. The only steps that are not quite straightforward are the second and third steps of building an explanation and using it to find a TOP.

The explanation that a case-based planner builds for a failure is a causal description of why that failure occurred. Each of the TOPs corresponds to one of the different descriptions that the planner can build. But these TOPs are not just descriptions of problems. They are descriptions of problems that are paired with the solutions that can be applied to fix the problems. The strategies under a TOP are those and only those alterations of the problem described by the TOP that can solve that problem. The strategies themselves are not specific repairs, they are the abstract descriptions of changes in the causality of the situation that the planner knows about. Finding a TOP that corresponds to a problem means finding the possible repairs that can be used to fix that problem.

Each TOP is stored in memory, indexed by the features of the explanation that describes the problem the TOP deals with. To get to the strategies that will deal with a problem the planner has to explain why it happened and then use this explanation to find the TOP and strategies that will fix the plan. This is a simple idea: the solution to a problem is based on the nature of the problem. It makes sense to index solutions to problems under descriptions of the problems themselves and use these descriptions to later access the appropriate solutions.

6.1 Noticing the failure

The first step in dealing with a failure is noticing it. There are three types of failures that we are concerned with here:

- Failures of a plan to be completed because of a precondition failure on some step.
- Failures of a plan to satisfy one of the goals that it was designed to achieve.
- Failures of a plan because of objectionable results in the outcome.

In terms of its domain, CHEF can notice that a plan has stopped when the shrimp cannot be shelled because it is too slippery, that a plan to make a soufflé fails because the batter hasn't risen and that a stir fry dish with fish fails because the fish has developed an iodine taste.

After CHEF has built a plan, it runs a simulation of it. This simulation is the program's equivalent of the real world and a plan that makes it to simulation is considered to be complete. The result of this simulation is a table of descriptions that characterize the states of the ingredients used in the plan. Any compound objects created out of those ingredients are also described.

For example, after running a plan to make a beef and broccoli dish the table of results includes descriptions of the taste, texture and size of the different ingredients as well as the tastes included in the dish as a whole (figure 6.1).

```
(SIZE OBJECT (BEEF2) SIZE (CHUNK))
(SIZE OBJECT (BROCCOLI1) SIZE (CHUNK))
(TEXTURE OBJECT (BEEF2) TEXTURE (TENDER))
(TEXTURE OBJECT (BROCCOLI1) TEXTURE (SOGGY))
(TASTE OBJECT (BEEF2) TASTE (SAVORY INTENSITY (9.)))
(TASTE OBJECT (BROCCOLI1) TASTE (SAVORY INTENSITY (5.)))
(TASTE OBJECT (GARLIC1) TASTE (GARLICY INTENSITY (9.)))
(TASTE OBJECT (DISH) TASTE (AND (SALTY INTENSITY (9.))
                                (GARLICY INTENSITY (9.))
                                (SAVORY INTENSITY (9.))
                                (SAVORY INTENSITY (5.))))
```

Figure 6.1: Section of result table for BEEF-WITH-BROCCOLI.

Once a simulation is over, CHEF checks the states on this table against the goals that it believes should be satisfied by the plan that it has just run. These goals take the form of state descriptions of the ingredients, the overall dish and the compound items that are built along the way. No matter what its object, each goal defines a particular TASTE or TEXTURE for that object. Goals have the same form as the states placed on the simulator's result table, allowing CHEF to test for their presence after a simulation. CHEF tests for the satisfaction of goals by comparing expected states against those on the table of results.

Most of the failures that CHEF is able to recognize are related to the final result of the plan rather than the steps that the plan goes through on the way to that result. This is because CHEF notices failures by looking at that final product rather than monitoring the plan as it is being executed. The only failures that CHEF recognizes that are related to the running of the plan rather than its effects are those that result from the inability to perform a step because the conditions required for that performance aren't satisfied.

The easiest failure for CHEF to notice is the failure of a plan to finish because of a blocked precondition on a particular step. When this occurs, the simulator stops execution of the plan and sets a flag that tells CHEF that the plan has failed because of a violated precondition. This is what happened in the case of the SHRIMP-STIR-FRY plan that CHEF created out of its memory of the FISH-STIR-FRY plan.

```
Inferring from -> Marinate the shrimp in the soy sauce,
 sesame oil, egg white, sugar, corn starch and rice wine.

RULE: "When things are marinated together they pick up tastes."
RULE: "Marinated things are in the bowl with other things."
RULE: "Liquids make things wet."
RULE: "Things in the same pan are linked together."
RULE: "Liquids make things wet."
RULE: "Things in the same pan are linked together."
RULE: "Solids marinated in liquids are hard to handle"


Unable to infer from -> Shell the shrimp.
 : failed  precondition.

RULE: "A thing has to be handleable in order to shell it."

Some precondition of step: Shell the shrimp.
 has failed.

Changing name of recipe SHRIMP-STIR-FRIED
to BAD-SHRIMP-STIR-FRIED
```

> One type of failure CHEF recognizes is the failure of a plan to run to completion because the preconditions for a step have not been met.

More often than not CHEF's plans run to completion. Even though a plan may run, this is no guarantee that it will run well or that it will succeed in doing all that it is supposed to do. After a plan finishes CHEF must check its outcome to be sure that it has not failed to achieve the desired results.

CHEF evaluates its results along two dimensions. First, it has to check for any of the plan's goals that might not have been achieved. Second, it has to check for any generally objectionable states that might also have resulted from the plan.

Each of CHEF's plans has a set of goals associated with it. These goals are generated by CHEF using the general role information attached to the general plan type and the specific ingredients of the plan itself. Each role specifies the expected contribution of its fillers and each ingredient provides the particulars of that contribution.

These goals take the form of state descriptions of the ingredients, the overall dish and the compound items that are built along the way. No matter what its object, each goal defines a particular TASTE or TEXTURE for that object. These goals all have the same form as the states placed on the simulator's result table, allowing CHEF to test for their presence after a simulation.

Once a plan has been run, the goals associated with the plan are searched for on the table of results built up by the simulator. If a goal is not present, then the plan has not succeeded in achieving it and is considered a failure. This is the second kind of failure that CHEF can recognize. It is the failure of a plan to achieve one of its goals. The failure in the beef and broccoli recipe is one of this type. CHEF finds the goal to have crisp broccoli associated with the plan, checks it against the states on the simulator's table of results and finds that the desired state is not there. Because the plan has failed to achieve one of its own goals, it is considered a failure (figure 6.2).

> The second type of failure that CHEF recognizes is the failure of a plan to achieve a goal it was designed to satisfy.

The final type of failure that CHEF can recognize is a failure that results from a state that has been included rather than excluded from the results of a plan. In this case, however, the state is one that the planner knows to be objectionable. Its inclusion in the results of a plan is a liability rather than an asset. In this situation, the plan may actually achieve all of the goals it is designed to but also results in states that are *a priori* objectionable.

To recognize these failures CHEF uses descriptions of states that it wants to avoid. Like positive goals, these states are of the same form as the

```
Checking goals of recipe -> BEEF-AND-BROCCOLI

Checking goal ->
 It should be the case that: The broccoli is now crisp.

The goal: The broccoli is now crisp.
is not satisfied.
It is instead the case that: The broccoli is now soggy.

Recipe -> BEEF-AND-BROCCOLI has failed goals.
```

Figure 6.2: Finding fault with BEEF-WITH-BROCCOLI.

states on the simulator's table of results so they can be tested for directly.

One example of this type of failure occurs as a result of CHEF's first attempt to build a stir fried fish dish. The plan CHEF creates achieves all of the goals that it was designed for but also results in a dish that has the taste of iodine. This taste is a by-product of the fish which was treated in the same way as the chicken that was originally in the dish. CHEF recognizes this by checking the states resulting from the plan against its knowledge of states to be avoided in general (figure 6.3).

```
Checking goals of recipe -> FISH-STIR-FRIED


Checking for negative features ->

Unfortunately: The dish now tastes a bad taste.
In that: The dish now tastes fresh, like iodine, like sea-food,
 like garlic, hot, oniony, sweet, nutty and salty.

Recipe -> FISH-STIR-FRIED has failed goals.
```

Figure 6.3: Finding fault with FISH-STIR-FRIED.

> The last type of failure CHEF can recognize is the occurrence of an objectionable state in the result of a plan.

6.2 Explaining the failure

Once a failure is noticed it has to be explained. This is because the explanation of a plan failure is used to access the TOP and strategies that can be applied. The best way to organize plan repairs is under the descriptions of the problems that they solve so that the problem itself is a pointer to the solution. And the best description in this case is a causal explanation of the problem. So the next step in dealing with a failed plan is to causally explain why the failure occurred.

> CHEF's explanation of a failure is a causal description of the steps and states that led to it.

In the case of a failure due to a precondition that was not satisfied, the explanation is of the events that led up to the state that violated that condition. In the case of a failure due to an unsatisfied goal, it is an explanation of why the steps that normally lead to the goal state did not do so in this plan. And in the case of a failure due to a result that includes an objectionable state, it is an explanation of why that state has come about.

In general, the explanation of a failure is aimed at finding out:

- *What state constitutes the failure?*
- *Why caused the failure?*
- *What goals were being planned for when the failure happened?*

By finding out the answers to these general questions, the planner can then find out how to respond to the failure while protecting the rest of the plan. This is the information that any planner would need in order to make an intelligent decision about how to react to a planning failure.

To build its explanations CHEF uses the trace left by the forward chaining of the simulator. The links built by the simulator are a very simple set of causal connections that reflect the requirements of the domain. Steps are connected to the states that follow from them by RESULT links. States lead into new steps by filling slots and by satisfying PRECONDITIONs. The tests on preconditions are limited to tests on the texture, taste and existence of ingredients as well as their amounts and the relationship of those amounts to other ingredients. Failures are traced back from the failed states themselves through the steps that caused them, back to the conditions that caused the steps to fail, and so on back to the step that caused the unexpected condition itself.

> CHEF constructs its causal explanation of failures by backchaining through the causal links built during the simulation of the failed plans.

It is important to note that we make no claims about the details of any process model involved with constructing these explanations. We are not claiming that we have solved or even made great advances in automatic diagnosis. We do, however, stand by our claim that the form of the diagnosis must be a causal description of the states and steps that actually lead to a failure. We have done some work in the use of case-based techniques in the construction of explanations ([Hammond 87] [Hammond and Huwitz 88]), but a detailed discussion of that work is beyond the scope of this book.

CHEF's movement through the causal network built up by the simulator is controlled by a set of explanation questions [Schank 86]. These questions tell CHEF when to chain back for causes and when to chain forward for goals that might be satisfied by a particular state or step. Each answer tends to be used as the starting point for the next part of the search. For example, the answer to the question of what step caused an undesired state is the starting point in searching for the answer to the question of what condition altered the expected outcome of that step.

CHEF has a different set of questions for different situations. For failures in the results of a plan, CHEF has seven questions aimed at identifying the steps and states that have combined to cause an objectionable state or block a desired one. For situations involving plans that cannot be completed because some precondition of a step is blocked, CHEF asks a somewhat different set of questions that are designed to identify the cause of the precondition violation. Both sets of questions, however, have the overall aim of diagnosing the problem so that the appropriate repair strategies can be found and applied.

> CHEF's search through the simulator's causal trace is guided by a set of explanation questions that focus on the relevant steps and states.

When a plan fails because of a faulty result CHEF first asks the questions that will determine the steps that caused the failure and then it asks the questions that will determine how those steps relate to the goals of the plan. The first set takes the form of backward chaining rules while the second takes the form of forward chaining rules.

The questions are:

- **What is the failure?**

  This identifies the particular problem state. In situations where the failure is an unsatisfied goal, the negation of the goal state serves as the answer. In situations where an objectionable state has come about, the state itself serves.

- **What is the preferred state?**

  Where a goal has not been achieved, the goal itself is the answer. Where an objectionable state has come about, the desired state of the object affected is focused on instead.

- **What was the plan to achieve the preferred state?**

  This question identifies the step that has actually caused the failure. The answer is found by chaining back from the failure to the step that actually caused it to come into being. To do this CHEF traverses a RESULT link back to the step.

- **What were the conditions that led to the failure?**

  With this question, CHEF is trying to identify the non-normative conditions that caused the step to go wrong. Using the step that caused the failure as a starting point, CHEF searches back along PRECONDITION links to any states that had to be true for the original inference of the failure to be made.

- **What caused the conditions that led to the failure?**

  This question identifies the actual cause of the non-normative conditions. Continuing to chain back, CHEF identifies the causes of the state that altered the predicted conditions and thus allowed the failure to result.

- **Do the conditions that caused the failure satisfy any goals?**

  This question directs CHEF's attention forward. It looks to the effects of the condition that led to the failure for any goals that it directly or indirectly satisfies.

- **What goals does the step which caused the condition enabling the failure satisfy?**

  This question is similar to the last one in that it directs CHEF's attention to the goals satisfied by the step that eventually led to the failure.

In explaining failures of a plan to complete, because of the failed preconditions of a step, CHEF uses a slightly different set of questions.

- **What was step that was blocked?**

  In this situation, CHEF begins by identifying the blocked step itself.

- **What was the condition that disabled the step?**

  Checking the preconditions on the step, CHEF chains back to find the one that has failed.

- **What caused the precondition to fail?**

  Next it chains back along RESULT links to the step that caused the state which in turn violated the precondition.

- **What goals does the step which caused the condition disabling the step satisfy?**

  This question directs CHEF to chain forward to the goals satisfied by the step which caused the violating state.

- **Do the conditions that caused the failure satisfy any goals?**

  Just as the last question looked forward to the goals satisfied by the step this question looks forward to the goals satisfied by the violating state itself.

- **What goals does the blocked step serve?**

  With this question, CHEF again chains forward to find the goals served by the step that was blocked.

The answers to these questions give CHEF the same flexibility and assurance in this situation that it gets from the explanation of failures rising out of the results of a plan. It has the extended causal chain that leads back from the blocked step to the state that blocked it and then back to the step that caused that state. This gives it the knowledge of where it can change the plan. It also has the understanding of what goals the different steps satisfy. This gives it the knowledge it needs to alter a step or state while maintaining goals that they serve.

> While CHEF asks different explanation questions in different situations, the questions it asks are always aimed at building a causal chain of the states and steps that led to the failure.

One good example of the kind of explanation that is built by CHEF is found in the case of the fallen strawberry soufflé. The problem is that the added liquid from the chopped strawberries disturbs the balance between the amount of liquid in the batter and the amount of whipped egg and flour used as leavening. Because there is too much liquid, the soufflé falls. One important aspect of this situation is that the condition that prevents the soufflé from rising is not just that there is too much liquid. It is that there is no longer a balance between the amount of liquid and the amount of leavening. When CHEF has to chain back to find the cause of this condition it has to check the two parts of the relationship against the normative case. The part that is irregular is then traced down as the cause of the imbalance.

```
ASKING THE QUESTION: 'What is the failure?'
ANSWER-> The failure is: It is not the case that: The batter
is now risen.

ASKING THE QUESTION: 'What is the preferred state?'
ANSWER-> The preferred state is: The batter is now risen.

ASKING THE QUESTION:
 'What was the plan to achieve the preferred state?'
ANSWER-> The plan was: Bake the batter for twenty five minutes.

ASKING THE QUESTION:
 'What were the conditions that led to the failure?'
ANSWER-> The condition was: There is an imbalance between the
whipped stuff and the thin liquid.
```

```
           ************ noting balance failure ************

Only one aspect of the imbalance:
 'There is an imbalance between the whipped stuff and the
 thin liquid' is unexpected.

The state:
 'There is whipped stuff in the bowl from the total equaling
 60 teaspoons' normally participates in the goal:
 The batter is now risen.

Only the other aspect of the imbalance:
 'There is thin liquid in the bowl from the strawberry equaling
 2.4  teaspoons' is an unexpected condition.

                     ************ ************

ASKING THE QUESTION:
 'What caused the conditions that led to the failure?'
ANSWER-> There is thin liquid in the bowl from the strawberry
equaling 2.4 teaspoons.
was caused by:
 Pulp the strawberry.

ASKING THE QUESTION:
  'Do the conditions that caused the failure satisfy any goals?'
ANSWER-> The condition:
 There is thin liquid in the bowl from the strawberry equaling 2.4
 teaspoons is a side effect only and meets no goals.

ASKING THE QUESTION:
  'What goals does the step which caused the condition enabling the
   failure satisfy?'
ANSWER-> The step:
 Pulp the strawberry.
establishes the preconditions for:
 Mix the strawberry with the vanilla, egg white, egg yolk, milk,
 sugar, salt, flour and butter.
This in turn leads to the satisfaction of the goals:
 The dish now tastes like berries.
```

This explanation gives CHEF the descriptors that will index to the planning TOP and repair strategies that will propose the appropriate set of solutions.

The fact that the CHOP step has the side-effect of producing liquid makes it a candidate for change. The fact that it exists to enable adding the strawberries to the batter, thus making the batter taste like berries, means that any change that is made to this step to avoid the side-effect has to include some addition that satisfies that goal. Likewise, the fact that the liquid is itself a side-effect that satisfies no goals means that the planner can add steps that remove that side-effect without having to worry about any goals that the condition served. The TOP and strategies that are found using these features reflect the constraints that they place on the type of repair that can be made to the plan.

> The explanation of *why* a failure has occurred is used to search for the planning TOP and repair strategies appropriate to the problem.

This is a simple idea: the solution to a problem is based on the nature of the problem. Because of this, it makes sense to index different sets of solutions by the descriptions of different sorts of problems and then use the descriptions of the problems to find the solutions that are appropriate.

6.3 Getting the TOP

CHEF's repair strategies are all stored under planning TOPs, structures that correspond to different planning problems. The TOPs themselves are stored in a discrimination network, indexed by the features of the explanations they correspond to. The strategies organized under a TOP describe the alterations to the failed plans described by the TOP. These alterations are designed to repair the failure without interfering with the other goals in any plan that the TOP describes. The TOPs include structures such as SIDE-EFFECT:DISABLED-CONDITION:BALANCE and SIDE-FEATURE:ENABLES-BAD-CONDITION. The strategies include changes such as REORDER the steps, REMOVE the condition, and SPLIT-AND-REFORM the step.

To get to a TOP, CHEF uses the answers to each of its explanation questions as an index through a discrimination network that organizes its TOP. The features that are important in this discrimination include the nature of the violated condition, the temporal relationship between the steps and the nature of the failure itself. The vocabulary for describing these features is discussed in Chapter 6.

> The answers to CHEF's explanation questions are used to index through a discrimination net to the TOP that corresponds to the situation described by those answers.

In the case of the strawberry soufflé failure, the condition violated in the plan was a balance requirement between two amounts and the condition that caused the imbalance was a side-effect rather than a goal state. These two facts were very important in discriminating down to the TOP that corresponds to the situation. If the condition that caused the imbalance had not been a side-effect or the requirement had not been one for a balance condition, different TOPs with different strategies would have been found.

```
Searching for top using following indices:

Failure = It is not the case that: The batter is now risen.
Initial plan = Bake the batter for twenty five minutes.
Condition enabling failure = There is an imbalance between
 the whipped stuff and the thin liquid.
Cause of condition = Pulp the strawberry.
The goals enabled by the condition = NIL
The goals that the step causing the condition enables =
 The dish now tastes like berries.

Found TOP TOP3 -> SIDE-EFFECT:DISABLED-CONDITION:BALANCE
TOP -> SIDE-EFFECT:DISABLED-CONDITION:BALANCE has 5
      strategies associated with it:

         ALTER-PLAN:SIDE-EFFECT
         ALTER-PLAN:PRECONDITION
         ADJUNCT-PLAN
         RECOVER
         ADJUST-BALANCE:UP
```

The TOP that is found to deal with the problem of the fallen soufflé is indexed so that it can be found using the explanation of any situation in which a side-effect of one step violates the conditions of a later step by causing an imbalance in a required relationship. Each of the strategies that is stored under SIDE-EFFECT:DISABLED-CONDITION:BALANCE is designed to deal with one aspect of this problem. If the problem had been different, a different TOP would have been found and a different set of strategies would have been suggested. The strategies under a TOP are limited by the types of changes CHEF is able to make and by the kinds of actions the domain allows. For instance, CHEF does not have the ability to have other actors perform tasks for it, so the strategy of having a step performed by a different actor is not available to it.

> Each TOP organizes a set of strategies that, if implemented, will repair any problem described by the TOP.

Each of the strategies indexed under SIDE-EFFECT:DISABLED-CONDITION:BALANCE is also under other TOPs that share features with it. Each strategy suggests an alteration to the initial plan that will cause a break in a particular part of the causal chain that leads to the failure. Each change suggested by a strategy is, in principle, sufficient to repair the plan. So they are used individually and are not designed to be used in concert. Each changes one link in the causal chain that leads to the failure. The strategies indexed under SIDE-EFFECT:DISABLED-CONDITION:BALANCE are:

ALTER-PLAN:SIDE-EFFECT: Replace the step that causes the side effect with one that does not. The new step must satisfy the goals of the initial step.

ALTER-PLAN:PRECONDITION: Replace the step that has the violated condition with a step that satisfies the same goals but does not have the same condition.

ADJUNCT-PLAN: Add a new step that is run concurrent with the step that has the violated condition. This new step should allow the initial step to satisfy the goal even in the presence of the precondition violation.

RECOVER: Add a new step between the step that causes the side-effect and the step that it blocks. This step should remove the state that violates the precondition.

ADJUST-BALANCE:UP: Adjust the imbalance between conditions by adding more of what the balance lacks.

Each of these five strategies suggests a change in the causal situation that will solve the current problem without affecting the other goals of the plan. They are those and only those changes that will alter the causal structure of the current faulty plan so as to remove that fault.

> The strategies stored under a TOP may also be stored under other TOPs. Each strategy under a TOP deals with a particular aspect of a planning problem that may occur in other planning situations.

If the features of the problem had been different, the TOP and the strategies found would also be different. For example, if the condition violated by the side-effect had not been a balance condition, CHEF would have found SIDE-EFFECT:DISABLED-CONDITION, a simpler TOP that lacks the ADJUST-BALANCE:UP strategy. Likewise, if the condition satisfied goals of its own, DIRECT-EFFECT:DISABLED-CONDITION:BALANCE would have been selected, a TOP that lacks both ALTER-PLAN:SIDE-EFFECT and RECOVER because strategies that remove the condition would alter any plan to no longer satisfy the goal achieved by the condition. So as the situation changes, the fixes that can be applied to it change and thus the TOP and strategies that are found to deal with it change as well.

> Different problem descriptions allow access to different TOPs and different TOPs organize different strategies. The causality of a situation determines the strategies that will be suggested to deal with it.

Once it has found a planning TOP, CHEF has access to a set of strategies that, if implemented, will repair its current problem. It may not be the case, however, that every abstract repair will have a real implementation in every situation. It may also be the case that the change suggested by one strategy will be better than those suggested by others. So CHEF must test each strategy and decide which to apply to the particular problem. It does this by generating the changes to the plan that the TOP's strategies suggest, choosing between those changes and then implementing the change it has chosen.

6.4 Applying the strategies

Once a TOP has been found, the strategies that are stored under it are applied to the problem at hand. For CHEF, applying a strategy means generating the specific change to the failed plan that is suggested when the abstract strategy is filled in with the specifics of the current situation. The idea here is to take an abstract strategy such as RECOVER and fill it in with the specific states and steps from the current problem. In this way a general strategy for repairing a plan becomes a specific change to the plan at hand.

> To apply a strategy, CHEF fills the framework the strategy defines with the particulars of the current situation, turning it into a specific change rather than just an abstract alteration.

Each strategy has two parts: a test and a response. The test under each strategy determines whether or not the strategy has an actual implementation in the current situation. The response is the actual change that is suggested. In most cases, the results of the test run by the strategy is used in the response. For example, one of CHEF's strategies is RECOVER, which suggests adding a new step between two existing ones that removes a side-effect of the first before it interferes with the second. The test on RECOVER checks for the existence of a step that will work for the particular problem. The response is a set of instructions that will insert that step between the two existing ones. The action that is returned when CHEF searches for the step described by RECOVER is used in building the response (figure 6.4). The general format of the strategies is to build a test and then use the response to that test in building the set of instructions that CHEF has to follow in order to implement the change directed by the strategy.

These strategies fall into four general classes of changes: some alter the sequence of events in a plan, some break single steps into multiple ones, some add new steps and others replace old steps with new ones. Each of these classes of response has a slightly different type of test associated with it. Those involving changes to the order of steps in a plan only test for conflicts that the reordering might cause. Strategies that split steps test the step to check for any problems that splitting it might cause. Strategies that add steps check a library of actions for the existence of the steps that they describe. This library has actions indexed by their effects and preconditions which makes it possible for CHEF to search for a particular

```
Asking question needed for evaluating strategy: RECOVER

ASKING ->
Is there a plan to recover from
 There is thin liquid in the bowl from the strawberry equaling 2.4
 teaspoons

There is a plan: Drain the strawberry.

Response: After doing step: Chop the strawberry
          Do: Drain the strawberry.
```

Figure 6.4: Test and Response for RECOVER strategy

action that has the effect described by a strategy. Similarly, the strategies that direct the planner to replace steps check this library for actions that meet their precondition and effect specifications.

These repair strategies make up the core of the strategies needed to deal with planning problems in general. They are not strategies that are related to the CHEF domain alone. Just as the planning TOPs are built out of a general vocabulary for describing different causal interactions, the repair strategies used by CHEF are general methods for altering plans. The vocabulary for describing TOPs is taken from a basic vocabulary of plan interactions and can describe a wide range of planning problems. Because the TOPs are products of the combination of these descriptors, however, each one is very specific. So the strategies stored under each can be equally specific. This means that the TOPs approach allows a planner to deal with a wide range of planning problems with very specific plan repairs.

This does not mean, however, that these strategies are in any way domain-specific. They are specific changes to plans that can be applied in response to specific problems that arise in all domains. And with the general descriptive powers of the TOPs vocabulary, a wide range of problems can be described at this level of specificity.

```
(def:strat recover
 bindings (*condition* expanswer-condition
           *step* expanswer-step)
 question (enter-text ("Is there a plan to recover from "
                        *condition*)
           test (search-step-memory *condition* nil)
           exit-text ("There is a plan" *answer*)
           fail-text ("No recover plan found"))
 response (text ("Response: After doing step: " *step* t
                 "           Do: " *answer*)
           action (after *step* *answer*)))
```

Figure 6.5: Definition of RECOVER strategy

> Each strategy has a test that can be run to check for the conditions that have to hold for the strategy to be implemented. Each strategy also has a response, which gives CHEF the actual changes that it has to make to implement the strategy.

In building the tests and responses during the application of a strategy to a particular problem, CHEF uses the answers to its explanation questions to fill in the specific steps and states that the strategy will test and possibly alter. The tests and responses are actually empty frames that are filled with the specifics of the current explanation. The strategy RECOVER, for example, uses the answer to the question of what condition caused the current failure to construct its test and the answer to the question of what step caused that condition to build its response. This is so it can find a step that will remove the condition and run it immediately after the condition arises. The definition of each strategy refers to the answers to the explanation questions that are important to it, making it possible to build the specific test and response at the appropriate time. Each definition begins with a binding of the existing explanation answers to variables that the strategy will then use to construct its query and response (figure 6.5). When the strategy is actually applied, the specific answers are inserted into the appropriate slots in the strategy structure.

> CHEF builds the changes suggested by a strategy by filling its framework in with the appropriate answers to its earlier explanation questions.

While each of the strategies that a TOP suggests for repairing a plan will result in a successful plan if implemented, there is no guarantee that an implementation will be found for a specific correction. In the Beef and Broccoli case, for example, one strategy that is suggested is ADJUNCT-PLAN. This directs the planner to find a step that can be run along with the original STIR-FRY step that will continuously remove the effects of stir frying the beef as they are created. While any such addition would repair the plan, because the liquid would be removed before it could affect the broccoli, CHEF does not have knowledge of such a step so the strategy cannot be implemented in this situation.

While not all strategies will be useful in all situations, most of the time many changes are suggested that the planner can make. In the example of the strawberry soufflé, the five strategies associated with the TOP end up generating four possible changes that will repair the plan. CHEF generates all possible changes so that it can compare the specific changes and choose which one to actually implement on the basis of the changes themselves rather than on the basis of the abstract strategies.

```
Applying TOP -> SIDE-EFFECT:DISABLED-CONDITION:BALANCE
to failure It is not the case that: The batter is now risen.
in recipe BAD-STRAWBERRY-SOUFFLE

Asking questions needed for evaluating strategy:
 ALTER-PLAN:SIDE-EFFECT

ASKING ->
Is there an alternative to
 Pulp the strawberry.
that will enable
 The dish now tastes like berries.
which does not cause
 There is thin liquid in the bowl from the strawberry equaling
 2.4  teaspoons

There is a plan: Using the strawberry preserves.

Response: Instead of doing step: Pulp the strawberry
          do: Using the strawberry preserves.

Asking questions needed for evaluating strategy:
 ALTER-PLAN:PRECONDITION
```

```
ASKING ->
Is there an alternative to
 Bake the batter for twenty five minutes.
that will satisfy
 The batter is now risen.
which does not require
 It is not the case that: There is thin liquid in the bowl from the
 strawberry equaling 2.4 teaspoons.

No alternate plan found

Asking questions needed for evaluating strategy:
 ADJUNCT-PLAN

ASKING ->
Is there an adjunct plan that will disable
 There is thin liquid in the bowl from the strawberry equaling
 2.4  teaspoons
that can be run with
 Bake the batter for twenty five minutes.

There is a plan: Mix the flour with the egg, spices, strawberry,
 salt, milk, flour and butter.

Response: Before doing step: Pour the egg yolk, egg white, vanilla,
 sugar, strawberry, salt, milk, flour and butter into a baking-dish
          Do: Mix the flour with the egg, spices, strawberry, salt,
  milk, flour and butter.

Asking questions needed for evaluating strategy:
 RECOVER

ASKING ->
Is there a plan to recover from
 There is thin liquid in the bowl from the strawberry equaling 2.4
 teaspoons

There is a plan: Drain the strawberry.

Response: After doing step: Chop the strawberry
          do: Drain the strawberry.

Asking questions needed for evaluating strategy:
 ADJUST-BALANCE
```

```
ASKING ->
Can we add more whipped stuff to BAD-STRAWBERRY-SOUFFLE

There is a plan: Increase the amount of egg white used.

Response: Increase the amount of egg white used.
```

The changes suggested by the different strategies are aimed at altering different aspects of a problem. Some change the steps that caused a particular condition, some add steps that will remove the condition itself and others change the circumstances that make the condition a problem. The next chapter will look at the different strategies CHEF uses in greater detail and discuss the TOPs that they are stored under.

Each of CHEF's strategies generates a change that is a combination of the abstract description of a repair provided by the strategy itself and the specifics of the failed plan. Because each TOP only stores those strategies that will repair the situation described by it and used to find it, any one of them will fix the plan if implemented. Because each TOP does have multiple strategies, however, CHEF must have not only a a mechanism for generating these changes, but also one for choosing between them.

6.5 Choosing the repair

Once all of the possible repairs to a failed plan are generated, CHEF has to choose which one it is going to implement. To do this CHEF has a set of rules concerning the relative merits of different changes. By comparing the changes suggested by the different strategies to one another using these heuristics, CHEF comes up with the one that it thinks is most desirable.

This set of heuristics is the compilation of general knowledge of planning combined with knowledge from the domain about what sort of changes will be least likely to have side-effects. Some of these heuristics are closely tied to the domain, such as "It is easier to add a preparation step than a cooking step". and "It is better to add something that is already in the recipe than something new". Others are more domain independent, such as "It is better to add a single step than to add many steps". and "It is better to replace a step than add a new step".

In the strawberry soufflé example, the final repair that is chosen is to add more egg white to the recipe. This change is generated by the strategy ADJUST-BALANCE:UP which suggests altering the down side of a relationship between ingredients that has been placed out of balance. This repair is picked because it is the least violent change to the plan that can be made and has the least likelihood of creating one problem as it solves another.

```
Deciding between modification plans suggested by strategies.

Comparing plan:
 After doing step: Chop the strawberry
              do: Drain the strawberry.

With plan: Increase the amount of egg white used.

Plan: Increase the amount of egg white used.
is better because: It is better to add more than to remove.

Comparing plan:
 Before doing step: Pour the egg yolk, egg white, vanilla,
 sugar, strawberry, salt, milk, flour and butter into a
 baking-dish
 do: Mix the flour with the egg, spices, strawberry, salt,
 milk, flour and butter.

With plan:
 Increase the amount of egg white used.

Plan: Increase the amount of egg white used.
is better because: It is better to add more than to add new.

Comparing plan:
 Instead of doing step: Pulp the strawberry
 do: Using the strawberry preserves.

With plan:
 Increase the amount of egg white used.

Plan: Increase the amount of egg white used.
is better because: It is better to add more than to replace.

Best plan suggested ->
 Increase the amount of egg white used.
```

> CHEF chooses between the competing changes suggested by different strategies using a set of repair heuristics designed to find the most reliable alteration.

Once a change is selected, CHEF actually implements the change using its procedural knowledge of how to add new steps, split steps into pieces, remove steps and add or increase ingredients. These functions are the same as those used to implement the plan changes made by the MODIFIER when it adds new goals to existing plans.

In the strawberry soufflé situation the final change is marginal, which is the best sort of change if it actually can repair the problem. The only difference between the original strawberry soufflé plan and the new one is that the new one has more egg white in it. This was the change generated by the strategy ADJUST-BALANCE:UP.

```
Changing name of recipe BAD-STRAWBERRY-SOUFFLE
to STRAWBERRY-SOUFFLE

Implementing plan -> Increase the amount of egg white used.
Suggested by strategy ADJUST-BALANCE:UP

New recipe is -> STRAWBERRY-SOUFFLE

               STRAWBERRY-SOUFFLE

          Two teaspoons of vanilla
          A half cup of flour
          A quarter cup of sugar
          A quarter teaspoon of salt
          A half cup of milk
          Two cups of milk
          One piece of vanilla bean
          A quarter cup of butter
          Five egg yolks
          Six egg whites
          One cup of strawberry
```

> CHEF implements the changes suggested by a strategy using the same alteration functions used by the MODIFIER to add new goals to plans.

Once a change is made, the plan is simulated again to assure that the change has led to the expected result. If another failure occurs, it is once again passed through the repair process of explaining the failure, finding the TOP and applying the appropriate strategy. Although past changes will not be marked explicitly, the fact that they participate in satisfying a goal will stop the REPAIRER from removing them. For example, after fixing a Fish and Peanuts recipe to solve the problem of the iodine taste of the fish, CHEF adds the step of marinating it in rice wine. Unfortunately, this causes the fish to become soggy. In trying to fix the new failure, CHEF recognizes that it cannot just remove the marinate step, because it satisfies a goal of keeping the fish tasting good. Instead of removing the step CHEF replaces it with another step that satisfies the same goal, removing the iodine taste of fish, but does not add any more liquid. Rather than marinating the fish in rice wine, it marinates it in crushed ginger.

If the plan is successful, it is then indexed in memory like any other plan, except it is marked by the fact that it avoids a particular kind of failure that can be used when that failure is predicted to occur at some later date.

```
New recipe is -> STRAWBERRY-SOUFFLE

If this plan is successful, the following should be true:

   The batter is now baked.          The batter is now risen.
   The dish now tastes like berries.  The dish now tastes sweet.
   The dish now tastes like vanilla.  The plan avoids the failure

And the following avoidance goals should be met:

   'It is not the case that: The batter is now risen.'
   caused by conditions:
        "Chopping fruits produces liquid."
        "Without a balance between liquids and leavening the batter
         will fall."
```

A repaired plan has associated with it the fact that it now avoids the failure that was repaired.

6.6 Storing the plan

Because CHEF uses its plans again and again, just building them is not enough. It also has to place them in memory so that they can be accessed again.

Storing a repaired plan in memory is no different from storing a plan that never failed at all, except that the repaired plan has an extra feature that can be used to index it: the fact that it avoids the failure from which the planner has recovered. By storing a repaired plan in terms of this feature, the later prediction of a similar failure can be used to find it.

Plans that run with no failures the first time through are stored in CHEF's plan memory by the positive goals that they achieve. Goals having to do with taste, texture and ingredients used are taken from the plan and used as indices for storing it. The type of dish that the recipe creates is also used as an index. The strawberry soufflé plan discussed in this chapter is stored under the fact that it is a SOUFFLE, includes strawberries, is sweet and has the taste of berries. It also is indexed by the only textural goal of the dish, that the batter is risen.

Plans that have failed and have been repaired are somewhat different in that they avoid a particular problem and should be indexed so that they can be used in situations where that problem will arise. To do this, CHEF generates a new token out of the name of the TOP that describes this failure and associates this token with CHEF's prediction of the failure. It then also uses this token to index the plan in memory. With this, CHEF's ANTICIPATOR can later predict this failure on the basis of the surface features that are associated with it, find this token and hand it to the RETRIEVER so it can find the plan in memory that it indexes. This token also has other information about the failure associated with it, but this is less important than the fact that the same token that is recalled when a failure is predicted is used to index the plan that avoids that failure in memory.

> CHEF stores a repaired plan in memory indexed by the fact that it avoids the problem that has just been fixed. The token used to do this indexing is also linked to CHEF's memory of the failure itself, so the prediction of a failure can be used directly to locate the plan that avoids it.

```
Searching for plan that satisfies -
   Include raspberry in the dish.
   Make a souffle.

 Collecting and activating tests.

  Fired: Is the dish SOUFFLE

  Fired: Is the item a FRUIT.

  Fruit + Souffle = Failure
    "Chopping fruits produces liquid."
    "Without a balance between liquids and leavening the batter
     will fall."
     Reminded of STRAWBERRY-SOUFFLE
     Fired demon: DEMON2

Based on features found in items: raspberry and souffle
Adding goal: Avoid failure of type
SIDE-EFFECT:DISABLED-CONDITION:BALANCE exemplified
by the failure 'The batter is now flat' in recipe
STRAWBERRY-SOUFFLE.

Placing goals in order of difficulty -
   Make a souffle.
   Avoid failure of type SIDE-EFFECT:DISABLED-CONDITION:BALANCE
   exemplified by the failure 'The batter is now flat' in recipe
   STRAWBERRY-SOUFFLE.
   Include raspberry in the dish.

Driving down on: Make a souffle.
 Succeeded -
Driving down on:
  Avoid failure of type SIDE-EFFECT:DISABLED-CONDITION:BALANCE
  exemplified by the failure 'The batter is now flat' in recipe
  STRAWBERRY-SOUFFLE.
```

```
 Succeeded -
Driving down on: Include raspberry in the dish.
 Failed trying more general goal.
  Driving down on: Include fruit in the dish.
   Succeeded -

Found recipe -> REC12 STRAWBERRY-SOUFFLE

Recipe exactly satisfies goals ->
    Avoid failure of type SIDE-EFFECT:DISABLED-CONDITION:BALANCE
exemplified by the failure 'The batter is now flat' in recipe
STRAWBERRY-SOUFFLE.
    Make a souffle.

Recipe partially matches ->
    Include raspberry in the dish.
         in that the recipe satisfies: Include fruits in the dish.
```

If a new plan is built out of one that avoids a failure, the fact that it too avoids the same failure is associated with it. When the new plan is stored in memory, it too is stored by the token which is related to the prediction of the failure. This means that any one failure can have many plans in memory that can be used to avoid it. Each one of these is indexed by the token related to the failure and is also indexed by the goals that it satisfies and any other failures that it also avoids. Every time a once failed plan is stored in memory, the token that is associated with the prediction of a failure is used to index it in memory. This closes the repair loop, allowing the prediction of a failure to provide the information needed to find the plan that will avoid it.

Chapter 7

Planning and Planners

Case-based planning suggests an approach to planning that is somewhat different than that taken by planners in the past. It suggests that planning is actually remembering and that many constructive tasks are actually recollection tasks. By definition a case-based planner has to be a learner. The learning done by a case-based planner is linked to its functions as a planner. A case-based planner learns by remembering, in that it stores past plans, past failures and past repairs for use in later planning.

Because so much of the emphasis in case-based planning is on memory use, it is not surprising that many ideas in case-based planning differ sharply from those in both machine learning and planning.

7.1 Case-based planning as planning.

Case-based planning differs from other planners in three areas: its initial plan building, its reaction to plan failures, and its vocabulary for describing and storing plans. While there is a great deal of overlap in these areas, given that the initial choice of a plan affects the way in which it is debugged and the way in which debugged plans are stored affects the way in which they are chosen for later use, it is important to tease apart these different areas in order understand how different planners handle them.

7.1.1 Building an initial plan.

A case-based planner builds new plans out of old plans that it is reminded of. It finds these past planning experiences by searching an episodic memory. This memory is organized by two sorts of indices: goals to be satisfied and failures to be avoided. Plans are organized around goals so that they can be retrieved when the goals that they satisfy are requested. But plans are not organized under goals alone. Plans are also organized under failures that the planner encountered when originally putting them together. Anticipated failures can then be avoided by finding plans that were constructed to deal with similar failures in the past.

In order to use its own memory organization, a case-based planner must begin the task of building a plan for a set of goals by considering how the goals will be interacting. By doing this, it can anticipate any failure that it has experienced before, and use this anticipation to search for a plan that solves the problem that it has predicted. It can also use the prediction of any positive interaction between goals to characterize its current set of goals in terms of an already existing exemplar in memory that can be accessed directly.

> The case-based approach to finding an initial plan is to *anticipate* problems so it can find plans that *avoid* them.

The *anticipate and avoid* approach to planning is different in many ways than the *create and debug* approach taken by past planners. The *create and debug* strategy is to plan for sets of goals by planning for each of the individual goals and then dealing with any interactions between plans as they arise. *Create and debug* planners store plans in terms of the individual goals that they satisfy. The same plan that is used when the planner is planning for a single goal alone is also suggested when the planner is planning for the same goal in conjunction with others. Because of this, *create and debug* planners have to debug the problems that are discovered in faulty plans rather than anticipating problems and then suggesting plans that are appropriate to all aspects of a goal situation in the first place. Even when the planner has the knowledge that would allow it to anticipate the problems that arise, it has to first build the faulty plan and later encounter the problem during a simulation or analysis of the plan itself. While this approach is reasonable in the case of a planner that lacks knowledge of a particular problem, it is unacceptable in those cases where a planner is faced with a problem that it has the knowledge to deal with.

While there have been many suggestions as to how a planner can deal with interactions between plans once they are discovered, they have all been implemented within the confines of this basic framework. Unfortunately, this framework itself stands in the way of the most effective method for dealing with plan interaction problems: anticipate them and start with a plan that already deals with them. This is not to say that such planners could not then recover from this kind of error, it is just that they would continue to make them even in the presence of rules and experiences that should allow them to anticipate and avoid them.

The *create and debug* strategy makes it impossible to organize complex plans dealing with goal interactions in a way that makes them accessible to the planner. Even if plans exist to deal with some set of goal interactions, they cannot be stored by the fact that they solve some goal interaction problem because that kind of feature is not included in the vocabulary used to index and organize the plans themselves. The planner has to constantly replan in situations involving interactions between goals, even when it has already designed plans that can effectively deal with these situations. While this does not mean that such planners are incapable of producing finished plans for goal interaction situations such as presented in this example, it does mean that they must constantly repeat the errors that they have made in the past.

The most straightforward, if not first, example of this approach was STRIPS [Fikes and Nilsson 71], a planner based on the ideas presented in GPS [Newell and Simon 72]. STRIPS built plans out of a series of operators that were stored in a table of preconditions and effects. Each goal that it planned for was viewed in terms of the difference between the current description of the world and the description provided by the goal itself. Each operator, when applied to STRIPS' understanding of the world, would add or delete states in accord with its effects. For STRIPS, planning consisted of building up operators one by one that would reduce the differences between the initial state of the world and that described by the goals that it was currently planning for.

Planning for many goals at once was no different for STRIPS than planning for a single goal. The multiple goals were translated into a set of states that had to obtain at the end of the plan execution and STRIPS planned for these each in its turn.

STRIPS could reuse complete plans and plan segments that it had built up during past planning experiences, but only when the current conjunct of goals was an exact match for those it had planned for in the past. The vocabulary it had for storing the plans and plan segments that it built was not sufficient to describe many of the similarities between different goal situations. In particular it could not describe problems having to do with goal and plan interactions. Without such a vocabulary to describe the similarity between different situations, STRIPS could not know that a past plan stored in its table of operators would be useful in a solving a present planning problem.

The problem with STRIPS was not in the level of generality of the indexing vocabulary that it used to access its initial plans and operators. The problem was instead in the type of vocabulary that it used. STRIPS only attended to surface features of the goals it was handed and did not concern itself with the interactions between them. Though there has been research that is aimed at improving the search performance of STRIPS and STRIPS-like planners, ([Korf 82] and [Minton 85]), none of it has been directed at developing a new vocabulary for plan storage.

Many of the problems that arose because of STRIPS were addressed by two later theories, HACKER [Sussman 75] and NOAH [Sacerdoti 75]. In particular, a way to avoid the combinatorics of a best-first search of a planning space of primitive operators was suggested in the form of hierarchical planning. Neither of these programs, however, suggested any reasonable alternative to the *create and debug* paradigm. In fact, HACKER and NOAH stand as the prime examples of this planning philosophy.

Sussman's HACKER was designed to learn by saving debugged plans for later use. HACKER would plan for a conjunct of goals by finding the plan segments in its answer library that achieved each of the individual goals and proposing an initial plan composed of each of these segments in an arbitrary order. Once the initial plan was created, HACKER would then run it in a *careful* mode. In this mode HACKER would examine the effects of each plan step and notice failures as they occurred. Bugs were both noticed and repaired by plan *critics* that had knowledge of planning problems in general as well as specific knowledge of the limited physics of the blocks world itself. Once a bug was detected and corrected, the resulting plan was generalized and added to a plan library for later use.

Like STRIPS, the intent in HACKER was to reuse past plans by storing them in a library, indexed by the goals they satisfied. Unfortunately, also like STRIPS, the indexing did not reflect the fact that a particular problem having to do with a goal interaction was solved by a particular plan. It was only by rebuilding the failed plan again that HACKER could recognize that it was in a similar situation and then make use of the alterations that it had devised earlier.

Like HACKER, Sacerdoti's NOAH built plans for multiple goal situations by combining the plans associated with each of the individual goals. Unlike HACKER, however, NOAH did not linearize its plans or run simulations to check for errors. NOAH instead assumed that the plan steps could be run in any order unless the specifics of the preconditions or effects of one step placed a constraint on the others. NOAH would notice such constraints while expanding each of its planning steps into more primitive actions and analyzing the resulting plan using critics similar to those suggested by Sussman in HACKER. This analysis took the place of the simulation that HACKER ran.

The choice of initial plan segments was approximately the same in NOAH as in HACKER. NOAH would find the plan steps associated with each of the individual goals it was given and compose its final plan out of them. While both NOAH and HACKER could manipulate the order of the plan steps they had, once they were chosen, they did not have the ability to choose new plan segments for the goals that they were planning for. Neither of them had the ability to make use of the context surrounding a goal to choose the plan to be used to achieve it. For example, NOAH would begin planning for the need to use many tools by forming a plan to go to the tool box for each one. Later it could merge this series of trips into one trip, but it could not access a plan such as going to the tool box and bringing it back. This is because to be useful this plan would have to be indexed by the fact that it is a good plan that *subsumes* [Wilensky 78] a large number of goals to have tools, but this kind of description is not included in HACKER and NOAH's vocabulary of simple goals.

A different approach to the problem of goal and plan interactions was proposed by Wilensky in PANDORA ([Wilensky 80] and [Wilensky 83]). While he suggested an alternative to dealing with planning problems once they arise, he did so within the confines of the *create and debug* paradigm.

PANDORA is a planner that reacts to interactions between plans and goals by introducing meta-level goals into the basic planning agenda. If, for example, the planner is given the goal to get a newspaper that is outside while it is raining, it notices the conflict between the goal to get the paper and the goal to remain dry. Once an interaction such as a *goal conflict* is detected, a meta-level goal to resolve this conflict is introduced into the planner's agenda and this is dealt with like any other goal.

PANDORA is not designed to reuse of any plans that it designs, so it must repeatedly confront and repair any planning failures. Even with a method of storing plans, however, its basic planning algorithm of finding and combining the plan segments for each of the individual goals it is given, independent of other goals or relevant states, firmly places it in the *create and debug* family. It has no mechanism or vocabulary for searching for plans related to a set of goals or even the goal interaction types that it uses to debug it own plans. Like STRIPS, HACKER and NOAH, it must repeat its failures and its debugging efforts because it has no way to effectively save its debugged plans for future use.

To sum up, although their response to the identification of an interaction between goals and plans is different, these planners have the same basic strategy for indexing into plans initially. They assume that the first step in planning for a set of goals is to find the best plans for each of the planner's individual goals and then mediate between them when the need arises. They assume that the final plan for a set of goals will rise out of a combination of the individual plans for each goal alone. They ignore the fact that often the best plan for a situation has less to do with surface features and more to do with the interactions that arises between them. Thus they have no vocabulary or mechanism for searching for plans using a characterization of goal situations as a whole or for searching for a plan that relates to the interaction between goals as opposed to just the individual goals alone.

There are two problems with the strategy of originally indexing to plans on the basis of single goals alone. First, the "best" plan for satisfying a single goal alone is not necessarily also the best one to use when satisfying that goal when it appears in conjunction with others. Second, there is no method by which these planners can effectively retrieve complex plans that have been built up in the past, because they begin by looking for plans related to individual goals first. These problems alone make it clear that a more abstract form of characterizing goals and indexing plans has to be found.

The first difficulty with the "each goal first" strategy used by the *create and debug* planners is the assumption that the best plan used to satisfy a goal in general is also the best one for dealing with the goal when it is one of many that have to be satisfied. NOAH for example could change a series of trips to its tool box into a single trip during which it would retrieve many tools. While this is a reasonable solution to the problem, it is not as effective or intelligent a plan as simply carrying back the entire tool box. The difference between the two plans of carrying back each of the tools as opposed to carrying back the tool box is subtle, to be sure, but it is not trivial. The plan to go to the box once, and carry back each of the tools is a solution that joins each of the original plans into a single structure. The plan to bring back the tool box, on the other hand, is a solution that adopts a plan that is different in kind than the original set of plans that it replaces. It is a plan for the overall situation rather than for each of the individual goals. It is itself a subsumption plan [Wilensky 78]. The point is that best plan for a satisfying a set of goals does not have to include each of the best plans for the individual goals.

The second problem with this "each goal first" strategy involves the reuse of existing plans. There seems to be no method, within the context of just searching for plans under individual goals, for storing and accessing complex plans that are the product of previously solved problems. At best, there have been suggestions, such as PANDORA's "canned plans", that the planner look for past solutions *after* it has run into planning difficulties [Wilensky 83]. In Wilensky's newspaper and rain situation for example, any solution to the problem of getting the newspaper without getting wet is lost when the planning is over. Even if it is saved as a "canned plan", the next time this situation is seen again, the same "each goal first" strategy will be used prior to the planner noticing the existence of this plan which is perfectly suited to the situation. It is only after the planner has tried and failed, attempting less useful plans, that it will be in a position to find the plan that was designed precisely for the situation that it is currently in. It can then only be found if the current situation includes *all* of the goals that were present when the canned plan was first built.

Because plans are indexed by goals and goals alone, features in the initial situation, which may in fact predict goals but not be goals themselves, are ignored in choosing a plan. Although the rain predicts the need to do something to avoid getting wet, it is not itself a goal and is thus ignored by any planner that indexed plans on the basis of goals alone. For such planners, it is only after the plan has been run or simulated, and the actual goals have arisen that a plan to deal with them can be activated. Because plans are indexed by goals alone, the other features in a situation, that are not goals but may predict that the planner will develop a goal, can not be used to search for plans. This forces these planners to simulate the world in order to tease out the goals that these surface features predict. But a dependence on simulation is basically a dependence on unconstrained inference.

This problem is far more severe than the first in that it undercuts the ability of a planner to learn from its own mistakes. Planners using this approach must constantly replan, using inappropriate sub-plans obtained from individual goals, before they can begin to search for the more appropriate solutions that they have previously built. There are of course straightforward solutions to this problem. Using a notion such as that of Wilensky's canned plans, it is possible to index a plan under each of the simple goals that it satisfies. These canned plans, stored under individual goals, could be found when all other goals originally satisfied by the plan are present in the current input. Unfortunately, this allows for the use of existing canned plans only in the case of those situations which are exactly like those that originally motivated their development. This same objection can be leveled against HACKER's use of conjuncts of goals to index complex plans. So while this addition to the basic "each goal first" strategy could be adapted to the reuse of some complex plans, it would not allow any but the most inflexible learning to occur.

A further problem with any approach that stores complex plans in terms of the conjunction of the individual goals that they solve is that, in many cases, the goals that are interacting may not all be in the initial input that the planner has to work with. This is certainly the case in Wilensky's newspaper-and-rain example where the goal to remain dry does not arise until the program has already begun to execute, or at least simulate, the plan. While the specific goal does not arise until the initial plan of going outside is in motion, the features that a planner could use to anticipate the conflict are present in the input. The fact that it is raining should have an effect on the choice of plan that the planner will use to get the paper. But, because the fact of rain is not itself a goal, it is not used to index any plans. A planner that can only index plans in terms of specific goals and conjuncts of goals can never make use of the presence of these features in the input and must instead rely on a simulation of some initial plan to expose problems by giving rise to particular goals or goal violations that will occur given the first order plan. It seems clear that any indexing process could be improved with the addition of a vocabulary that includes all of the features that participate in the choice of a plan. This includes descriptions of relevant states in the world and predictions of possible conflicts that the plans may resolve as well as the goals that the plans satisfy.

Case-based planning suggests dealing with these problems by storing plans under the goal interactions that they deal with and by associating these interactions with the features that predict them. When these features arise in planning the planner is able to immediately predict the possibility of a problem and then use that prediction to access a plan that deal with it. Rather then repeating the same mistake over again a case-based planner is able to anticipate it, and by anticipating it avoid it.

7.1.2 Debugging failed plans.

A case-based planner can anticipate and thus avoid failures having to do with plan interactions. It can only do this, however, with the interactions it has seen before. In order to plan effectively it must be able to recover and learn from those failures that it hasn't seen before and isn't able to anticipate. So, like *create and debug* planners it has to have knowledge of how to identify and repair faulty plans that have failed due to unforeseen interactions between steps.

While there are technical differences between the way case-based planning handles plan failures and the way programs such as NOAH or PANDORA deal with them, the most important difference between them is that a case-based planner treats its mistakes as *expectation* failures as well as *planning* failures. Planning is a test of its understanding of the world. Planning failures are indicators of where that understand has broken down and where it has to be fixed. They tell CHEF when it needs to learn.

A planning failure occurs when a plan does not satisfy some goal that it was designed to deal with. For example, in the plan created by CHEF for a beef and broccoli dish, the fact that the broccoli ended up soggy was a *planning* failure because soggy broccoli is a bad state that any planner wants to avoid. An *expectation* failure is different. It occurs when an expected event does not come about or when an event for which there was no expectation does. In the beef and broccoli example, there is an *expectation* failure that occurs at the same time as the planning failure, because CHEF did not anticipate that the broccoli would end up begin soggy.

CHEF responds to *plan* failures by building a causal explanation of why the failure has occurred and then using that explanation to access replanning strategies designed for the situation in general. It responds to *expectation* failures by again using that explanation to add new inference rules which allow it to anticipate the problem that it previously was unable to foresee. It first asks itself, "What went wrong with the plan?" and then asks "What went wrong with the planning?"

It is important to note that there is not a one to one correspondence between planning failure and expectation failure. It is possible to have the expectation that a plan will fail and have this expectation confirmed when it does or violated when it doesn't. CHEF, however, is concerned only with the sub-set of expectation failures that correspond to planning failures. In fact, CHEF is only concerned with planning failures that can be described in terms of domain level states. It is not able to recognize, for example, failures of overall strategy that lead to resource problems. This lack of ability is not a theoretical problem, but instead reflects CHEF's lack of a complete vocabulary for describing planning problems.

Of the planners already discussed, none deal with the failures they encounter as expectation failures. While STRIPS and HACKER do save plans, they do not change the inferences they make that would allow them to anticipate the problems that the plans were designed to deal with. The plans they save can only be used when the planner is confronted with goals that have surface features in common with the past situation. But surface features alone do not account for many of the similarities between different situations in which a single plan is applicable. In the beef and broccoli situation, for instance, neither of these planners could save the final plan in a way that would make it useful to the later problem of planning of chicken and snow peas, because the similarity between the two problem situations is not in the individual goals, but in way in which they interact.

There are also differences between CHEF and these past planners in the way they deal with planning failures as planning failures alone. CHEF's approach to planning failures has three parts: first it explains why the failure has occurred, next it finds the TOP and general repair strategies that are associated with that type of failure, and finally it uses the strategy which has the best implementation, given the specifics of the problem and circumstances surrounding it. In the beef-and-broccoli example, this means explaining that the soggy broccoli is the product of stir frying it with the liquid from the meat, seeing this as an instance of the TOP SIDE-EFFECT:DISABLED-CONDITION:CONCURRENT, and then searching for an implementation of each of that TOP's strategies before choosing to SPLIT-AND-REJOIN the single step of stir-frying into a series of steps.

CHEF's approach to failure recovery draws a great deal from the tradition established by Sussman and Sacerdoti by their use of planning critics and then extended by Wilensky. Both Sussman and Sacerdoti suggested that planners need to know about planning error in general to intelligently debug faulty plans. With this knowledge, a planner would not have to perform the tedious backtracking and replanning that a STRIPS-like planner has to do when it hits a dead end. Instead, it would be able to apply one of a set of planning critics, each having knowledge of a specific problem and the means to solve it, thus repairing the faulty plan by changing only the steps that participate in the failure. The only difference between the two views of planning critics suggested by Sussman and Sacerdoti had to do with when the critics were applied. Sussman's HACKER would apply its critics while running a fully expanded plan in a careful mode while Sacerdoti's Noah would have its critics check for plan interactions at each stage of expansion down to primitive planning steps.

There are difficulties with the critics approach presented by both Sussman and Sacerdoti, however. The first stems from the fact that they both wrote planners that functioned in somewhat impoverished domains, Sussman working in a blocks world and Sacerdoti working in a world where the problem task was the building of simple machines such as pumps. Unfortunately, in such worlds, there is usually only one plan for each goal and the effects of each plan tend to be those and only those that directly satisfy the goal being planned for. Because of this, only a limited vocabulary was needed to describe the problems the critics were confronted with and each problem required only a single transformation to solve it. As a result the critics suggested by both Sussman and Sacerdoti only begin to scratch the surface of what is needed to deal with complex domains.

One critic suggested by Sussman, *prerequisite-clobbers-broher-goal*, has the repair REORDER. This is used to repair bugs such as putting a block on top of a block that has to be moved. But this is not a precise enough description of the situation. It does not capture the fact that the state doing the "clobbering" is a state the planner is directly planning for rather than a side-effect. The difference is that a side-effect can be recovered from by adding a step that removes it where a desired effect is a state that the planner's wants to have maintained for some duration. A problem due to a side-effect can be dealt with by removing that side-effect but problems due to desired effects have to be planned around while maintaining that effect. This distinction is not captured in the vocabulary used by either Sussman or Sacerdoti and it is a distinction that has an effect on how the planner should react to the different bugs.

This lack of depth in the planner's domain has more of an effect than just limiting the number of critics or the level of detail used to describe them. It also disguises the fact that there is not a one to one correspondence between problems that can be recognized and ways in which they can be solved. This assumption of a correspondence between problems and solutions, however, is implicit in the entire critics approach. Critics are units that contain both a description of a problem and a description of how the planner should deal with it. A more reasonable approach is to first diagnose a problem and then decide between alternative solutions that can be applied to solve it.

The major problem with critics is the same quality that makes them so seductive: their unity. The notion of a set of general purpose rules for debugging plans, rules that are independent of the planning knowledge of any domain, is appealing in its elegance. But it ignores the fact that often a planner has to use domain knowledge to choose between the applicability of different repair strategies suggested by the debugging rules. Even in the block tower case, it is difficult to see how critics alone could deal with a choice between reordering the plans or using an alternative plan for the second step that would allow the plan to move the already built two block tower as a unit. The choice between these different plans has to be based on information in the domain itself (*i.e.*, the difficulty of individual plans, their existence, and other interactions) as well as information about the general advisability of using the different strategies (*i.e.*, is it better to reorder existing plans or replace steps). The structure of the knowledge in critics, however, makes it difficult to compare different strategies or to see how the specifics of the planner's domain would affect the choice between them.

While the idea of making use of domain independent knowledge of planning itself to debug plans is a powerful idea, the structure that Sussman and Sacerdoti gave it, that of critics, is highly limited. This is a problem inherent to the notion of using a single structure for both the diagnosis and treatment of a bug: there is no place to put the possibility of multiple treatments or to be able to recognize a problem that has no treatment at all.

In an effort to remedy these problems with critics, Wilensky has suggested the idea of *meta-planning* ([Wilensky 80] and [Wilensky 83]). Rather than representing abstract planning knowledge in a set of critics, Wilensky has represented it in the form of meta-goals and meta-plans that are identical in form to the specific goals and plans of the planner's domain. When confronted with a problem stemming from plan interactions, a goal to deal with that interaction is spawned and the general planning mechanism deals with it directly. This allows the planner to notice a problem, insert a goal to deal with it into its general planning agenda, and then find plans to deal with it. Wilensky has taken the same knowledge that Sussman and Sacerdoti stored in critics, and has divided it into diagnostic knowledge which recognizes problems and prescriptive knowledge which solves them.

In an example done by Wilensky's PANDORA, the planner tries to get a newspaper that is outside in the rain. On simulating the plan, the planner sees that going outside in the rain will make it get wet. Getting wet, however, is the violation of a P-GOAL [Schank and Abelson 77] to remain dry. This violation means that there is a conflict between the goal to get the paper and the P-GOAL to remain dry. Seeing this the planner builds the meta-goal RESOLVE-GOAL-CONFLICT and hands this back to itself for further planning. RESOLVE-GOAL-CONFLICT has a set of meta-plans associated with it, including one that has the planner look under the violated goal to stay dry for a canned plan. Here it finds the plan USE-RAINCOAT and adds this to the steps it has to take in getting the newspaper. Rather than having a critic to deal with this situation Wilensky diagnoses the problem and then prescribes a treatment, splitting the knowledge used in the critics of HACKER and NOAH into two more flexible units. The major advantage to this approach is that a meta-planner would be able to suggest many different solutions to a single problem where a planner using critics would have only the single solution suggested by the critic that recognized the problem.

While the meta-planning idea of splitting the repairing of plan bugs into diagnosis and prescription is a step forward, there is a problem in what PANDORA considers to be a diagnosis. PANDORA is able to analyze the newspaper and rain situation down to the level of GOAL-CONFLICT. This means that the planner knows that there is a problem in the plan to get the newspaper, but is unable to identify why the conflict has arisen. This information is contained in the event simulator that it runs in order to detect planning problems, but the simulator's assessment of the problem is not handed back to the planner. The simulator is only interested in the states that the planner passes though while running a plan, and is not interested in why those states occur. The information given back to the planner is simply that there is some threat to the P-GOAL to remain dry, but it is unable to identify the conditions which cause this threat. For example, the feature in the input situation that has determined the need for some alteration of the initial GET-NEWSPAPER plan (*e.g.*, it is raining) is never used by the planner itself in either characterizing the input problem or deciding on a plan to deal with it.

Without a causal description of what has led up to the violation of the P-GOAL, there is no way to know where to alter the existing plan. The plans that are available are only those associated with the P-GOAL itself. In this case, the P-GOAL is the goal to remain dry, which has the plan of using a rain coat associated with it. But what if a different set of circumstances causes the violation of this goal? If, for example, the planner has to go into a flooded basement, it will again be told by the simulator that it will have a conflict between its initial plan and the P-GOAL to remain dry. Again, it will build the meta-goal and again it will try the normal plan to remain dry, use a rain coat. But here using a rain coat makes no sense, because the rain coat will not do anything to alter the causal circumstances that led to the planner getting wet. Because the planner does not have a full description of the causality that led up to the failure, it is unable to appropriately alter the circumstances. Without a description of these circumstances, only the most general strategies and plans can be reliably suggested for repairing a bug.

The causality behind a problem, the reason why it has happened, is not used by PANDORA to decide what to do about it. While Wilensky has given PANDORA more flexibility in dealing with bugs than HACKER or NOAH, by splitting its planning knowledge into separate diagnosis and prescription stages, he has not changed the level of description of those bugs that would have allowed the use of even more specific and powerful strategies. Like HACKER and NOAH, PANDORA does not have the vocabulary needed to describe the details of a bug. While they can describe *what* has happened, they cannot describe *why* it has happened. But without the knowledge of why something has happened, a planner cannot make the best decisions about how to stop it from happening in the present or how to avoid having it happen again in the future.

The difference between the CHEF approach and that of PANDORA is the level of description that each uses in building a diagnosis of a problem. There is no doubt that dividing the knowledge used to debug plans into separate diagnostic and prescriptive organizations is a plus. As argued earlier in discussing problems with NOAH and HACKER, this sort of division is necessary for the planner to adequately decide between competing debugging strategies. For PANDORA a diagnosis consists of a description of the failure alone, in Wilensky's newspaper and rain example, a description that begins and ends with the planner seeing the violation of a particular P-GOAL, stay dry. For CHEF, a diagnosis includes the states and steps that causally led to the failure, as well as the positive goals that were being planned for by those states and steps. With this information, CHEF is able to suggest strategies tailored to the exact situation and choose between them making use of its abstract knowledge of planning combined with its concrete knowledge of its domain.

In building PANDORA, Wilensky argued that HACKER and NOAH did not go far enough in taking seriously the role of goal and plan interactions, the main source of planning failures. He argued that the way to deal with problems rising out of goal and plan interactions is to elevate them to the status of goals themselves. He argued, in fact, that the basic structure of the planner should reflect the fact that it will often be encountering failures due to these interactions. This argument is continued in CHEF, and extended to include the argument that a planner needs to have a rich causal description of *why* a failure has occurred rather than just a description of *what* the failure is.

CHEF uses a vocabulary of causal interactions to describe its own planning failures. It then uses these descriptions to find very specific strategies for dealing with the failures.

7.1.3 Storing plans for later use.

Once a case-based planner has built and debugged a plan it tries to store it in memory indexed by the features that will allow the planner to access it in similar situations. While this is basically what any planner that saves its plans does, the notion of "similar" is somewhat different for a case-based planner than for other planners.

For example, like STRIPS and HACKER, CHEF indexes the plans it builds in terms of the particular goals that they satisfy. The basic vocabulary of plan indexing is the vocabulary of the planner's domain. For instance, the beef and broccoli plan built by CHEF is indexed by the foods that it includes (*e.g.*, beef, broccoli and garlic), the tastes that it exhibits (*e.g.*, savory, lightly sweet, spicy) and by the type of dish that it is, (stir-fry). It is also indexed by a generalization of the features that it exhibits, allowing this beef and broccoli plan to also be stored as a more general meat and vegetable plan. These surface features, are used as the initial vocabulary for storing plans in a discrimination network.

Unlike other planners, CHEF also uses descriptions of goal and plan interactions to index its plans. The plan interactions that CHEF encounters on the way to building a working plan, such as the liquid from the beef leading to the soggy broccoli, are as much a part of why a particular set of step was chosen as is the initial surface goals. When a plan is stored, it is stored by a description of the negative goal interactions that it avoids. Later, when CHEF infers that a set of goals is going to lead to a problem, a plan to deal with that problem can be accessed because the plan is indexed by the fact that it avoids problems of this sort. This indexing allows CHEF to use the prediction of a problem to find a plan that deals with it. The plan for beef and broccoli, designed to deal with the interaction between the two major ingredients is indexed as an example of a SIDE-EFFECT:DISABLED-CONDITION:CONCURRENT plan. It can later be accessed when the need for such a plan is inferred. Like any other vocabulary item based on a plan satisfying a goal, CHEF uses the fact that a plan successfully avoids a problem to store the plan for later use when a goal to avoid the same or similar problem arises.

CHEF stores plans by the goals they satisfy and the problems that they avoid. This allows it to find plans that achieve the goals it is planning for while avoiding the problems it predicts will arise while doing so.

In summary, CHEF begins the task of planning by making inferences based on past experiences as to what might go wrong in planning for a set of goals. It then searches its memory for a plan that best satisfies the goals it has and best avoids the failures that is able to anticipate. Ingredient critics for modifying initial plans are organized around the type of plan to be modified and the goal to be added, allowing CHEF to have different plans for a single goal indexed by context. Any failures that CHEF encounters are explained, using CHEF's causal rules for the domain. This explanation tells CHEF how to repair the plan and also tells it which features can be marked as predictive of similar failures in the future. CHEF then stores its final plan in terms of the goals that it satisfies as well as any problems that it encountered so that it may be used to avoid similar problems in the future. CHEF has a closed experiential loop, encountering a problem, solving it and then storing the final plan so that it can be applied to later instances of the problem.

7.2 Case-based planning as learning.

A case-based planner is a planner, but it is a planner that learns. The learning it does, however, is not *concept learning* via induction, (*e.g.*, [Lebowitz 80], [Michalski and Larson 78] and [Winston 70]), or even *explanation driven learning* (*e.g.*, [DeJong 83] and [Mitchell 83]) of the form that emerged in recent years. It differs from past theories in three ways. First, the categories CHEF forms are functional categories that help in later planning. Second, the process of credit assignment used for deciding which features of a situation will be included as part of a new category is based on a causal analysis of the situation. And finally, the motivation for building a new category is provided by the needs of the planner. This means that CHEF only learns when it recognizes that its understanding of which plans are appropriate to a situation is faulty.

> Learning from cases differs from other types of learning in *what* is learned (functional categories), *how* it is learned (though causal analysis of failures) and *when* it is learned (when the planner fails).

7.2.1 Functional categories

Initial work on learning was based on the idea that a program could build up categories of feature conjunctions by viewing repeated instances of members of those categories. These programs built categories defined by those features included in all instances of a class that they were shown. Some of these programs took the step of building generalizations of features into the category being defined. These generalizations were the product of taking different features from two or more examples and finding a single description that would cover them all. The source of this description was often a semantic hierarchy in which the two features shared a common abstraction or a disjunction of the two features that allowed either one as part of the category description.

The best known program of this class was built by Patrick Winston. His program was given descriptions of compound objects in a blocks world and would learn concepts like ARCH and STACK by seeing repeated instances of members of these categories and instances of "near misses", objects that lacked only one feature for determining membership. By viewing members of the categories, the program could build up a feature list that defined what was sufficient for membership. By viewing "near misses" it could identify the features in that list that were necessary requirements for membership.

After learning a category, the program could identify members of the category it had just constructed. But that identification required the use of all of the features used in the definition. Identifying an object as an ARCH did not mean that the program could then make any further conclusions about the object, because all of the features that were included in the definition were used in the recognition. The categories that the program built were functionless. Although they could be used to recognize objects of a particular class, no other features could then be attributed to that object as a result of that identification.

This is an inherent property of the concept learning paradigm, because the task itself is to learn the features that *define* a category. The feature lists that concept learners build up do not distinguish between the features of an object that can be observed and tested for and the features of an object that the learner would want to infer from the fact that it has identified that object.

An example of where the concept learning paradigm goes wrong is pointed out in Schank, Collins and Hunter [Schank, Collins and Hunter In press.]. They discuss the problem of learning the categories of edible and inedible mushrooms. The task is not to learn the definition of edible and inedible, but to learn the features of each that could be to classify new instances. These features include the shape, color, smell and texture. Although the goal is to be able to determine whether particular mushrooms are poisonous or not, the tests that should be built to classify them can not depend on a direct examination of this feature. The idea is to be able to predict when a mushroom is inedible on the basis of a set of features, not to define what features have to be present for it to be inedible. The second task is all too easy, the class of inedible mushrooms has the necessary and sufficient condition that each member of that class is inedible. But this is not a particularly good test to use when picking mushrooms.

In this case, a functional categorization of mushrooms has to be based on recognition tests that allow a user to infer the edibility of the mushrooms tested on the basis of other observable features. A functionless category would be one that just defines the two classes of edible and inedible mushrooms on the basis of these individual features alone.

Although the task of concept learners is building categories, the categories they build lack any function, because they use all of the features that define the category to test for membership. What they need is the notion of the difference between features that *predict* membership and those that *result* from membership. The predictive features are used to classify, while the resulting features are used to make inferences that react to that classification.

For a category to be functional, it needs to be constructed somewhat like an "IF-THEN" rule. The left side, the "IF", has the features that are used to recognize a category. The right side, the "THEN", has the response or inferences that are appropriate for the category.

CHEF builds categories as well. CHEF's categories are descriptions of different planning situations. These situations are recognized on the basis of features in its input. The response to recognizing a situation is to find a plan that is indexed by the description of the category it defines. The categories that CHEF learns are functional, the "IF" is the set of goals that predict a planning problem, the "THEN" is the plan or plans that can be used to deal with it.

The categories that CHEF builds are composed of features that can predict problems and plans that can be used to respond to them. When CHEF builds a new category, the predictive features are used to recognize problem situations, while the plans related to that problem are used to solve it. The categories that CHEF builds are actually categories that define when it is appropriate to use certain plans.

For example, at one point CHEF builds a bad strawberry soufflé that falls because strawberries have too much liquid in them to be put into a standard soufflé . CHEF solves this problem by adding extra egg to the soufflé that balances out the extra liquid. But now it has a plan for a situation that has to be distinguished from the normal soufflé situation. It has the problem of figuring out which features in the current situation should be used to define that category. The problem is to find the features that predict the failure so that the plan that deals with it can be accessed. Because this category is going to be used later, it has to include only those features that will be apparent to the planner when it is making it choice of which plan to use in a new planning situation. So it has to include only those features that will be in its input.

The input for CHEF is the goals it has to satisfy, so the categories it forms are recognized through an examination of those features. In this case, the goal to include strawberries and the goal to make a soufflé are blamed for the problem because strawberries have a high liquid content and soufflés are sensitive to liquids. These features are generalized and a new category is formed. The category defines those situations in which this new soufflé plan with added egg to compensate for extra liquid is appropriate. It is recognized when the planner has the goal to build a soufflé and a goal to include a high moisture fruit in that soufflé . By doing a little bit of causal reasoning, the planner also is able to recognize this situation when it has the goal to make a soufflé and a goal to include any liquid spice. The category is not just the features that are used to recognize it. It also includes the plans that are designed to deal with it. The planner's recognition of this situation allows it to find the past plan it built, the strawberry soufflé plan, that can be modifier to fit the exact needs of other aspects of the situation.

Unlike concept learners, the categories that CHEF builds are functional. They have two parts to them: the features that allow it to recognize a situation and the responses that it has to deal with the situation. It uses these categories to differentiate between the different planning situations it faces and the different planning responses it should have.

> CHEF learns *functional* categories that consist of tests for recognizing new instances of situations it has already encountered and plans for reacting to those situations.

7.2.2 Credit assignment

One of the biggest problems in learning is that of credit assignment. That is, given a set of features that make up a situation, how does a learner decide which of those features should be included in the new category, functional or otherwise, that is being learned.

In inductive learning systems, the problem of credit assignment becomes a question of features repetition. Here, the question of relevance is reduced to the question of persistence, the relevant features being those that persist from example to example. The features that persist through a series of examples end up being included in the definition of the category being formed. As an inductive learner looks at more and more examples, its definition of the category it is building becomes more and more precise. The assumption being that the relevant features will have to be included in all examples and extraneous features will have at least one example in which they are not present.

In the case of Winston's program, features such as the size of the blocks and their shape were weeded out of the definition of ARCH by having it look at examples of arches in which these features varied. By getting one example in which the top block of the arch was triangular and one in which it was square, the program was able to remove the shape requirement on the top block from its definitional list. The program could not look at a single example and decide which features were relevant to any new category it was forming but it was able to constantly narrow the field of features by noticing those features that did and did not appear in repeated examples.

There are many problems with this approach to credit assignment. Most of these problems rise out of the substitution of the notion of relevance with the idea of repetition. Instead for figuring out the features in a situation that are relevant and then building a new category on that basis, these learners give up on that task and wait until the constant repetition of certain features points out which ones are constant if not relevant. Because of this, none of these learners can glean anything from single instances. They cannot learn about a class of situations from a instance of that situation because they are not designed to even understand the situations they look at all. These programs were in the position of being able to build up classifications of objects that they had no individual understanding of.

The second problem with this type of learning is the inability of these learners to weed out features that reoccur but are not relevant. Because they have no notion of relevance, they are content to build and maintain categories with spurious features. These features are maintained when the learner is given examples of a class that include spurious features. For example, Mike Lebowitz's IPP could learn categories of actions such as "IRA bombings" which would contain information about the location of the bombing and who took responsibility for the action. Unfortunately, because the program had no notion of the relevance of particular features it would also include features like the number of people killed, thinking that if it was an IRA attack, two people would always be killed. In some ways this was a reasonable generalization to make, in that this is what happened in every story the program read. In other ways, however it is quite unreasonable, because the number of people killed is not linked to the organization doing the killing in any coherent way. It was just a feature of the episodes the program read that did not vary between readings.

The final problem with this approach to credit assignment lies in the need to tell these learners what they are learning as they are learning it. Because these systems build up categories by matching new example against old definitions, each example has to be identified with the category it is a member of. Each example that Winston's program looked at was identified as an ARCH, a STACK or a "near miss" of one of its categories. Without this, the program would not know which category to try to fit the new example to, and might fit it to the wrong one thus ruining the definition by altering it to fit a non-instance.

Lebowitz's IPP tried to get around this problem by building new categories for pairs of examples that had any features at all in common. Once a category was built, it would have a certainty factor added to it that required more that one non-example to undercut. But this meant a trade-off between having to hand feed examples to the program and having to weed out the propagation of spurious generalizations that provided a stream of erroneous predictions.

CHEF tries to avoid these problems by taking a different approach to credit assignment. CHEF does not wait for repetitions of similar situations, which is to say similar planning failures, to indicate which features should be used to predict those failures. Instead, CHEF decides which features are relevant to a situation, and thus predictive of the failure, using a causal description of the situation. By back-chaining using a set of causal rules, CHEF can describe why a failure has occurred. The features that participated in the failure are included in this description and are assigned the blame for causing it. These features are then used to define the predictive side of the new category. The plan that is built in response to the failure is used as the reactive side.

The only features that CHEF includes in a category are the features that are actually relevant to the problem, in that they caused it and can now be used to predict it. These are the features that should predict the problem and are the features that define the situation in which the use of the repaired plan is most appropriate.

In the case of the strawberry soufflé mentioned earlier, the causal explanation is that the liquid from the strawberries caused an imbalance in the relationship between liquid and leavening in the plan which in turn caused the soufflé to fall. The features that are included in the new category are derived from this explanation. The goal to include a high moisture fruit and the goal to make a soufflé define the predict side of the category. The new plan that uses more egg to compensate for the added liquid becomes the reactive side.

By using an explanation of why a failure has occurred, CHEF is able to focus on the features that are relevant to that failure. It does not have to see repetitions of the failure because it understands the event and its understanding is able to tell it which features are truly relevant. It not only rejects features such as the fact that strawberries are red or the soufflé has sugar in it, it does not even consider them, because these features did not participate in causing the failure. A feature that does not participate in a failure simply has no relevance in defining the situation that will later predict it.

By using explanations to focus in on the relevant features of a situation, CHEF avoids all of the problems of credit assignment through repetition. It does not have to see repeated instances of a problem to figure out how to predict it. It does not have to rely on getting the right examples to figure out which features of a problem are relevant. It is not fooled by irrelevant features. And it does not have to be told what category a situation is a member of because it does not have to match between situations at all.

> Unlike programs doing inductive generalization, CHEF is able to build new categories on the basis of single examples. It does so by using a causal description of why the situation is different than expected to pick out the features that are relevant to the new category.

CHEF's approach to credit assignment is by no means unique. There are many learning programs that are now *explanation driven*, that is, doing the assignment of credit using an explanation of the events in an episode.

DeJong [DeJong 83] has recently proposed a set of programs that all fall within the same general design. A learner is presented with a plan, builds up a causal explanation of the reason behind each step in the plan, and then saves only those steps that actually participate in achieving the goals of the plan. Each step is then generalized to the level of the rules that explained the reason behind the step.

This is a somewhat different task than the one addressed by CHEF. Instead of explaining planning failures so as to predict and avoid them in the future, DeJong is interested in explaining successful plans so as to weed out extraneous steps. It is the fact that he is explaining successes that causes most of his problems. Instead of having to explain why a single failure, which amounts to a single state, has occurred, DeJong is forced to explain why each step in his plan is taking place. His program is forced to run a huge, detailed simulation of every plan it sees. DeJong's programs have to explain entire plans from beginning to end, a task which amounts to the equivalent of building the plan up from scratch.

Because the explanation task is so difficult, the input to DeJong's programs is overly detailed. This gives the programs very short inference chains to build. The level of detail is so minute that it is arguable that the entire task of building the explanation has been side-stepped altogether. So, as with learners in the concept learning paradigm, DeJong's programs have to be hand fed the planning examples that they look at. A plan that lacks the detail cannot be explained and thus cannot be used.

The difference between this approach to explanation and that in CHEF is that CHEF only explains when it has to. It assumes that the modifications it makes to existing plans, modifications that are designed to maintain the integrity of the plan, will not add new failures to the already successful plans. Because the cost of explanation is so high, it only builds one when it is forced to: in order to diagnose the causes of a failure. Because it does not examine its successful plans for extraneous steps as DeJong's programs do, it can miss plans that are more complex than they need to be. But because it begins with plans that have minimal complexity and uses a modification method that adds only those steps required for new goals, it does not run into situations in which it adds more complexity to a plan than is needed.

One point of argument here centers around this notion that a planner should be constructing efficient plans. Under DeJong's view of the world, a problem solver should always be attempting to generalize its solutions and remove unnecessary steps. Under our view, this goal is one of the many that a planner has to trade-off. Other such goals include reducing planning time, reducing execution time, maximizing certainty of execution as well as reducing resource use.

Because of the high cost of explanation, we argue that the planner should wait until it has an explicit goal that requires an explanation before building one. We further argue that any such goal is going to come out of a failure, either at the level of the domain or at the planning level of the meta-goals mentioned above. When a plan becomes too complex to execute or uses extreme amounts of a resource, then it makes sense to do a causal analysis of the structure of the plan so as to make it more efficient. To do so without such a goal requires tht the planner violate other meta-goals such as reducing planning time.

While CHEF uses the same basic notion of credit assignment through explanation as do DeJong's programs, they differ in what they try to explain. DeJong's programs build explanations for every new plan they look at, while CHEF only builds them when it is forced to by its own failures.

> CHEF differs from other programs doing *explanation driven learning* in that it waits until it is forced to build an explanation to do so.

7.2.3 Why doesn't CHEF generalize its plans.

CHEF does not form generalizations. Instead, it saves specific plans, indexed by the most general features it can associate with them. Why does it do this rather than just construct general plans that it can then instantiate?

The reason behind this is simple, the needs of the planner drive the learning done by CHEF, and the needs of the planner center around the notion of *transformation* or *modification* of existing plans rather than instantiation of generalized plans.

We have already argued the utility of this approach. The planner can construct new plans in the absence of a deep domain model. Given a domain model, it can avoid the combinatorics of search through operator combinations by using the model only when confronted with failure. And it can learn from those failures to use those and only those domain facts that will allow it to avoid similar failures in the future.

Using this approach, CHEF is able to achieve breadth by having implicit generalization in the indices it uses. It is able to achieve depth for those goals it has seen before because it saves the exact plans that satisfy them.

7.2.4 When to learn

Most programs that learn have no reason for learning. They learn because their task is learning. This is true of all of the learning programs mentioned so far. Even Mike Lebowitz's IPP, though it was associated with a parser, did not use the generalizations it learned in parsing. Because of this, there has been little said about when a program should learn or what it should do with what it has learned.

The problem here has to do with when programs or theories are actually called upon to learn. Most learning systems, even those designed to learn functional categories, do not take their own knowledge into account in deciding when to learn. They either learn by analyzing their own output or by looking at examples handed to them by a tutor, passively taking in and processing the new information. None of them are designed to say, "I don't need to learn this because I already know it."

CHEF, on the other hand, does the bulk of its learning from its own failures, so it always is trying to learn in those situations where it needs it the most. In CHEF, the decision of *when* to learn is linked to the planner's abilities. When those abilities are shown to be lacking, the planner's failure tells the learner that it is time correct the planner's understanding of the world. In CHEF, the decision about what examples to look at and what those examples will tell the program is taken away from the user and placed in the hands of the program. As a result, the planner decides what it needs to be learning on the basis of its own performance.

The problem of having an external source of examples is obvious when looking at the work on concept learning. The categories that are learned are functionless. They are definitional lists that cannot be used for any task. Although the programs actually run and build up new categories, it is not at all clear that the task they perform is of any use to other processes such as planning and understanding. But if a new concept is of no use, what is the point of learning it at all?

The argument is less apparent for the theories and programs that have recently grown out the *explanation driven learning* paradigm but it is there none the less. In DeJong's work, for example, the task is to examine and learn new plans. But because plans are handed to the program and are not integrated into the memory of an active planner, DeJong has ignored the issues of memory, indexing and reminding that have to be addressed by any planner that reuses plans. His stress is on the moment of learning rather than the use of what is learned. Because he does not consider the eventual use of his plans, he cannot reasonably say that his programs are learning useful things.

The approach in CHEF is to integrate a learning system into a case-based planner. The learning CHEF does is always in service of its planning needs. When CHEF recognizes that a category is not detailed enough to capture an important distinction, it calls on its learning abilities. As a result, the learning CHEF does is not confined to the plans it builds. When

CHEF learns a new plan, it also learns the circumstances in which that plan is applicable. When it builds a plan to avoid a failure, it also learns the features that predict that failures so that it can anticipate the situation in which the new plan will be most useful. And when it figures out how to solve a problem it recalls the solution it used so that it can make the same repair again to a similar plan.

> CHEF only learns when it is forced to by its own inabilities. It learns when it fails and its failures tell it what it has to learn and what it should do with the new knowledge.

CHEF only builds new categories when it has encountered a failure in applying the ones it already has. In the Beef-and-Broccoli example, its definition of the category of dishes with meat and vegetables fails to capture the difference between the initial case of Beef-and-Green-Beans and the new case of Beef-and-Broccoli. The distinction here is that the first situation can be planned for with a plan in which the two main ingredients can be cooked together and the second cannot. Because the planner starts off by seeing the second situation as another case of the category that describes the first, it fails. This failure tells it that it must now add a new category, in the form of inference rules that anticipate a problem and thus alter the plans that will be suggested. The features that make up this new category, the combination of meat and crisp vegetables, are determined through a causal analysis of what caused the failure. Plans are stored in terms of this new category and rules are built to recognize it, making it making it possible for CHEF to notice that new input is best described by this category and then use that description to find the appropriate plan to handle the situation.

> Unlike learners that do not use what they learn to do other tasks, CHEF learns only when that learning will make it function better as a planner.

Although CHEF is learning a new category in this example, its learning is functionally motivated. It starts with some categories and only expands them when they fail to capture distinctions in the world that affect its ability to plan. Its function as a planner gives it a motivation to learn from failures that other learning systems, using either induction or explanation, have lacked. It differs further from inductive learners in that it makes use of a causal model of the world to focus in on the features that should be included in the *new* category it is building. It also differs from programs doing explanation driven learning in that it has an initial focus of attention and resources on the features in the *old* category that are problematic and need to be explained that a learner trying to "explain" an entire episode does not.

The idea behind case-based planning is simple: plan and learn from experience. It differs from most planners in that it learns and from most learners in that it plans. But it is different from both in that it is based on the notion that intelligent behavior rises out a memory of experiences in the world. It differs in that it uses its own past cases of dealing with problems to guide it rather than a base of rules.

Building a plan is a test of its understanding of the world. Any failure of a plan is a failure of that understanding. Any time a plan has to be altered, it is an indication that the planner's understanding has to be altered as well. There are two halves to the task of case-based planning: build plans that succeed and learn from those that don't.

Chapter 8

Case-based Planning

8.1 CHEF as a program

In the course of generating the examples used in this book, CHEF created twenty-one new recipes starting from a data-base of ten initial plans. Many recipes that lie well within the range of CHEF's abilities were never created because they were nothing more than minor variations of existing plans that had little of value to say about CHEF's abilities. In general, the situations that CHEF planned for served one of two functions. Some were situations that caused CHEF problems, prompting it to explain and fix the problems and thus learn to recognize when to predict them. Others were situations designed to test the knowledge CHEF built earlier, while dealing with its own failures.

CHEF began with ten basic recipes:

- BEEF-WITH-GREEN-BEANS
- CHICKEN-WITH-PEANUTS
- PORK-SHREDS-WITH-HOISIN-SAUCE
- BROCCOLI-WITH-TOFU
- GINGER-CHICKEN
- VANILLA-SOUFFLE
- BEEF-WITH-CARROTS

- PORK-DUMPLINGS
- ANTS-CLIMB-A-TREE
- PEPPER-SOUFFLE

The recipes that CHEF created on its own were all based on these initial recipes or on the recipes that it derived from them. These new recipes were created in response to goals given to CHEF by the user.

BEEF-AND-BROCCOLI: In response to a request for a stir fry dish with beef and broccoli, CHEF created BEEF-AND-BROCCOLI out of BEEF-WITH-GREEN-BEANS. The first version of this failed, teaching CHEF about the interaction between crisp vegetables and meats.

CHICKEN-AND-SNOW-PEAS: This recipe was built in response to a request for a stir fry dish with chicken and snow peas. Reminded of the past problem involving crisp vegetables and meats, CHEF used the BEEF-AND-BROCCOLI recipe as its baseline plan. It modified the original recipe by replacing the beef with chicken and the broccoli with snow peas.

BROCCOLI-STIR-FRY: In response to a request for a broccoli stir fry dish with soy sauce, CHEF again predicted the problem of soggy vegetables. As a result, it again used the BEEF-AND-BROCCOLI recipe as its baseline plan. It altered the plan by removing the beef.

CHICKEN-AND-BROCCOLI: When asked to build a recipe for chicken and broccoli, CHEF was again reminded of the potential problems of crisp vegetables and meat. It used this prediction to find the CHICKEN-AND-SNOW-PEAS plan and modified it to include the broccoli.

STRAWBERRY-SOUFFLE: In response to a request to build a strawberry soufflé, CHEF modified a vanilla soufflé to include strawberries. The additional liquid from the fruit caused the soufflé to fall. The plan was repaired through the addition of extra egg white.

RASPBERRY-SOUFFLE: When requested to make a raspberry soufflé, CHEF was reminded of the problem of making a soufflé with fruit. It used this reminding to find the STRAWBERRY-SOUFFLE plan that was known to deal with the problem. It modified this plan by replacing the strawberries with raspberries.

KIRSCH-SOUFFLE: When asked to make a kirsch soufflé, CHEF was again reminded of the failure of the STRAWBERRY-SOUFFLE, because the failure was caused by an excess of liquid. As a result, CHEF used the STRAWBERRY-SOUFFLE as its baseline recipe and modified it by replacing the strawberries with kirsch.

CHOCOLATE-SOUFFLE: When asked to make a chocolate soufflé in the context of knowing only about strawberry soufflés, CHEF created a CHOCOLATE-SOUFFLE out of the STRAWBERRY-SOUFFLE. This recipe included too much egg white. This resulted in a dry soufflé. CHEF modified the recipe to include less egg white.

DUCK-DUMPLINGS: When asked to make a dumpling dish with duck, CHEF modified its PORK-DUMPLING recipe to include duck rather than pork. The resulting recipe was too greasy and CHEF had to modify it again by adding a step to remove the fat from the duck before it is placed in the dumplings. A critic that adds the de-fatting step to duck dishes was then stored under the concept DUCK.

DUCK-PASTA: When asked to build a plan for a pasta dish with duck, CHEF anticipated the problem with duck encountered while making duck dumplings but could not find a pasta dish that avoided it. In order to deal with the problem, CHEF built a dish out of ANTS-CLIMB-A-TREE by replacing the pork with duck and then added the step of removing the duck fat that the new duck critic suggests.

CHICKEN-DUMPLINGS: When asked to make a dumpling dish with chicken, CHEF created the dumplings out of its DUCK-DUMPLINGS recipe. As it removed the duck from the recipe, it reversed the effects of the critic it had built, removing the step having to do with the duck fat.

BEEF-PASTA: When asked to make a pasta dish with beef, CHEF modified its ANTS-CLIMB-A-TREE recipe by replacing the pork with beef with no ill effects.

FISH-STIR-FRIED: When asked to make a stir fry dish with fish, CHEF modified its GINGER-CHICKEN recipe. The plan failed and CHEF discovered the problem of the iodine taste of stir fried fish. This problem was solved by marinating the fish in rice wine.

SHRIMP-STIR-FRIED: When asked to make a shrimp dish, CHEF predicted the problem of the iodine taste of the sea-food coming out during the stir frying. It used this prediction to find and modify its

FISH-STIR-FRY dish. Unfortunately, the MARINADE step interfered with the SHELL step that CHEF had to add to the dish. This problem was solved by reordering the two steps. In response to this problem, CHEF constructed a new critic to recognize and repair this interaction.

SHRIMP-AND-GREEN-PEPPER: When asked again to make a shrimp dish with green pepper, CHEF predicted the problem of the iodine taste of sea-food and the problem with the ordering of the MARINADE and SHELL steps that can occur in shrimp dishes. Using these predictions, it found the SHRIMP-STIR-FRIED plan that avoids these problems. It modified this recipe to include green pepper.

HOT-BEEF: In response to a request to make a hot beef dish, CHEF built HOT-BEEF out of its BEEF-WITH-CARROTS recipe. In building this dish, CHEF added salt to the beef as it was stir frying which dries it out. CHEF repaired the plan by putting the salt in after the cooking is over. Because the salt was put in to bring out the taste of the hot pepper it marked adding pepper to a meat plan as predictive of this problem.

HOT-CHICKEN: When asked to make a hot chicken dish, CHEF was reminded of the problem of adding salt along with red pepper and useed this reminding to find the HOT-BEEF recipe that already dealt with the problem. It then altered the plan by replacing the beef with chicken.

FISH-AND-PEANUT: When asked to make a fish dish with peanuts, CHEF modified the FISH-STIR-FRIED to include peanuts. This plan was modified to include peanuts, but this required the further addition of salt to bring out the taste of the nuts. Unfortunately, the salt also brought out the taste of the iodine in the fish. CHEF repaired this by adding more rice wine. Unfortunately, the added liquid ruined the texture of the fish. In a last repair, CHEF replaced some of the rice wine with crushed ginger, a step that masked the taste of the iodine but did not add additional liquid to the dish.

PEANUT-AND-SHRIMP: When asked to create a recipe for shrimp and peanuts, CHEF predicted the problem of the seafood taste of shrimp interacting badly with the added salt. It also recalled the problems involved with the ordering of MARINADE and SHELL steps. To deal with the first set of problems, CHEF chose the FISH-AND-PEANUT recipe as its initial plan instead of any of its shrimp dishes. After modifying the plan to include shrimp and adding a SHELL step,

CHEF applied the critic it had constructed earlier to correctly order the MARINATE and SHELL steps.

BROCCOLI-SOUFFLE: In response to a request for a soufflé that included broccoli, CHEF created a recipe for broccoli soufflé out of its PEPPER-SOUFFLE plan. It did this by adding broccoli to the existing plan.

As CHEF learned these new recipes, it learned the features that predict the problems it encountered, (*e.g.*, crisp vegetables stir fried with meats, high moisture fruits in soufflés, seafood in stir frying and duck in general). It also learned a small set of critics that it could apply to situations in which it could not find an appropriate plan to deal with the problems it predicts (*e.g.*, remove fat from duck, marinate seafoods and reorder any case of a SHELL step following a MARINATE in making shrimp). The features that predict problems were necessary for CHEF to be able to anticipate failures and thus search for the plans that avoid them. The critics gave CHEF the flexibility to deal with a predicted problem when it could not find a plan that both avoided the problem and satisfied its other goals.

8.2 CHEF's gains

As a planner CHEF proposes a somewhat new approach to planning that allows it to avoid some of the problems of past systems. Most of these advances center around CHEF's reuse of its own plans and the mechanism it has for storing and recalling them when it predicts a failure. Other advances lie in the areas of plan repair and learning.

CHEF is designed to recall and modify old plans rather than build up new ones from scratch. This is a clear gain for CHEF, because it can avoid repeating much of the work it has done before. Because it has the results of past planning cached in memory, it can recall them and thus avoid repeating the same processing. Because CHEF has knowledge of the similarities between goals, it is able to make use of plans that at least partially satisfy its current goals even if they do not fully satisfy them. Because it has a notion of the relative difficulty of adding new goals to existing plans, it is able to choose the plan among competing plans that will minimize its own efforts.

The big advantage in CHEF, however, is its ability to predict problems and find the plans in memory that will deal with them. Because it associates its memory of past failures with the features that predict them, it is able to anticipate problems before they occur. Because it also indexes plans by the problems that they deal with, it is then able to find the appropriate plan in memory that will solve the problem that it has predicted.

This ability means that CHEF is able to avoid many of the mistakes that other planner's have to repeat over and over again because they have no way to describe or store these plans such that they will be available in the appropriate circumstances. In part, CHEF's ability to do this is the result of the notion of reusing plans in the first place. But even within this approach, the reuse of plans that avoid problems is not practical unless a planner stores its plans in terms of the problems that they avoid and then learns the features in its planning situations that predict that problem so the planner knows when to search for the plan in the first place. The crucial fact is that CHEF indexes plans by the problems that they avoid as well as the goals that they satisfy.

In situations where CHEF is unable to predict a problem and has to deal with a failure directly, it also has some advantages over past planners. The most apparent of these is its ability to characterize plan failures with a causal explanation of why they occurred and then use that characterization to find the repair strategies that will fix the faulty plan.

The vocabulary that CHEF uses to build up these causal descriptions is a vocabulary of interactions that characterizes steps and states in terms of the problems they cause and the goals that they satisfy. CHEF builds up its explanations by back chaining from failure states to their antecedent causes and then forward chaining to the goals that those antecedents satisfy. These explanations are then used to access planning TOPs which correspond to different problem descriptions and which store the replanning strategies that can be used to solve the problems described.

This vocabulary includes distinctions between the side-effects and desired effect of a action and between the required preconditions, satisfaction conditions and maintenance conditions on an action. This level of description allows CHEF to distinguish between situations that past planner's could not tell apart. This allows it to then access and apply a greater range of strategies than past planners have had access to.

CHEF's response to its own failures is two-fold: it repairs the plan and then it repairs the faulty knowledge that allowed it to build the plan in the first place. Because it treats planning failures as expectation failures and adds inference links from the features that caused the failure in the present case to a memory of that failure that can be activated if those features arise in later circumstances. This is the process that builds up the data-base CHEF later use to predict failures so that they can be avoided. In conjunction with building up the inferential ability to predict problems, CHEF also stores the plans that it creates to avoid them by the fact that they do so. CHEF's treats failures as opportunities to learn. An encounter with a failure always results in learning a new plan to avoid it and learning the features that predict it so the problem can be anticipated and the new plan applied before CHEF fails again.

Most of CHEF's planning ability is supported by its learning ability. In this area CHEF also stands as a gain over past systems.

CHEF's learning is driven by the explanations it builds of the problems it encounters. CHEF determines which features of a situation should be assigned the blame for a failure by looking at the causal explanation it builds of the situation. In doing this, CHEF avoids many of the problems that systems that learn through inductive generalization cannot. Unlike inductive learning programs that have to see repeated examples of a class, CHEF can create new categories of planning situations with only one example. Because its criterion for the relevance of a feature is based on the role that the feature plays in actually causing problems, it is able to weed irrelevant features out of the generalizations it builds immediately. And because CHEF does not have to be presented with repetitions of a problem situation in order to learn it, it does not have to be tutored with the "appropriate" examples as inductive learners are.

But the most interesting contribution that CHEF makes in the area of learning is in the integration of learning with planning.

CHEF is essentially a planner that learns only when failures indicate that its knowledge of the world is faulty. Because of this, CHEF's learning is always motivated by its needs as a planner and the concepts it builds are always designed to satisfy those needs. CHEF does not learn new concepts for the sake of learning alone. It learns them so that it can plan better and this requirement puts a constraint on when it learns and the form of what it learns.

CHEF's failures indicate where its understanding of the world is not detailed enough to discriminate between situations in which different plans are needed. What it learns in these situations are the features it needs to perform this discrimination. So it learns what amount to functional categories which are composed of the features that predict failures and the plans that avoid them. Its learning does not consist of building up lists of the features that *define* the different categories it is concerned with. It is interested instead, in learning the features that will allow it to *predict* problems so that it can then find the plans that solve them.

This is very different from the task of learners that are built for learning alone. These learners are doing learning in a vacuum and do not apply the concepts they have learned to independent tasks. Because they do not learn in service of a task, they have no constraints on the form of what they learn or what is done with the concepts they learn. So they have nothing to say about memory organization or the difference between the features in a concept that are used to recognize it as opposed to the features that should be inferred by the fact that it has been recognized.

Learning systems that learn in service of no other function, may learn sophisticated concepts, but do not question how the concepts should be organized for use. Although they may learn descriptive categories or even plans, they are more concerned with the moment of learning than the use to which what they have learned will be put to. They ignore the problems of memory organization, indexing and failure prediction that CHEF addresses directly. When CHEF learns a plan it learns the steps that are required to run it, but it also learns the situations in which that running is appropriate.

As a planner, CHEF stands as an improvement over past systems in that it reuses past processing and uses what it learns about the features that caused past problems to predict and avoid them in the future. It also uses a more detailed description of its domain to better diagnose and treat the problems that it cannot predict and avoid. As a learner, CHEF gains in that it uses a causal model of its domain to focus in on the features of a situation that it has to learn about. This allows it avoid many of the problems inherent to the syntactic nature of learning via inductive generalization and thus learn about its world faster and in a more knowledge directed manner. Because its learning is within the context of the needs of a planning system it also makes use of a more interesting model of what learning is. Instead of viewing learning as the amassing of feature lists that define categories, it models learning as the creation of functional categories in memory that allow a planner or understander to both recognize new situation and then react to them in the appropriate way.

8.3 The real difference

Although there are technical gains that CHEF makes in some areas of planning, the real difference between CHEF and other planner's is not really a technical one. It is much more a difference in view point as to what the task of planning is at all.

CHEF's approach to planning is to treat planning tasks as memory problems. Planning as a closed loop in which past successes and failures guide present processing and memories of current solutions and even failures are stored for later use. As much as is possible, CHEF goes to its memory of its own experiences to perform planning tasks. Instead of simulating plans in order to recognize problems, it tries to predict problems by recalling past situations similar to its current one. Instead of building plans up from primitive steps, it searches its memory for those plans that satisfy as many of its goals as possible. Instead of throwing plans away after execution, it saves them for future planning. And instead of treating failures as planning problems alone, it treats them as opportunities to learn so it can improve its understanding of its world and its ability to manipulate it.

For CHEF, planning is a test of its own understanding and its understanding is built out of the planning experiences it has.

Appendix A

A Causal Vocabulary for TOPs

Each of CHEF's TOPs corresponds to a causal configuration that describes a failure. The vocabulary that is used to build up these configurations and define the TOPs is one of causal interactions between steps and states. This vocabulary differs from those used by past planner's to describe the problems they encounter primarily in that it distinguishes the effects of steps that lead to satisfied goals from those that do not. It also distinguishes problems that cause a plan to halt from those that allow the plan to run to completion but ruin the result.

CHEF's causal vocabulary is based on four classes of things that it knows about:

- OBJECTS, which are physical objects such as the ingredients and the utensils used in the CHEF domain.
- STATES, which are features of the OBJECTs such as TASTE, TEXTURE and SIZE.
- STEPS, which are actions taken on OBJECTs with the aim of altering some STATEs.
- GOALs, which are STATEs that the planner is trying to achieve. Unlike other STATEs, GOALs are hypothetical STATEs that actual STATEs are tested against.

With the exception of a distinction between certain types of STATEs, the bulk of CHEF's vocabulary has to do with relationships between these OBJECTs, STATEs and STEPs. One important aspect of the relationships that CHEF uses to describe causal configurations is that they depend on the presence of goals. Many of the relationships change as the planner's goals change, even if the causality of the situation does not. If a STATE satisfies a goal, that fact is reflected in the description of any problems that result from it. If the goal it satisfies is no longer part of the planner's overall goal structure, the description of the situation will change to reflect this. CHEF's descriptions of causal situations depend on its goals because it has to use these description to find appropriate changes to make to its plans, and these changes cannot be such that they violate the goals already met by these plans.

> The vocabulary used to describe planning TOPs is based on the different relationships that can hold between OBJECTs, STATEs, STEPs and GOALs.

One of the most powerful distinctions that CHEF's vocabulary makes use of is the distinction between different relationships between STATEs and the STEPs that cause them. CHEF understands three types of relationships:

- DESIRED-EFFECTS are states that result from steps that satisfy the planner's goals. This satisfaction can either be the direct result of the state matching a goal state or the indirect result of the state enabling a later step that satisfies a goal.
- SIDE-EFFECTS are the results of steps that do not satisfy any goals either directly or indirectly.
- DEVELOPING-SIDE-EFFECTS are side-effects that occur during the running of a step rather than as a final result.

All of the effects of a step are linked to it by RESULT links that lead from the step to the state and RESULT-OF links that lead from the state back to the step.

The effect of distinguishing between these different relationships lies in the types of strategies that each will allow. Problems having to do with SIDE-EFFECTs can be solved by making changes to a plan that remove the effects in one way or another while those having to do with DESIRED-EFFECTs cannot. Likewise, those states that are DEVELOPING-SIDE-EFFECTS can be dealt with using adjunct steps that can be added to a plan to remove the effects of the steps as they are produced.

CHEF recognizes three types of preconditions for STEPs:

- REQUIRED-PRECONDITIONs are those states that have to hold for a step to be run at all.
- SATISFACTION-CONDITIONs are those states that have to hold as a step is entered for its desired effects to result.
- MAINTENANCE-CONDITIONs are those states that have to hold during the entire running of a step for its desired effects to result.

STATEs that meet the preconditions of a STEP have ENABLES links going from the STATEs to the STEP. The STEP has ENABLED-BY links going from it back to the STATEs. For example, the STATE representing the texture of the crushed strawberries in a strawberry soufflé plan is linked to the MIX step by an ENABLES link and the MIX step points back to it by an ENABLED-BY link.

Along with the relationships between STATEs and STEPs there are relationships between OBJECTs and STATEs and OBJECTs and STEPs. An OBJECT can link into a STEP in two ways:

- As a STEP-OBJECT, which means that the STEP acts on the OBJECT in order to change a STATE related to it.
- As an INSTRUMENT, which means that the STEP uses the OBJECT in order to enable a STATE change in another OBJECT.

The STATEs that CHEF knows about are actually features of OBJECTs. The different STATEs describe the TASTE, TEXTURE and SIZE of the OBJECTs as they are modified by the STEPs in the plan. Each STATE is not only the RESULT of a STEP, it is also a feature of an object. The texture of strawberries after they are chopped is the RESULT of the CHOP step but it is also a feature of the strawberries.

CHEF only recognized two types of relationships between an OBJECT and the STATEs that define their features:

- DESIRED-FEATURE is a feature of an OBJECT that satisfies or enables the satisfaction of a goal.

- SIDE-FEATURE is a feature that is incidental to the satisfaction of any current goals. It is not UNDESIRED in that it does not necessarily cause problems. It just doe not satisfy any goals.

There three relationships that a STATE can have with a GOAL:

- A SATISFY relationship exists when one STATE matches the preconditions of a step or the final GOAL of a plan.
- A VIOLATE or BLOCK relationship exists when a particular STATE of an object is supposed to SATISFY a GOAL or step precondition but does not.
- A DISABLE relationship exists when a state VIOLATEs the satisfaction conditions of a step.

STEPs, can only relate to one another in terms of their running order in the plan. CHEF only requires two relationships to describe its failure situations:

- Two STEPs are SERIAL when they are run at different times.
- Two STEPs are CONCURRENT when they are run at the same time.

Like other features that CHEF uses to describe situations, the time sequence of two STEPs determine the strategies that can be applied to different problems involving the interactions between them.

The last set of features that CHEF uses to describe situations has to do with nature of the STATEs it has to deal with rather than the relationship between STATEs and either STEPs or OBJECTs. The distinction here however, still makes use of the notion of "relationship" in that it points to the fact that some states are themselves relationships between many STATEs at once. CHEF understands two sorts of STATEs:

- A BALANCE STATE is defined as a relationship that has to hold between two or more STATEs.
- AN ABSOLUTE STATE is the feature of a single OBJECT.

By noticing this distinction CHEF is able to suggest strategies in cases of violated BALANCE STATEs that it is not able to suggest in cases of violated ABSOLUTE STATEs.

> The vocabulary of TOPs is one of causal interactions. It describes the relationships between OBJECTs, STATEs, STEPs and GOALs and makes distinctions between those that serve goals and those that do not. It distinguishes between these different TOPs because the different problems described by them require different repair strategies.

All of the features in CHEF's TOPs are described by this vocabulary, but there are structures that could be built by this vocabulary that are not included in CHEF's knowledge base. This it is only a reflection of the fact that they were not needed to deal with the problems in the CHEF domain.

Appendix B

CHEF's Simulator

CHEF runs a plan by putting it through a simulator that runs each step of the plan and produces a symbolic representation of the results that would entail if the step were actually performed in the real world. The simulator computes the results of each step and tests for the conditions that have to be present for running later steps and determining their effects. During the simulation, the results of each step are accessible to the simulator. After the simulation the final states produced by the plan are handed back to CHEF for comparison against its goals.

CHEF's simulator is forward chainer that uses two sets of rules associated with the steps in its domain. The first are PRECONDITION rules that test for the conditions that have to be true for a step to be performed at all. The second are RESULT rules that describe the effects of each step as it is run. Before running a step, CHEF uses the PRECONDITION rules for that step to test for the presence of the conditions required for its running. If they are present, it runs the step by asserting it and firing the inferences associated with the RESULT rules related to the step.

The conditions that PRECONDITION rules test for include the existence of the objects of the step, their texture and their accessibility. These rules look at the results of earlier steps and at the ingredients to test for characteristics that may be a product of the plan itself or be inherent properties of the ingredients. For example, the rule associated with the MIX step tests for the existence of the ingredients that are to be mixed and tests their texture (Figure B.1). Any ingredient that is the object of a MIX step has to have a MIX-TEXTURE, which is defined as being either LIQUID, POWDER, VERY-SOFT or GROUND. Any object that is one of these textures can be combined with other ingredients using a MIX step. In searching for the states that satisfy the conditions of this and other PRECONDITION tests, the simulator looks at its own record of the results of past steps and at the definitions of the ingredients themselves. The information about the texture of a piece of meat that has been ground earlier in a plan would be on the simulator's record of results, while the same texture information about soy sauce would be found in the definition of soy sauce itself.

```
(def:precon mix
 vars (?var1 ?var2)
 bindings (?var1 object ?var2 with)
 test (and (exists object ?var1)
           (exists object ?var2)
           (texture object ?var1 texture (mix-texture))
           (texture object ?var2 texture (mix-texture)))
 text "A thing has to be chopped or soft in order to mix it.")
```

Figure B.1: Definition of preconditions on MIX.

The conditions that are tested for by the precondition rule associated with a step are the conditions that have to be true for the step to be run at all, not the conditions that have to obtain for the step to be successful. If the conditions required by a step's PRECONDITION rule are satisfied, the step can be run and it results computed. If, however, they are not satisfied, the simulator cannot continue and the plan has to be halted at that point. If this occurs, the simulator reports this halt to CHEF and the planner recognizes this as a failure.

```
(def:precon shell
 vars (?var1)
 bindings (?var1 object)
 test (and (exists object ?var1) (handleable object ?var1))
 text "A thing has to be handleable in order to shell it.")
```

Figure B.2: Precondition tests associated with SHELL.

For example, in building a recipe for stir fried shrimp out of an existing plan for stir fried fish, CHEF has to add a new step, SHELL, to the plan. The PRECONDITION test on SHELL looks for two conditions: the shrimp has to exist and it has to be handleable (figure B.2). Any object soaked in liquid or ground to a pulp is not longer handleable. Unfortunately, CHEF adds the SHELL step after an already present MARINATE step, which has the result that the shrimp is no longer handleable because it is too slippery. When the simulator tries to run the SHELL step, the tests for its running fail and the simulator halts execution. After this happens, the simulator communicates the halt to CHEF and the plan is set for eventual repair.

```
Inferring from -> Marinate the shrimp in the soy sauce,
 sesame oil, egg white, sugar, corn starch and rice wine.

RULE: "When things are marinated together they pick up tastes."
RULE: "Marinated things are in the bowl with other things."
RULE: "Liquids make things wet."
RULE: "Things in the same pan are linked together."
RULE: "Liquids make things wet."
RULE: "Things in the same pan are linked together."
RULE: "Solids marinated in liquids are no longer handleable"

Unable to infer from -> Shell the shrimp.
 : failed  precondition.

RULE: "A thing has to be handleable in order to shell it."

Some precondition of step: Shell the shrimp.
 has failed.
```

> The simulator's PRECONDITION rules test for the conditions that have to be true for a step to be run at all.

Because the steps in CHEF's domain are fairly robust, that is they are rarely stopped by failed preconditions, it is usually the case that each step in a plan can be executed. This means that the simulator can run the step by firing the RESULT rules associated with it. The definition of these rules includes the step that it relates to, the results that can be inferred and the conditions that have to be true for those results to come about. The conditions tested for by the RESULT rules are different than those tested for by the PRECONDITION rules. They describe the conditions under which an inference can be made from the fact that a step has been run but never stop the running of any step. With different conditions, there are different effects, so rules that account for the effects have to test for the conditions under which their firing is appropriate.

Most steps have a rule related to them that describes the effects of their running under normal circumstances. These normative rules have very simple tests associated with them that check the initial states of the objects and the time of the step itself. They allow the simulator to infer most of the changes to ingredients that CHEF is trying to plan for. For example, STIR-FRY has a rule associated with it that allows the simulator to infer the texture change of any solid stir fried for over two minutes and another that allows the simulator to infer changes in the taste of the dish (figure B.3).

```
(def:infer stir-fry
 vars (?var1 ?var2)
 text "Stir-fried things are cooked."
 item-test (stir-fry object ?var1 time ?var2)
 var-tests (?object (i:feature '?var1 'texture 'solid)
            ?time (i:gt '?var2 '(2)))
 action (s-cooked object ?var1 cooked (cooked)))

(def:infer stir-fry
 vars (?var1 ?var2 ?var3)
 text "The dish picks up the taste of sthings that are stir-fried."
 item-test (stir-fry object ?var1 time ?var2)
 var-tests (?time (i:gt '?var2 '(2)))
 evals (?var3 (i:expand (i:get '?var2 'taste)))
 action (taste object (dish) taste ?var3))
```

Figure B.3: Definition for two normal STIR-FRY rules.

Most steps result in changes to the ingredients that they are acting on. A CHOP step will change the size and texture of an item, a STIR-FRY step will change the texture and taste and a MARINADE will change the taste. Some steps, such as MARINADE, ADD and MIX, because they move items around, change the location of items. Other steps, such as STIR-FRY, change the tastes and textures of the dish as a whole. Still others. such as MARINATE, change the handleability of items, making it impossible for some other steps to be run on them once the step is completed.

But not all steps result in just changes to the items that they function on. Some actually create new items while "destroying" the ingredients that they act on. Often a MIX will result in a batter that uses up the flour, milk and sugar it acted on. A FILL step will result in a dumpling, which is a compound object combining the OBJECT of the FILL and the ingredients that it is filled WITH (figure B.4). Just as a new item is created the original ingredients that go into making it are "destroyed", used up by in the process of making the new item.

```
(def:infer fill
 vars (?var1 ?var2)
 text "Filling a skin makes a dumpling."
 item-test (fill object ?var1 with ?var2)
 var-tests (?var1 (i:feature '?var1 'texture 'mix-texture)
           ?var2 (i:isa '?with 'skin))
 action (and (exists object (dumpling))
             (not (exists object ?var1))
             (not (exists object ?var2))
             (contains contains ?var2 object (dumpling))))
```

Figure B.4: Definition for normal FILL rule.

> The simulator's RESULT rules allow it to infer changes to ingredients and the overall dish as well as infer the creation of new items out of old ones.

While the simulator to be able to infer the results of actions in normal circumstances it also has to be able to infer the results of steps under conditions that the that the planner might not have anticipated. To do this, the simulator has rules that allow it to infer the results of steps in irregular situations. These are the situations in which states that are not planned for arise to interfere with the plan. There is no structural difference between the rules that are applicable in the normative and non-normative situations. The only difference is that the states described by one are those that the planner wants and the states that are described by the other are those that it wishes to avoid. In the absence of goals that the planner is trying to achieve, however, there is no difference in form of these rules. They are just rules that are for different situations that predict different results

One example of these rules is a stir fry rule that allows the inference that crisp vegetables will become soggy when stir fried in liquid. This rule states that any crisp vegetable, if it is stir fried for more than 2 minutes in a pan that has liquid in it, will become soggy (figure B.5). This rule, combined with the rule that beef that is stir fried will produce liquid in proportion to its weight, makes it possible for the simulator to infer that broccoli stir fried with beef will end up being soggy.

```
(def:infer stir-fry
 vars (?var1 ?var2)
 text "Stir-frying in too much liquid makes vegetables soggy."
 item-test (stir-fry object ?var1 time ?var2)
 var-tests (?var1 (i:and (i:isa '?var1 'vegetable)
                         (i:feature '?var1 'texture 'crisp))
            ?var2 (i:gt '?var2 '(2)))
 test (in-pan object (liquid))
 action (texture object ?var1 texture (soggy)))

(def:infer  stir-fry
 vars (?var1 ?var2 ?var3)
 text "Meat sweats when it is stir-fried."
 item-test (stir-fry object ?var1 time ?var2)
 var-tests (?var1 (i:isa '?var1 'meat) ?var2 (i:gt '?var2 '(2)))
 evals (?var3 (i:solid-liquid '?var1))
 action (in-pan object (thin-liquid amount ?var3) source ?var1))
```

Figure B.5: Rules used to infer soggy broccoli.

To run a plan the simulator tests and runs each step in turn. The precondition tests for each step are fired and the step is continued only if the tests are true. The result rules for each step are then run in order of least to most specific. The results of each rule are placed on a table of results (figure B.6), with new state information for each ingredient overwriting old information. Conflicts between results are resolved by having the later rules overwrite the results of earlier ones. As new tests are made for following steps, the simulator first checks its table of results for a state being tested for and then checks the defaults on the ingredient in question. To test if a piece of beef has a GROUND texture, the simulator first checks its table of results for a statement of the beef's texture and if it fails to find such a statement it checks the default texture on the concept BEEF. This allows the effects of a CHOP step that grinds the meat and thus changes its texture to be noticed by a later mix step that requires that the beef be ground.

> The simulator is able to infer the results of actions in both normative and non-normative situations. This allows it to infer the existence of states that CHEF is planning for as well as those that count as failures.

```
(SIZE OBJECT (BEEF2) SIZE (CHUNK))
(SIZE OBJECT (BROCCOLI1) SIZE (CHUNK))
(SIZE OBJECT (GARLIC1) SIZE (NUBB))
(TEXTURE OBJECT (BEEF2) TEXTURE (TENDER))
(TEXTURE OBJECT (BROCCOLI1) TEXTURE (SOGGY))
(TEXTURE OBJECT (GARLIC1) TEXTURE (SOGGY))
(TASTE OBJECT (BEEF2) TASTE (SAVORY INTENSITY (9.)))
(TASTE OBJECT (BROCCOLI1) TASTE (SAVORY INTENSITY (5.)))
(TASTE OBJECT (GARLIC1) TASTE (GARLICY INTENSITY (9.)))
(TASTE OBJECT (DISH) TASTE (AND (SALTY INTENSITY (9.))
                                (SWEET INTENSITY (7.))
                                (GARLICY INTENSITY (9.))
                                (SAVORY INTENSITY (9.))
                                (SAVORY INTENSITY (5.))))
```

Figure B.6: Section of Result Table for BEEF-WITH-BROCCOLI.

In the beef and broccoli situation, the rules about stir frying meat and the rules about stir frying crisp vegetables allow the simulator to produce the result of soggy broccoli. But this isn't all the simulator infers about the situation. It also makes inferences along the way about the effects of the CHOP, MARINATE and ADD steps. In this way it simulates changes in the ingredients and the overall dish that will later be compared to the planner's own goals.

```
Inferring from ->
   Chop the garlic into pieces the size of matchheads.

RULE: "Chopping things makes them smaller."
RULE: "Chopping things small makes them change texture."

Inferring from -> Shred the beef.

RULE: "Chopping things makes them smaller."

Inferring from ->
   Marinate the beef in the garlic, sugar, corn starch,
   rice wine and soy sauce.

RULE: "When things are marinated together they pick up tastes."
RULE: "Marinated things are in the bowl with other things."
```

```
RULE: "Liquids make things wet."
RULE: "Things in the same pan are linked together."
RULE: "Liquids make things wet."
RULE: "Things in the same pan are linked together."
RULE: "Solids marinated in liquids are no longer handleable"
RULE: "Liquids in a marinade are absorbed by the solids"

Inferring from -> Chop the broccoli into pieces the size of chunks.

RULE: "Chopping things makes them smaller."

Inferring from ->
   Stir fry the spices, rice wine and beef for one minute.

RULE: "Stir-fried things are in the pan with other things."
RULE: "The dish picks up the taste of things that are stir-fried."

Inferring from ->
   Add the broccoli to the spices, rice wine and beef.

Inferring from -> Stir fry the spices, rice wine, broccoli and beef
for three minutes.

RULE: "Stir-fried things are in the pan with other things."
RULE: "The dish picks up the taste of things that are stir-fried."
RULE: "Meat sweats when it is stir-fried."
RULE: "Things in the same pan are linked together."
RULE: "Stir-fried things are cooked."
RULE: "Cooked things change texture."
RULE: "Cooked things change texture."
RULE: "Stir-frying in too much liquid makes vegetables soggy."

Inferring from ->
   Add the salt to the spices, rice wine, broccoli and beef.

RULE: "Adding salt enhances the flavor of the dish."
```

The final product of a simulation is a table results that describes the states of the original ingredients, the overall dish and any compound items that were created during execution. This table includes the new tastes and textures that have developed and describes not only the states that the planner was trying to achieve but also those that it might not have anticipated and may very well be trying to avoid. Along with the states on the result table, the simulator creates links between the states and the steps that caused them. Other links leading back from the steps to the conditions that enabled their results are also built. These include links to states actually caused by steps during their execution that had some effect on other aspects of the outcome of the step.

The final product of a simulation of a plan is a table of results that is given back to CHEF for testing against the planner's goals.

Once the table of results has been built for a plan, CHEF is given access to it and it can then check the final states of the ingredients and the overall dish against the goals that it thinks the plan should accomplish.

Appendix C

CHEF's Recipes

While the intent behind CHEF was to demonstrate a set of planning ideas rather than develop an automatic cookbook, CHEF did create actual recipes along the way. Working from an initial base of ten plans it created twenty-one new recipes on the basis of user requests. Other recipes within the ability of CHEF to create were neglected because they lacked any theoretical interest.

In creating these recipes, CHEF had to deal with a wide range of plan failures, which resulted in its learning more about its domain and the problematic features in it. Each failure was repaired using CHEF's planning TOPs and repair strategies.

This appendix includes the recipes that CHEF started with (pages 237 - 246) ([Chen 82], [Rombauer and Becker 64] and [Schrecker 76]) and those that it created on its own (pages 247 - 266). All of the recipes included here have gone through CHEF's simulation of its "cooking world" without failure. While they may not be up to human standards they have at least passed the test of a machine's hallucination of the world.

All of the following recipes are actual output from the CHEF program.

C.1 CHEF's initial recipes

C.1.1 BEEF-WITH-GREEN-BEANS

```
                    BEEF-WITH-GREEN-BEANS

          A half pound of beef
          Two tablespoons of soy sauce
          One teaspoon of rice wine
          A half tablespoon of corn starch
          One teaspoon of sugar
          A half pound of green bean
          One teaspoon of salt
          One chunk of garlic

Chop the garlic into pieces the size of matchheads.
Shred the beef.
Marinate the beef in the garlic, sugar, corn starch, rice wine
 and soy sauce.
Stir fry the spices, rice wine and beef for one minute.
Add the green bean to the spices, rice wine and beef.
Stir fry the spices, rice wine, green bean and beef for three
 minutes.
Add the salt to the spices, rice wine, green bean and beef.
```

C.1.2 CHICKEN-WITH-PEANUTS

```
                    CHICKEN-WITH-PEANUTS

          A half cup of peanut
          One pound of chicken
          One tablespoon of soy sauce
          A half teaspoon of sugar
          One teaspoon of sesame oil
          One teaspoon of rice wine
          One egg white
          One tablespoon of corn starch
          Two green peppers
          Ten pieces of garlic
          One chunk of ginger
          Five pieces of red pepper
          Two scallions

Bone the chicken.
Chop the chicken into pieces the size of chunks.
Marinate the chicken in the corn starch, sugar, egg white,
 rice wine, sesame oil and half the soy sauce.
Chop the green pepper into pieces the size of chunks.
Chop the ginger and garlic into pieces the size of matchheads.
Chop the red pepper into pieces the size of nubbs.
Shred the scallion.
Add the scallion to the egg white, spices, rice wine and chicken.
Stir fry the green pepper for a half minute.
Add the spices to the green pepper.
Stir fry the spices and green pepper for a half minute.
Add the egg white, spices, rice wine and chicken to the spices and
 green pepper.
Stir fry the spices, green pepper, egg white, rice wine and chicken
 for two minutes.
Add the peanut to the spices, green pepper, egg white, rice wine
 and chicken.
Add the remaining soy sauce to the egg white, spices, rice wine,
 vegetables and chicken.
Stir fry the egg white, spices, rice wine, vegetables and chicken
 for one and a half minutes.
```

C.1.3 PORK-SHREDS-WITH-HOISIN-SAUCE

```
                 PORK-SHREDS-WITH-HOISIN-SAUCE

          One pound of pork
          Ten scallions
          One tablespoon of soy sauce
          One teaspoon of rice wine
          One teaspoon of sesame oil
          One egg white
          One chunk of ginger
          One tablespoon of water
          Two tablespoons of hoisin

Shred the pork.
Chop the scallion into pieces the size of pieces.
Marinate the pork and scallion in the egg white, sesame oil,
 rice wine, soy sauce and water.
Chop the ginger into pieces the size of matchsticks.
Stir fry the ginger for a half minute.
Add the egg white, spices, rice wine, water and pork to the ginger.
Add the hoisin to the egg white, water, spices, rice wine and pork.
Stir fry the egg white, water, spices, rice wine and pork for
 three minutes.
```

C.1.4 BROCCOLI-WITH-TOFU

```
                BROCCOLI-WITH-TOFU

          A half pound of tofu
          Two tablespoons of soy sauce
          One teaspoon of rice wine
          A half tablespoon of corn starch
          One teaspoon of sugar
          One pound of broccoli
          Six pieces of red pepper

Chop the tofu into pieces the size of chunks.
Marinate the tofu in the sugar, corn starch, rice wine and
 soy sauce.
Chop the broccoli into pieces the size of chunks.
Stir fry the red pepper, tofu, spices and rice wine for one minute.
Add the broccoli to the spices, tofu and rice wine.
Stir fry the tofu, spices, rice wine and broccoli for two minutes.
```

C.1.5 GINGER-CHICKEN

```
                    GINGER-CHICKEN

          One pound of chicken
          One tablespoon of soy sauce
          A half teaspoon of sugar
          One teaspoon of sesame oil
          One egg white
          One tablespoon of corn starch
          Ten pieces of garlic
          One chunk of ginger
          Two scallions

Bone the chicken.
Chop the chicken into pieces the size of chunks.
Marinate the chicken in the corn starch, sugar, egg white, sesame
 oil and half the soy sauce.
Chop the garlic and ginger into pieces the size of matchheads.
Shred the scallion.
Add the scallion to the egg white, spices and chicken.
Stir fry the garlic and ginger for a half minute.
Add the egg white, spices and chicken to the garlic and ginger.
Stir fry the spices, egg white and chicken for two minutes.
Add the remaining soy sauce to the spices, egg white and chicken.
Stir fry the egg white, spices and chicken for a half minute.
```

C.1.6 VANILLA-SOUFFLE

```
                VANILLA-SOUFFLE

          Two teaspoons of vanilla
          A half cup of flour
          A quarter cup of sugar
          A quarter teaspoon of salt
          A half cup of milk
          Two cups of milk
          One piece of vanilla bean
          A quarter cup of butter
          Five egg yolks
          Five egg whites

Mix the flour with the sugar and salt.
Mix the milk with the mixture of sugar, salt and flour.
Boil the milk and vanilla bean for less than a half minute.
Remove the vanilla bean from the milk.
Mix the mixture of milk, sugar, salt and flour with the milk.
Simmer the mixture of milk, sugar, salt and flour for five minutes.
Whip the egg yolk.
Add the butter and mixture of egg yolk to the mixture of milk,
 sugar, salt and flour.
Cool the mixture of egg yolk, milk, sugar, salt, flour and butter.
Whip the egg white.
Add the vanilla and mixture of egg white to the mixture of egg yolk,
 milk, sugar, salt, flour and butter.
Pour the mixture of spices, egg, milk, salt, flour and butter into a
 nine inch baking-dish.
Bake the batter for twenty five minutes.
```

C.1.7 BEEF-WITH-CARROTS

```
                 BEEF-WITH-CARROTS

          Three carrots
          One pound of beef
          One and a half teaspoons of soy sauce
          A half teaspoon of sugar
          One teaspoon of sesame oil
          One teaspoon of rice wine
          One egg white
          One tablespoon of corn starch
          Ten pieces of garlic
          Two scallions

Shred the beef.
Marinate the beef in the corn starch, sugar, egg white, rice wine,
 sesame oil and soy sauce.
Shred the carrot.
Chop the garlic into pieces the size of matchheads.
Shred the scallion.
Add the carrot and scallion to the egg white, spices, rice wine
 and beef.
Stir fry the garlic for a half minute.
Add the egg white, spices, rice wine, beef and carrot to the garlic.
Stir fry the egg white, spices, rice wine, carrot and beef for
 three minutes.
```

C.1.8 PORK-DUMPLINGS

```
          PORK-DUMPLINGS

     Fifteen scallions
     A half chunk of ginger
     One pound of ground pork
     A quarter cup of soy sauce
     One and a half tablespoons of sesame oil
     A half teaspoon of szechwan pepper
     One egg
     One and a half teaspoons of salt
     70 jiaoz skins

Chop the scallion into pieces the size of matchheads.
Chop the ginger into pieces the size of matchheads.
Mix the scallion and ginger with the salt, egg, szechwan pepper,
 sesame oil, soy sauce and ground pork.
Fill the jiaoz skin with the mixture of salt, egg, spices and
 ground pork.
Boil the bunch of dumplings filled with the salt, egg, spices and
 ground pork for twenty minutes.
```

C.1.9 ANTS-CLIMB-A-TREE

```
                    ANTS-CLIMB-A-TREE

          Fifteen scallions
          A half chunk of ginger
          One pound of ground pork
          A quarter cup of soy sauce
          One and a half tablespoons of sesame oil
          A half teaspoon of szechwan pepper
          One egg
          One and a half teaspoons of salt
          One pound of noodles

Chop the scallion into pieces the size of matchheads.
Chop the ginger into pieces the size of matchheads.
Mix the scallion and ginger with the salt, egg, szechwan pepper,
 sesame oil, soy sauce and ground pork.
Stir fry the mixture of salt, egg, spices and ground pork for
 five minutes.
Boil the noodles for three minutes.
Serve the mixture of salt, egg, spices and ground pork over
 the noodles.
```

C.1.10 PEPPER-SOUFFLE

```
                PEPPER-SOUFFLE

          Two green peppers
          A half cup of flour
          A quarter teaspoon of salt
          A half cup of milk
          Two cups of milk
          Three pieces of red pepper
          A quarter cup of butter
          Five egg yolks
          Six egg whites

Mix the flour with the salt.
Mix the milk with the mixture of flour and salt.
Boil the milk and red pepper for less than a half minute.
Remove the red pepper from the milk.
Mix the mixture of milk, salt and flour with the milk.
Simmer the mixture of milk, salt and flour for five minutes.
Whip the egg yolk.
Add the butter and mixture of egg yolk to the mixture of milk,
 salt and flour.
Cool the mixture of egg yolk, milk, salt, flour and butter.
Whip the egg white.
Pulp the green pepper.
Add the green pepper and mixture of egg white to the mixture of
 egg yolk, milk, salt, flour and butter.
Pour the mixture of green pepper, egg, milk, salt, flour and butter
 into a nine inch baking-dish.
Bake the batter for twenty five minutes.
```

C.2 The recipes CHEF created

From these basic plans CHEF created the following new recipes.

C.2.1 BEEF-AND-BROCCOLI

```
                BEEF-AND-BROCCOLI

          A half pound of beef
          Two tablespoons of soy sauce
          One teaspoon of rice wine
          A half tablespoon of corn starch
          One teaspoon of sugar
          A half pound of broccoli
          One teaspoon of salt
          One chunk of garlic

Chop the garlic into pieces the size of matchheads.
Shred the beef.
Marinate the beef in the garlic, sugar, corn starch, rice wine
 and soy sauce.
Chop the broccoli into pieces the size of chunks.
Stir fry the broccoli for three minutes.
Remove the broccoli from the pan.
Stir fry the spices, rice wine and beef for three minutes.
Add the broccoli to the spices, rice wine and beef.
Stir fry the spices, rice wine, broccoli and beef for a half minute.
Add the salt to the spices, rice wine, broccoli and beef.
```

In this recipe, CHEF learned about the problem of stir frying meats with crisp vegetables. The plan itself is indexed by the fact that it solves the problem and the goals are marked as predictive of the problem.

C.2.2 CHICKEN-AND-SNOW-PEAS

```
              CHICKEN-AND-SNOW-PEAS

          A half pound of chicken
          Two tablespoons of soy sauce
          One teaspoon of rice wine
          A half tablespoon of corn starch
          One teaspoon of sugar
          A half pound of snow pea
          One teaspoon of salt
          One chunk of garlic

Chop the garlic into pieces the size of matchheads.
Bone the chicken.
Shred the chicken.
Marinate the chicken in the garlic, sugar, corn starch, rice
 wine and soy sauce.
Chop the snow pea into pieces the size of chunks.
Stir fry the snow pea for three minutes.
Remove the snow pea from the pan.
Stir fry the spices, rice wine and chicken for three minutes.
Add the snow pea to the spices, rice wine and chicken.
Stir fry the spices, snow pea, rice wine and chicken for a
 half minute.
Add the salt to the spices, snow pea, rice wine and chicken.
```

In building this recipe, CHEF used information learned while creating its BEEF-AND-BROCCOLI dish. Because it was asked to build a plan for another stir fry dish with a crisp vegetable and meat, it predicted a problem due to the interaction of these goals. With this prediction it found and then modified the BEEF-AND-BROCCOLI it had built previously.

C.2.3 BROCCOLI-STIR-FRIED

```
                    BROCCOLI-STIR-FRIED

          Four tablespoons of soy sauce
          One teaspoon of rice wine
          A half tablespoon of corn starch
          One teaspoon of sugar
          A half pound of broccoli
          One teaspoon of salt
          One chunk of garlic

Chop the garlic into pieces the size of matchheads.
Chop the broccoli into pieces the size of chunks.
Stir fry the broccoli for three minutes.
Add the spices and rice wine to the broccoli.
Stir fry the spices, rice wine and broccoli for a half minute.
Add the salt to the spices, rice wine and broccoli.
```

In this recipe, CHEF predicted the same sort of problem that it saw in building BEEF-AND-BROCCOLI, because it was asked to make a dish with broccoli and extra soy sauce. The fact that there is added liquid reminded it that the failure solved by the BEEF-AND-BROCCOLI plan was actually one of liquid interacting with the vegetable. The BEEF-AND-BROCCOLI plan was found and modified to include only broccoli. The form of the initial plan was maintained and all of the liquid is added to the dish after the broccoli is stir fried.

C.2.4 CHICKEN-AND-BROCCOLI

```
            CHICKEN-AND-BROCCOLI

        A half pound of chicken
        Two tablespoons of soy sauce
        One teaspoon of rice wine
        A half tablespoon of corn starch
        One teaspoon of sugar
        A half pound of broccoli
        One teaspoon of salt
        One chunk of garlic

Chop the garlic into pieces the size of matchheads.
Bone the chicken.
Shred the chicken.
Marinate the chicken in the garlic, sugar, corn starch, rice
 wine and soy sauce.
Chop the broccoli into pieces the size of chunks.
Stir fry the broccoli for three minutes.
Remove the broccoli from the pan.
Stir fry the spices, rice wine and chicken for three minutes.
Add the broccoli to the spices, rice wine and chicken.
Stir fry the spices, rice wine, chicken and broccoli for a
 half minute.
Add the salt to the spices, rice wine, chicken and broccoli.
```

Once again, the planner made the same prediction of a failure on the basis of the texture of a vegetable. Because the CHICKEN-AND-SNOW-PEA plan built out of the original BEEF-AND-BROCCOLI recipe is indexed under the fact that it avoids the this problem as well, it was picked as the initial plan.

C.2.5 STRAWBERRY-SOUFFLE

```
                STRAWBERRY-SOUFFLE

          Two teaspoons of vanilla
          A half cup of flour
          A quarter cup of sugar
          A quarter teaspoon of salt
          A half cup of milk
          Two cups of milk
          One piece of vanilla bean
          A quarter cup of butter
          Five egg yolks
          Six egg whites
          One cup of strawberry

Mix the flour with the sugar and salt.
Mix the milk with the mixture of sugar, salt and flour.
Boil the milk and vanilla bean for less than a half minute.
Remove the vanilla bean from the milk.
Mix the mixture of milk, sugar, salt and flour with the milk.
Simmer the mixture of milk, sugar, salt and flour for five minutes.
Whip the egg yolk.
Add the butter and mixture of egg yolk to the mixture of milk,
 sugar, salt and flour.
Cool the mixture of egg yolk, milk, sugar, salt, flour and butter.
Whip the egg white.
Add the vanilla and mixture of egg white to the mixture of egg yolk,
 milk, sugar, salt, flour and butter.
Pulp the strawberry.
Mix the strawberry with the spices, egg, milk, salt, flour
 and butter.
Pour the mixture of egg, spices, strawberry, salt, milk, flour
 and butter into a nine inch baking-dish.
Bake the batter for twenty five minutes.
```

In building this plan, CHEF learned about the problem of liquid in soufflés. Here it encountered and repaired the problem of a soufflé that falls because of too much liquid.

C.2.6 RASPBERRY-SOUFFLE

```
RASPBERRY-SOUFFLE

        Two teaspoons of vanilla
        A half cup of flour
        A quarter cup of sugar
        A quarter teaspoon of salt
        A half cup of milk
        Two cups of milk
        One piece of vanilla bean
        A quarter cup of butter
        Five egg yolks
        Six egg whites
        One cup of raspberry

Mix the flour with the sugar and salt.
Mix the milk with the mixture of sugar, salt and flour.
Boil the milk and vanilla bean for less than a half minute.
Remove the vanilla bean from the milk.
Mix the mixture of milk, sugar, salt and flour with the milk.
Simmer the mixture of milk, sugar, salt and flour for five minutes.
Whip the egg yolk.
Add the butter and mixture of egg yolk to the mixture of milk,
 sugar, salt and flour.
Cool the mixture of egg yolk, milk, sugar, salt, flour and butter.
Whip the egg white.
Add the vanilla and mixture of egg white to the mixture of egg yolk,
 milk, sugar, salt, flour and butter.
Pulp the raspberry.
Mix the raspberry with the spices, egg, milk, salt, flour and
 butter.
Pour the mixture of egg, spices, salt, raspberry, milk, flour and
 butter into a nine inch baking-dish.
Bake the batter for twenty five minutes.
```

In this plan, CHEF made use of its knowledge of the difficulties of using high moisture fruit in making soufflés to anticipate the past problem. It then used this prediction to find the STRAWBERRY-SOUFFLE plan that avoids it.

C.2.7 KIRSCH-SOUFFLE

```
                KIRSCH-SOUFFLE

          Two teaspoons of vanilla
          A half cup of flour
          A quarter cup of sugar
          A quarter teaspoon of salt
          A half cup of milk
          Two cups of milk
          One piece of vanilla bean
          A quarter cup of butter
          Five egg yolks
          Six egg whites
          One tablespoon of kirsch

Mix the flour with the sugar and salt.
Mix the milk with the mixture of sugar, salt and flour.
Boil the milk and vanilla bean for less than a half minute.
Remove the vanilla bean from the milk.
Mix the mixture of milk, sugar, salt and flour with the milk.
Simmer the mixture of milk, sugar, salt and flour for five minutes.
Whip the egg yolk.
Add the butter and mixture of egg yolk to the mixture of milk,
 sugar, salt and flour.
Cool the mixture of egg yolk, milk, sugar, salt, flour and butter.
Whip the egg white.
Add the vanilla and mixture of egg white to the mixture of egg yolk,
 milk, sugar, salt, flour and butter.
Mix the kirsch with the spices, egg, milk, salt, flour and butter.
Pour the mixture of egg, spices, salt, milk, flour and butter into
 a nine inch baking-dish.
Bake the batter for twenty five minutes.
```

At this point, CHEF understands that it is liquid and not just fruit that causes planning problems with soufflés. As a result, it also anticipated and avoided a fallen soufflé when building a recipe to include the liqueur kirsch in a soufflé.

C.2.8 CHOCOLATE-SOUFFLE

```
                    CHOCOLATE-SOUFFLE

          Two teaspoons of vanilla
          Five teaspoons cocoa
          A half cup of flour
          A quarter cup of sugar
          A quarter teaspoon of salt
          A half cup of milk
          Two cups of milk
          One piece of vanilla bean
          A quarter cup of butter
          Five egg yolks
          Five egg whites

Mix the flour with the sugar and salt.
Mix the milk with the mixture of sugar, salt and flour.
Boil the milk and vanilla bean for less than a half minute.
Remove the vanilla bean from the milk.
Add the cocoa to the milk.
Mix the mixture of milk, sugar, salt and flour with the milk.
Simmer the mixture of milk, sugar, salt and flour for five minutes.
Whip the egg yolk.
Add the butter and mixture of egg yolk to the mixture of milk,
 sugar, salt and flour.
Cool the mixture of egg yolk, milk, sugar, salt, flour and butter.
Whip the egg white.
Add the vanilla and mixture of egg white to the mixture of egg yolk,
 milk, sugar, salt, flour and butter.
Pour the mixture of spices, egg, milk, salt, flour and butter into
 a nine inch baking-dish.
Bake the batter for twenty five minutes.
```

In planning for a CHOCOLATE-SOUFFLE, CHEF created a soufflé with too little rather than too much liquid. This resulted in a dry soufflé that CHEF repaired by decreasing the eggs in the recipe.

C.2.9 DUCK-DUMPLINGS

```
DUCK-DUMPLINGS

Fifteen scallions
A half chunk of ginger
One pound of duck
A quarter cup of soy sauce
One and a half tablespoons of sesame oil
A half teaspoon of szechwan pepper
One egg
One and a half teaspoons of salt
70 jiaoz skins

Chop the scallion into pieces the size of matchheads.
Chop the ginger into pieces the size of matchheads.
Bone the duck.
Clean the fat from the duck.
Grind the duck.
Mix the scallion and ginger with the salt, egg, szechwan pepper,
 sesame oil, soy sauce and duck.
Fill the jiaoz skin with the mixture of salt, egg, spices
 and duck.
Boil the bunch of dumplings filled with the salt, egg, spices and
 duck for twenty minutes.
```

In building this recipe, CHEF learned about the problem of duck fat. It built a new plan and anticipation links. It also built a new critic that adds a step to remove the fat from the duck. This critic was then stored under the concept DUCK, indexed by the problem it solves.

C.2.10 DUCK-PASTA

```
                DUCK-PASTA

          Fifteen scallions
          A half chunk of ginger
          One pound of duck
          A quarter cup of soy sauce
          One and a half tablespoons of sesame oil
          A half teaspoon of szechwan pepper
          One egg
          One and a half teaspoons of salt
          One pound of noodles

Chop the scallion into pieces the size of matchheads.
Chop the ginger into pieces the size of matchheads.
Bone the duck.
Clean the fat from the duck.
Grind the duck.
Mix the scallion and ginger with the salt, egg, szechwan pepper,
 sesame oil, soy sauce and duck.
Stir fry the mixture of salt, egg, spices and duck for five minutes.
Boil the noodles for three minutes.
Serve the mixture of salt, egg, spices and duck over the noodles.
```

In building a plan for a pasta dish with duck, CHEF anticipated the problem with duck but could find a pasta dish that avoided it. As a result, it built a dish out of ANTS-CLIMB-A-TREE and added the step of removing the duck fat that its new DUCK critic suggests.

C.2.11 CHICKEN-DUMPLINGS

```
CHICKEN-DUMPLINGS

Fifteen scallions
A half chunk of ginger
One pound of chicken
A quarter cup of soy sauce
One and a half tablespoons of sesame oil
A half teaspoon of szechwan pepper
One egg
One and a half teaspoons of salt
70 jiaoz skins

Chop the scallion into pieces the size of matchheads.
Chop the ginger into pieces the size of matchheads.
Bone the chicken.
Grind the chicken.
Mix the scallion and ginger with the salt, egg, szechwan pepper,
 sesame oil, soy sauce and chicken.
Fill the jiaoz skin with the mixture of salt, egg, spices and
 chicken.
Boil the bunch of dumplings filled with the salt, egg, spices and
 chicken for twenty minutes.
```

In this dish, there was no anticipation of a problem, and CHEF created the dumplings out of its DUCK-DUMPLINGS recipe. As it removed the duck from the recipe, it reversed the effects of the critic it has built, removing the step having to do with the duck fat.

C.2.12 BEEF-PASTA

```
        BEEF-PASTA

    Fifteen scallions
    A half chunk of ginger
    One pound of beef
    A quarter cup of soy sauce
    One and a half tablespoons of sesame oil
    A half teaspoon of szechwan pepper
    One egg
    One and a half teaspoons of salt
    One pound of noodles

Chop the scallion into pieces the size of matchheads.
Chop the ginger into pieces the size of matchheads.
Grind the beef.
Mix the scallion and ginger with the salt, egg, szechwan pepper,
 sesame oil, soy sauce and beef.
Stir fry the mixture of salt, egg, spices and beef for five minutes.
Boil the noodles for three minutes.
Serve the mixture of salt, egg, spices and beef over the noodles.
```

For this recipe, CHEF just modified its ANTS-CLIMB-A-TREE recipe with no ill effects.

C.2.13 FISH-STIR-FRIED

```
                    FISH-STIR-FRIED

          One pound of fish
          One tablespoon of soy sauce
          A half teaspoon of sugar
          One teaspoon of sesame oil
          One egg white
          One tablespoon of corn starch
          Ten pieces of garlic
          Five pieces of red pepper
          Two scallions
          One tablespoon of rice wine

Chop the fish into pieces the size of chunks.
Marinate the fish in half the soy sauce, sesame oil, egg white,
 sugar, corn starch and rice wine.
Chop the garlic into pieces the size of matchheads.
Chop the red pepper into pieces the size of nubbs.
Shred the scallion.
Add the scallion to the egg white, spices, rice wine and fish.
Stir fry the garlic and red pepper for a half minute.
Add the egg white, spices, rice wine and fish to the garlic
 and red pepper.
Stir fry the spices, egg white, rice wine and fish for two minutes.
Add the remaining soy sauce to the spices, egg white, rice wine
 and fish.
Stir fry the egg white, spices, rice wine and fish for a
 half minute.
```

In this recipe CHEF discovered the problem of the iodine taste of stir fried fish. It understands that this is a feature of seafood in general. This problem was solved by marinating the fish in rice wine.

C.2.14 SHRIMP-STIR-FRIED

```
                SHRIMP-STIR-FRIED

          One pound of shrimp
          One and a half teaspoons of soy sauce
          A half teaspoon of sugar
          One teaspoon of sesame oil
          One egg white
          One tablespoon of corn starch
          Ten pieces of garlic
          Five pieces of red pepper
          Two scallions
          One tablespoon of rice wine

Shell the shrimp.
Marinate the shrimp in half  the soy sauce, sesame oil, egg white,
 sugar, corn starch and rice wine.
Chop the garlic into pieces the size of matchheads.
Chop the red pepper into pieces the size of nubbs.
Shred the scallion.
Add the scallion to the egg white, spices, shrimp and rice wine.
Stir fry the garlic and red pepper for a half minute.
Add the egg white, spices, shrimp and rice wine to the garlic
 and red pepper.
Stir fry the spices, egg white, shrimp and rice wine for
 two minutes.
Add the remaining soy sauce to the spices, egg white, shrimp and
 rice wine.
Stir fry the egg white, spices, shrimp and rice wine for a
 half minute.
```

CHEF predicted the problem of the iodine taste of the sea-food coming out during the stir frying. It used this prediction to find the FISH-STIR-FRY dish in which the fish is marinated in rice wine. Unfortunately, the MARINADE step interfered with the SHELL step that CHEF had to add to the dish. This problem was solved by reordering the two steps.

C.2.15 SHRIMP-AND-GREEN-PEPPER

```
                 SHRIMP-AND-GREEN-PEPPER

          Three green peppers
          One pound of shrimp
          One and a half teaspoons of soy sauce
          A half teaspoon of sugar
          One teaspoon of sesame oil
          One egg white
          One tablespoon of corn starch
          Ten pieces of garlic
          Five pieces of red pepper
          Two scallions
          One tablespoon of rice wine

Shell the shrimp.
Marinate the shrimp in half the soy sauce, sesame oil, egg white,
 sugar, corn starch and rice wine.
Shred the green pepper.
Chop the garlic into pieces the size of matchheads.
Chop the red pepper into pieces the size of nubbs.
Shred the scallion.
Add the green pepper and scallion to the egg white, spices, shrimp
 and rice wine.
Stir fry the garlic and red pepper for a half minute.
Add the egg white, spices, shrimp, rice wine and green pepper to
 the garlic and red pepper.
Stir fry the spices, egg white, shrimp, rice wine and green pepper
 for two minutes.
Add the remaining soy sauce to the spices, egg white, shrimp, rice
 wine and green pepper.
Stir fry the egg white, spices, shrimp, rice wine and green pepper
 for a half minute.
```

Here CHEF predicted the problem of the iodine taste of sea-food and the problem with the ordering of the MARINADE and SHELL steps. It found and modified the SHRIMP-STIR-FRIED plan on the basis of both these predictions.

C.2.16 HOT-BEEF

```
        HOT-BEEF

    Three carrots
    One pound of beef
    One and a half teaspoons of soy sauce
    A half teaspoon of sugar
    One teaspoon of sesame oil
    One teaspoon of rice wine
    One egg white
    One tablespoon of corn starch
    Ten pieces of garlic
    Two scallions
    One piece of red pepper
    One teaspoon of salt

Shred the beef.
Marinate the beef in the corn starch, sugar, egg white, rice wine,
 sesame oil and soy sauce.
Shred the carrot.
Chop the garlic into pieces the size of matchheads.
Shred the scallion.
Add the carrot and scallion to the egg white, spices, rice wine
 and beef.
Stir fry the red pepper and garlic for a half minute.
Add the egg white, spices, rice wine, beef and carrot to the red
 pepper and garlic.
Stir fry the spices, egg white, rice wine, beef and carrot for
 three minutes.
Add the salt to the spices, egg white, rice wine, beef and carrot.
```

In building a hot beef dish out of BEEF-WITH-CARROTS, CHEF added salt to the beef as it was stir frying. This dried the beef out. CHEF repaired the plan by putting the salt in after the cooking is over. Because the salt is put in to bring out the taste of the hot pepper CHEF marked adding pepper to a meat plan as predictive of this problem.

C.2.17 HOT-CHICKEN

```
                    HOT-CHICKEN

          Three carrots
          One pound of chicken
          One and a half teaspoons of soy sauce
          A half teaspoon of sugar
          One teaspoon of sesame oil
          One teaspoon of rice wine
          One egg white
          One tablespoon of corn starch
          Ten pieces of garlic
          Two scallions
          One piece of red pepper
          One teaspoon of salt

Bone the chicken.
Shred the chicken.
Marinate the chicken in the corn starch, sugar, egg white,
 rice wine, sesame oil and soy sauce.
Shred the carrot.
Chop the garlic into pieces the size of matchheads.
Shred the scallion.
Add the carrot and scallion to the egg white, spices, rice wine
 and chicken.
Stir fry the red pepper and garlic for a half minute.
Add the egg white, spices, rice wine, chicken and carrot to the
 red pepper and garlic.
Stir fry the spices, egg white, rice wine, chicken and carrot for
 three minutes.
Add the salt to the spices, egg white, rice wine, chicken and
 carrot.
```

Predicting problems that will result from adding red pepper and thus salt to the chicken, CHEF found and modified its HOT-BEEF recipe.

C.2.18 FISH-AND-PEANUT

```
                    FISH-AND-PEANUT

          One cup of peanut
          One pound of fish
          One tablespoon of soy sauce
          A half teaspoon of sugar
          One teaspoon of sesame oil
          One egg white
          One tablespoon of corn starch
          Ten pieces of garlic
          Five pieces of red pepper
          Two scallions
          One teaspoon of salt
          One tablespoon of rice wine
          One chunk of ginger

Chop the fish into pieces the size of chunks.
Marinate the fish in half the soy sauce, sesame oil, egg white,
 sugar, corn starch, ginger and rice wine.
Chop the garlic into pieces the size of matchheads.
Chop the red pepper into pieces the size of nubbs.
Shred the scallion.
Add the peanut and scallion to the egg white, spices, rice wine
 and fish.
Stir fry the spices and salt for a half minute.
Add the egg white, spices, rice wine, fish and peanut to the spices.
Stir fry the spices, egg white, rice wine, fish and peanut for
 two minutes.
Add the remaining soy sauce to the spices, egg white, rice wine,
 fish and peanut.
Stir fry the egg white, spices, rice wine, peanut and fish for a
 half minute.
```

Predicting the taste problem with fish, CHEF modified FISH-STIR-FRIED to include peanuts. It added salt to bring out the taste of the nuts. Unfortunately, the salt also brought out the taste of the iodine again. CHEF repaired this by adding more rice wine. The added liquid in turn ruined the texture of the fish. In a last repair, CHEF replaceed some of the rice wine with crushed ginger, a step that masks the taste of the iodine but does not add additional liquid to the dish.

C.2.19 PEANUT-AND-SHRIMP

```
                PEANUT-AND-SHRIMP

          One cup of peanut
          One pound of shrimp
          One tablespoon of soy sauce
          A half teaspoon of sugar
          One teaspoon of sesame oil
          One egg white
          One tablespoon of corn starch
          Ten pieces of garlic
          Five pieces of red pepper
          Two scallions
          One teaspoon of salt
          One tablespoon of rice wine
          One chunk of ginger

Shell the shrimp.
Marinate the shrimp in half the  soy sauce, sesame oil, egg white,
 sugar, corn starch, ginger and rice wine.
Chop the garlic into pieces the size of matchheads.
Chop the red pepper into pieces the size of nubbs.
Shred the scallion.
Add the peanut and scallion to the egg white, spices, shrimp and
 rice wine.
Stir fry the spices and salt for a half minute.
Add the egg white, spices, shrimp, rice wine and peanut to the
 spices.
Stir fry the spices, egg white, shrimp, rice wine and peanut for
 two minutes.
Add the remaining soy sauce to the spices, egg white, shrimp,
 rice wine and peanut.
Stir fry the egg white, spices, shrimp, rice wine and peanut for
 a half minute.
```

In building a recipe for shrimp with peanuts, the previous problem of the added salt increasing the iodine taste of the sea-food was recalled. The problem with the ordering of the MARINADE and SHELL steps was also activated. But this later problem has a critic associated with it, so CHEF used the FISH-AND-PEANUT recipe instead of one of its shrimp plans. After modifying the recipe to include shrimp and the SHELL step, the MARINATE and SHELL steps are reordered.

C.2.20 BROCCOLI-SOUFFLE

```
                BROCCOLI-SOUFFLE

          A half pound of broccoli
          A half cup of flour
          A quarter teaspoon of salt
          A half cup of milk
          Two cups of milk
          Three pieces of red pepper
          A quarter cup of butter
          Five egg yolks
          Six egg whites

Mix the flour with the salt.
Mix the milk with the mixture of flour and salt.
Boil the milk and red pepper for less than a half minute.
Remove the red pepper from the milk.
Mix the mixture of milk, salt and flour with the milk.
Simmer the mixture of milk, salt and flour for five minutes.
Whip the egg yolk.
Add the butter and mixture of egg yolk to the mixture of milk,
 salt and flour.
Cool the mixture of egg yolk, milk, salt, flour and butter.
Whip the egg white.
Pulp the broccoli.
Add the broccoli and mixture of egg white to the mixture of egg
 yolk, milk, salt, flour and butter.
Pour the mixture of egg, milk, salt, flour, butter and broccoli into
 a nine inch baking-dish.
Bake the batter for twenty five minutes.
```

CHEF created a recipe for broccoli soufflé out of its plan for PEPPER-SOUFFLE.

Bibliography

[Car79] J. Carbonell. *Subjective Understanding: Computer Models of Belief Systems.* PhD thesis, Yale University, 1979.

[Car81] J. Carbonell. A computational model of analogical problem solving. In *The Proceedings of the Seventh International Joint Conference on Artificial Intelligence*, Vancouver, B.C., August 1981.

[Car83] J. Carbonell. Derivational analogy and its role in problem solving. In *The Proceedings of the Third Annual Conference on Artificial Intelligence*, Washington, DC, August 1983. AAAI.

[Che62] J. Chen. *Joyce Chen Cook Book.* J. B. Lippincott, New York, NY, 1962.

[Dea85] T. Dean. Temporal imagery: An approach to reasoning about time for planning and problem solving. Technical Report 433, Yale University Department of Computer Science, October 1985.

[DeJ83] G. DeJong. An approach to learning from observation. In *Proceedings of the International Machine Learning Workshop*, pages 171–176, Monticello, IL, June 1983. University of Illinois.

[DeJ3a] G. DeJong. Acquiring schemata through understanding and generalizing plans. In *The Proceedings of the Eighth International Joint Conference on Artificial Intelligence*, Karlsrhue, Germany, August 1983a. IJCAI.

[FI85] P.E. Friedland and Y. Iwasaki. The concept and implementation of skeletal plans. *Journal of Automated Reasoning*, 1:161–208, 1985.

[FN71] R. Fikes and N. Nilsson. STRIPS: A new approach to the application of theorem proving to problem solving. *Artificial Intelligence*, 2, 1971.

[GH83] M. Gick and K. Holyoak. Schema induction and analogical transfer. *Cognitive Psychology*, 15:1–38, 1983.

[GL85] D. Gentner and R. Landers. Analogical reminding: A good match is hard to find. In *Proceedings of the International Conference on Systems, Man and Cybernetics*, Tuscon, AZ, November 1985.

[Ham83] K.J. Hammond. Planning and goal interaction: The use of past solutions in present situations. In *The Proceedings of the Third Annual Conference on Artificial Intelligence*, pages 148–151, August 1983.

[Ham84] K. Hammond. Indexing and causality: The organization of plans and strategies in memory. Technical Report 351, Yale University Department of Computer Science, December 1984.

[Ham87] K. Hammond. Learning and re-using explanations. In *Proceedings of the Fourth international Conference on Machine Learning*, Irvine, CA, June 1987. ML.

[HH88] K. Hammond and N. Hurwitz. Extracting diagnositic features from explanations. In *Proceedings of the 1988 AAAI Symposium on Explanation-Based Learning*, Stanford, CA, August 1988. AAAI.

[Kor82] R. Korf. A program that learns to solve rubik's cube. In *The Proceedings of the Second Annual Conference on Artificial Intelligence*, pages 164–167, Pittsburg, PA, August 1982. AAAI.

[KS84] J.L. Kolodner and R.L. Simpson. A experience and problem solving: A framework. In *Proceedings of the Sixth Annual Conference of the Cognitive Science Society*, Boulder, CO, August 1984.

[KSS85] J.L. Kolodner, R.L. Simpson, and K. Sycara. A process model of case-based reasoning in problem-solving. In *The Proceedings of the Ninth International Joint Conference on Artificial Intelligence*, Los Angeles, PA, August 1985. IJCAI.

[Leb80] M. Lebowitz. *Generalization and Memory in an Integrated Understanding System.* PhD thesis, Yale University, October 1980.

[Mil85] D. Miller. Planning by search through simulations. Technical Report 423, Yale University Department of Computer Science, October 1985.

[Min85] S. Minton. Selectively generalizing plans for problem-solving. In *The Proceedings of the Ninth International Joint Conference on Artificial Intelligence*, pages 313–315, Los Angeles, CA, August 1985. AAAI.

[Mit79] T. Mitchell. An analysis of generalization as a search problem. In *The Proceedings of the Sixth International Joint Conference on Artificial Intelligence*, 1979.

[Mit83] T. Mitchell. Learning and problem solving. In *The Proceedings of the Eighth International Joint Conference on Artificial Intelligence*, Karlsrhue, Germany, August 1983. Computers and Thought Award Lecture.

[ML78] R. Michalski and J. Larson. Selection of most representative training examples and incremental addition of vli hypothesis: The underlying methodology and the description of programs esel and aq11. Technical Report 867, Computer Science Department, University of Illinois, Urbana, 1978.

[NS72] A. Newell and H. Simon. *Human Problem Solving.* Prentice-Hall, Englewood Cliffs, NJ, 1972.

[RB64] I. Rombauer and M. Becker. *The Joy of Cooking.* New American Library, New York, NY, 1964.

[Sac74] E.D. Sacerdoti. Planning in a hierarchy of abstraction spaces. *Artificial Intelligence*, 5:115–135, 1974.

[Sac75] E.D. Sacerdoti. A structure for plans and behavior. Technical Report 109, SRI Artificial Intelligence Center, 1975.

[Sch76] E. Schrecker. *Mrs. Chiang's Szechwan Cookbook.* Harper and Row, New York, NY, 1976.

[SA77] R. Schank and R. Abelson. *Scripts, Plans, Goals and Understanding.* Lawrence Erlbaum Associates, Hillsdale, New Jersey, 1977.

[Sch82] R. C. Schank. *Dynamic memory: A theory of learning in computers and people.* Cambridge University Press, 1982.

[Sch84a] R. Schank. Explanation: A first pass. Technical Report 330, Yale University Department of Computer Science, September 1984.

[Sch84b] R. Schank. The explanation game. Technical Report 307, Yale University Department of Computer Science, March 1984.

[Sch86a] R. Schank. *Explanation Patterns: Understanding Mechanically and Creatively.* In preparation, 1986.

[SCH86b] R.C. Schank, C.G. Collins, and L. Hunter. Transcending inductive category formation in learning. *Behavioral and Brain Sciences*, 9:639–686, 1986. 45 pages.

[Sim85] R.L. Simpson. *A Computer Model of Case-based Reasoing in Problem Solving.* PhD thesis, Georgea Institute of Technology, 1985.

[SR85] R. Schank and C. Riesbeck. Explanation: A second pass. Technical Report 384, Yale University Department of Computer Science, July 1985.

[Sus75] G.J. Sussman. *A computer model of skill acquisition*, volume 1 of *Artificial Intelligence Series.* American Elsevier, New York, 1975.

[Tat77] A. Tate. Generating project networks. In *The Proceedings of the Fifth International Joint Conference on Artificial Intelligence*, pages 888–893, Cambridge, Ma, U.S.A, August 1977. IJCAI.

[TH85] P. Thagard and K. Holyoak. Discovering the wave theory of sound: Inductive inference in the context of problem solving. In *The Proceedings of the Ninth International Joint Conference on Artificial Intelligence*, pages 610–612, Los Angeles, CA, August 1985. AAAI.

[Wil78] R. Wilensky. *Understanding Goal-Based Stories.* PhD thesis, Yale University, 1978. Research Report #140.

[Wil80] Robert Wilensky. Meta-planning. Technical Report M80 33, UCB College of Engineering, August 1980.

[Wil83] R. Wilensky. *Planning and Understanding: A Computational Approach to Human Reasoning.* Addison-Wesley Publishing Company, Reading, Massachusetts, 1983.

[Win70] P. Winston. Learning structural descriptions from examples. Technical Report 231, AI Laboratory, Massachusetts Institute of Technology, 1970. Reprinted in P.Winston, Ed. and The Psychology of Computer Vision, 1975, McGraw-Hill.

Index

Abelson, R. 108, 197, 269
Abstracting xi
Adaptation xiv, 79, 81
Adjunct plans 41, 102, 104, 112, 116, 120, 122, 135, 172, 177
ADJUNCT-PLAN:PROTECT 102, 116–117, 120–121, 124, 126
ADJUNCT-PLAN:REMOVE 116
Adjust balance 102, 104, 117, 135, 172–173, 180
ADJUST-BALANCE:DOWN 102
ADJUST-BALANCE:UP 121
ALTER-ACTOR 136
ALTER-FEATURE 102, 125, 127, 136
ALTER-ITEM 102, 125, 135
ALTER-PLACEMENT:AFTER 102, 136
ALTER-PLACEMENT:BEFORE 102, 135
ALTER-PLAN:PRECONDITION 60, 102, 104, 110, 116, 127, 135, 172
ALTER-PLAN:SIDE-EFFECT 41, 60, 102, 104, 110, 112–113, 116, 122, 133, 135, 172
ALTER-TIME:DOWN 102, 128, 135
ALTER-TIME:UP 102, 128, 135
ALTER-TOOL 102, 129, 135
Analogy 68, 130
ANTICIPATOR 24, 29, 183
ANTS-CLIMB-A-TREE 214–215, 245, 256, 258
ASSIGNER 23–29, 58
ATRANS 108
Backtracking 36, 50, 108, 195
Backward chaining 43, 165, 206
Becker, M. 269
BEEF-AND-BROCCOLI 45–48, 51, 55–56, 59, 74, 85, 96, 115, 214, 247
BEEF-AND-GREEN-BEAN 35
BEEF-PASTA 215, 258
BEEF-WITH-BROCCOLI 160, 163, 233
BEEF-WITH-CARROTS 213, 216, 243, 262
BEEF-WITH-GREEN-BEANS 213–214, 237
Best-first search 189
Birnbaum, L. viii
Blocked-Goals 60, 110, 114, 118, 122–127, 146, 161, 165, 167
BROCCOLI-SOUFFLE 217, 266
BROCCOLI-STIR-FRY 214
Bugs xv, 4–5, 39, 44, 186
Carbonell, J. 136, 267
Cases x, xi, xii, xiii, xiv, xvi, 1, 8, 30, 33, 55, 79, 87, 94, 109, 122, 139–141, 144–145, 154, 174, 187, 193,

201, 212, 225
Categories 62, 64, 114, 201–207, 210–212, 219
Category membership 202
Causal reasoning xvii, xviii, 6, 8, 36–40, 43–44, 50, 54–57, 64, 70, 91, 93, 103–107, 110, 112–116, 120, 122, 129–136, 139–140, 156, 158–159, 164–168, 172–175, 194, 198–201, 204, 206–208, 211, 218–223, 226
Causal configurations 40, 91, 103, 112–114, 129–132, 222
Chapman, D. 28
Chen, J. 267
CHICKEN-AND-BROCCOLI 214, 250
CHICKEN-AND-PEANUTS 59
CHICKEN-AND-SNOW-PEAS 214, 248
CHICKEN-DUMPLINGS 215, 257
CHICKEN-STIR-FRIED 48
CHICKEN-WITH-PEANUTS 213, 238
CHOCOLATE-SOUFFLE 215, 254
Classification 203, 205
Clobbering 196
CMU xx
Collins, G. viii, 202, 270
ConFlicting goals 109, 174, 190, 193, 197
Constraints 170, 190, 220
Counter-Planning 136
Creativity xiv
Credit assignment 8, 88, 136, 202
Critics xvii, 7, 15, 17, 33–34, 39, 59–63, 88, 97–101, 111, 140–141, 144–158, 189–190, 195–198, 201, 215–217, 255–257, 265
Dean, T. 267
Debugging 186, 191
DeJong, G. 7, 55, 201, 207–210, 267
DESIRED-EFFECT TOPs 40, 112, 119–121
Desired-Effects 223
DESIRED-FEATURE TOPs 114, 123, 126, 224
DEVELOPING-SIDE-EFFECT 223
Diagnosis xvii, 111, 122, 129–130, 140, 157, 165, 197, 199
Disable 40–41, 52, 104, 112, 115, 119, 123, 132, 167
Discrimination 12, 14, 50–52, 63, 70, 76, 78–80, 83, 88, 89, 113, 170–171, 200, 219
Discriminators 76
Domain specific 144, 175
DUCK-DUMPLINGS 61–62, 215, 255, 257
DUCK-PASTA 215, 256
Episodic memory xvii, 4, 10–11, 18, 45, 68–69, 105–108, 131, 187, 206–207, 212
Expectations viii, 2, 5–7, 109, 143, 194, 218
Expectation failure 5, 146, 165
Experiences xii, xiii, xvii, 2, 4, 6–9, 30, 63, 70–71, 74, 80–81, 89, 187–188, 201, 212, 221
Explanation 2, 6–10, 20, 32, 35–40, 43–44, 49, 54–57, 60, 63–64, 68, 93, 103–104, 108, 113, 132–134, 140, 158–159, 164–171, 176, 182, 194–195, 201, 206–213, 218
Explanation-driven 7, 55
Failure xvi, xvii, xviii, 1–10, 16, 18–32, 35–63, 67–71, 74,

78, 80–87, 90–112, 115–132, 136, 139–141, 144–146, 156–176, 179, 182–195, 198–201, 204, 206–222, 225, 228–229, 232, 236, 249
Failure anticipation 4, 10, 24–25, 28, 30–31, 37, 45, 48, 56, 60, 78, 86–87, 90, 187, 193, 215, 219, 231, 234, 253, 255
Failure avoidance xvii, xviii, 1–10, 14, 18, 21–32, 36, 43, 45–55, 58–59, 62–65, 68–75, 81, 84–101, 119–120, 129, 138–143, 156–158, 162–163, 170, 182–189, 192–194, 199–201, 206–211, 215–220, 231, 234, 250, 252–253, 256
Failure driven xvi
Faulty plans xvii, 2, 4–6, 19–20, 32, 35–36, 42, 54, 59, 66, 70, 100, 110, 123, 126, 140, 166, 173, 187, 194–195, 201, 218
Feedback xvi, 2
Fikes, R. 4–5, 188, 267
First principles x, xi, xii, xiii, xix, 1, 153, 196, 208, 217
FISH-AND-PEANUT 216, 264
FISH-STIR-FRIED 163, 215–216, 259, 264
FISH-STIR-FRY 97, 124, 161, 216, 260
FISH-WITH-PEANUTS 133
Friedland, P. 267
Functional descriptions 3, 9, 28, 72, 140–143, 147–148, 152, 154, 156, 162, 199, 219
Generalization 31, 43–44, 49–57, 64, 72, 109, 189, 200, 202, 204, 206–209, 219
Gentner, D. 68, 268
GET-NEWSPAPER 198
Gick, M. 68, 268
GINGER-CHICKEN 213, 215, 241
Goal abandonment 82
Goal conflict 197
Goals xv, xvi, xvii, 2–8, 11–40, 43–53, 56–59, 63, 69–104, 108–130, 134–148, 151–173, 181–204, 207–209, 214, 217–218, 221–227, 231, 233, 235, 247
GPS 188
HACKER 39, 122, 132, 189
Holyoak, K. 68, 268, 270
HOT-BEEF 97, 216, 262
HOT-CHICKEN 216, 263
Hunter, L. 202, 270
Hurwitz, N. viii, 268
Hypothetical 222
If-then rules 203
Implementation xiii, xvi, 17, 51, 69, 71, 76, 129, 131, 173–174, 177, 195
Indexing x, xii, xiv, xv, xvi, xvii, 1–3, 6–7, 11–14, 17–23, 27, 29–32, 39, 44–46, 49–54, 58–72, 76–78, 81, 84–85, 89, 97–107, 113–114, 117–123, 128–132, 139, 141, 143–144, 158–159, 169–174, 182–185, 188–193, 200–203, 209–210, 218, 220, 247, 250, 255
Indices 4, 17, 50–51, 107, 116, 128, 183, 187, 209
Induction 7, 64, 201, 205, 207, 211, 219
Inference 6, 24, 36–38, 56, 108, 110, 131, 157, 166, 192, 194, 201, 203, 208, 211,

218, 227, 229, 231, 233
Instantiation 41, 209
Integrate xvii, 4, 14, 32, 140, 148, 210, 219
Iwasaki, Y. 267
JPL xix
Kass, A. ix
KIRSCH-SOUFFLE 215, 253
Knowledge-Based 7
Knowledge-Intensive 140
Kolodner, J. 268
Korf, R. 4, 189, 268
Labeling xii
Landers, R. 68, 268
Larson, J. 7, 201, 269
Leake, D. ix
Least-commitment planning xv
Lebowitz, M. 7, 201, 205–206, 209, 268
Linearization assumption 190
Lytinen, S. viii
Machine generated plans xix
Marks, M. viii
Martin, C. ix
Matching 11–14, 19, 24, 28, 32–33, 44, 50, 53, 59, 63, 72, 76–83, 86, 90, 147, 151–153, 188, 206–207, 223, 225
McDermott, D.viii, xv, xvi
Memory viii, xii, xiii, xiv, xvii, xviii, 1–14, 17–19, 22–34, 39, 44–59, 62–72, 75–110, 130, 138, 146, 153, 158–161, 182–187, 200–201, 210–212, 216–221, 265
Memory organization 1, 4–5, 11, 21, 62, 66–70, 75–76, 84, 90–91, 101–102, 106, 132, 187, 199, 206, 220
Merging plans 15, 148–151, 154–156, 190, 201
Meta-goals 197–198, 208
Meta-level reasoning 190
Meta-planning 197
Meta-plans 197
Michalski, R. 7, 201, 269
Miller, D. 268
Minton, S. 189, 269
Mitchell, T. 7, 55, 201, 269
MODIFIER 15–18, 22, 28, 98, 124, 138–157, 181
Modifiers 39, 97
Mutual-goal-pursuit 109
Myths about memory 66
Network 56, 70, 76–78, 91, 113, 165, 170, 200
Newell, A. 188, 269
Nilsson, N. 4–5, 188, 267
NOAH 5, 39, 132, 189–191, 194, 197
Non-normative features 166, 231
Observable features 203
Owens ix
P-GOAL 197
PANDORA 5, 132, 190, 192, 194, 197
PEANUT-AND-FISH 153
PEANUT-AND-SHRIMP 153, 216, 265
PEPPER-SOUFFLE 214, 217, 246, 266
Plan construction 2, 4, 31, 92, 165, 187, 202–203, 216
Plan execution 157
Plan interaction xvii, 2, 4–8, 15, 21, 27–29, 39–40, 45–51, 58–60, 74, 81, 84, 86–87, 96, 99, 102, 108–110, 113, 124, 126, 129, 136, 138–139, 156, 175, 187–200, 214, 216, 218, 222, 225–226, 248

Plan modification xvii, xviii, 1–3, 10–18, 22, 26, 28, 32–34, 39, 41, 43, 45, 47, 51, 57, 59, 62–63, 70–72, 75, 77, 82, 84, 86–87, 97–102, 136, 138–156, 201, 208–209, 214–217, 224, 248–249, 258, 261, 263
Plan repair xvii, xviii, 1–10, 15, 18–23, 27–32, 36–39, 42, 49–51, 54–55, 59–63, 69–70, 74, 80, 85, 97, 99–114, 122–123, 128–141, 146, 157–159, 164–165, 169–186, 189–190, 194–198, 201, 206, 211, 214, 216–218, 226, 229, 236, 251, 254, 262, 264
Planners xv, 2, 4–6, 32, 84, 123, 136, 186–195, 200, 212, 218
Planning viii, x, xv, xvi, xvii, xviii, xix, 1–12, 17–33, 36, 39, 45, 49, 54–57, 62–65, 68, 70–71, 75, 84–85, 92, 95, 99, 103, 105–114, 119, 121, 129–141, 146, 164, 169–170, 173, 175, 179, 186–212, 217–223, 232, 236, 253
PORK-DUMPLING 214–215, 244
PORK-SHREDS-WITH-HOISIN-SAUCE 213, 239
Preconditions 110, 114–115, 119, 121, 125, 132–133, 161, 165, 167, 174, 188, 190, 218, 224–225, 228
Prediction 4–5, 8, 23–31, 45–46, 50, 53, 55–63, 84, 90, 92, 96, 99, 101, 109, 130–131, 141, 158, 183–187, 193, 200, 206, 214–216, 220, 248, 250, 252, 260
Predictors 129
Preparation steps 179
Prioritizing goals 82
Problem detection 189–190, 198
Problem recognition demons xix, 44, 146, 236
Problematic features 35, 68, 80–82, 99–100, 131, 134, 140, 144, 146, 212, 236
Propagation of activation 206
RASPBERRY-SOUFFLE 214, 252
Recipes xvi, xix, 32–35, 45, 47–49, 52, 57, 72, 75, 91, 95, 99–100, 133, 152, 162, 179, 182–183, 213–217, 228, 236–237, 247–250, 253–259, 263, 265
Recognition 40, 110, 130, 149, 196, 198, 202–204, 220, 224
RECOVER 3, 5, 18, 21, 59, 71, 102, 104, 108, 117–118, 121, 130, 183, 188, 193, 195
Relationships between plan steps 70, 147, 223
Reminding xii, 9–10, 26, 54–57, 66, 68, 96, 109, 187, 210, 214–216, 249
REMOVE-FEATURE 60–61, 102, 124–125, 136
REORDER 39, 60, 102, 110, 117–118, 121–123, 132, 135, 170, 196
REPAIRER 19–24, 27–29, 138–140, 157, 182
Replacement 112, 131, 147, 153
Replacing 82, 125, 133, 155, 214
Replanning 6, 36, 108, 188, 192, 194–195, 218
Representation xviii, 4, 6–8, 11–12, 15, 18, 20–23, 27, 39,

44–45, 54, 67, 69–72, 110–113, 122, 137, 171, 175, 186, 188–196, 199–200, 218, 222–223, 226
RESOLVE-GOAL-CONFLICT 197
Retrieval xii, xiii, 4, 7, 12, 14–19, 27, 30, 34, 47, 49, 68, 72, 75, 79–80, 85, 87, 106, 187, 191
RETRIEVER 10–19, 22, 25, 27–28, 50, 78, 130, 138–140, 156–157, 183
Reuse xviii, 1–4, 7–11, 28–29, 32, 49, 60, 64, 146, 188–193, 210, 217
Riesbeck, C. viii, 9, 270
Riesbeck, M. viii
Rombauer, I. 269
Rule-Based xii, 1, 11
Sacerdoti, E. xv, 4–5, 39, 110, 122, 131–132, 189, 195–197, 269
Schank, R. iv, viii, x, xiv, xvi, 6, 9, 39, 108–109, 165, 197, 202, 269
Scheduling 132
Schrecker, E. 269
Seifert, C. viii
Semantic 56, 72, 202
SHRIMP-AND-GREEN-PEPPER 216, 261
SHRIMP-STIR-FRIED 215–216, 260
SHRIMP-STIR-FRY 161
SIDE-EFFECT TOPs 40, 41, 60, 102, 104, 110, 112–122, 132, 133, 135, 172, 170, 195, 200
SIDE-FEATURE TOPs 123–125, 126, 129, 130, 170, 225
Simon, H. 188, 269
Simpson, R. 268, 270
Simulation xv, xvi, xix, 9, 20, 28, 35–37, 99, 157, 160–166, 182, 187, 190, 192–193, 197–198, 208, 221, 227
Situated Activity xx
SLOW-DOWN 137
Soloway, E. viii
Specialization 41, 142
SPEED-UP 137
SPLIT-AND-REFORM 41, 60, 102, 116, 120, 128, 135, 170
SPLIT-AND-REJOIN 195
Stanford xix
STEP-PARAMETER TOPs 127,128
Storage xi, xiv, xvii, 2–8, 14, 17–21, 27, 31, 39–40, 44, 49–53, 59–72, 75–78, 85, 88, 91, 97–113, 116, 118–120, 126, 129, 131–132, 139–140, 146, 148, 153, 159, 170, 172–175, 179, 183–189, 192–193, 197, 200–201, 211, 215, 218–221, 255
Stored 71, 173, 185, 200
STORER 18–24, 27, 29
Strategies xvii, xviii, 6, 21–23, 36–43, 60, 69–70, 101–107, 110–137, 158–159, 164–165, 169–181, 194–199, 218, 223, 225–226, 236
Strategy 20, 39, 41, 60–61, 67, 102–105, 111–113, 122, 124, 129, 131, 133–136, 172–182, 187–188, 191
STRAWBERRY-SOUFFLE 52–54, 57, 117, 214–215, 251
STRIPS 41, 188–191, 194–195, 200
STYLE-STIR-FRY 142
Substitution xvi, 86, 147, 153
SUBSUMPTION 190
Sussman, G. xvi, 4–5, 39, 110, 121–

122, 131–132, 189–190, 195–197, 270
Sycara, K. 268
Symbolic Processing 227
Tate, A. 4, 270
Thagard, P. 68, 270
Thematic x, xi, xii
TOPS xviii, 39–43, 50, 70, 103–105, 108–134, 158–159, 164, 169–179, 182–183, 195, 218, 222–223, 226, 236
Transformational planning xv, xvi, 196, 209
USE-RAINCOAT 197
VANILLA-SOUFFLE 213, 242
Variation 132, 213
Violation 165, 172, 193, 197
Wilensky, R. 4–5, 131–132, 136, 190–199, 270
Winston, P. 7, 201–202, 205–206, 270
Yale iv, viii, xiv, xvi, xix, xx

Printed in Dunstable, United Kingdom

91897626R00170